# GOSPEL GRACE

## The Modern-day Controversy

Mark W. Karlberg

Wipf and Stock Publishers
*Eugene, Oregon*

Wipf and Stock Publishers
199 West 8th Avenue, Suite 3
Eugene, OR 97401

http://www.wipfandstock.com


Gospel Grace
By Karlberg, Mark W.
Copyright@2003 by Karlberg, Mark W.
ISBN: 1-59244-352-4




*All rights reserved.* No part of this publication may be reproduced, stored in a retrieval system, or transmitted in any form or by any means, electronic, mechanical, photocopy, recording, or otherwise, without the prior permission of the publisher and author. The only exception is brief quotation in printed reviews and articles. (First rights belong to the original publishers of the articles and reviews here republished.)

*To my friends at
Park Woods Orthodox Presbyterian Church
Overland Park, Kansas*

*Whose witness and stand for the Gospel of Christ
Are etched in history*

*May your tribe increase!*

**Soli Deo gloria**

**Permission to republish material was granted by:**

*Christian Research Network*
*Foundations*
*Journal of the Evangelical Theological Society*
*Trinity Journal*

## Collection of Republished Articles

CHAPTER 2: "A (New) Systematic Theology for Our Times: A Review Article," *Foundations: A Journal of Evangelical Theology* 45 (2001) 23-41.

CHAPTER 5: *John Piper on the Christian Life: An Examination of His Controversial View of "Faith Alone" in* Future Grace (Great Bromley: CRN [Christian Research Network], 1999).

CHAPTER 6: *The Changing of the Guard: Westminster Theological Seminary in Philadelphia* (Unicoi, TN: The Trinity Foundation, 2001).

## Collection of Republished Book Reviews

Michael S. Horton's *Covenant and Eschatology*, in *Trinity Journal* 24 (2003) 125-129.

Willem J. Van Asselt's *The Federal Theology of Johannes Coccceius (1603-1669)*, in the *Journal of the Evangelical Theological Society* 45 (2002) 734-738.

**NOTE ON SELECTED WEBSITES**: My previously published book, *Covenant Theology in Reformed Perspective*, is available online at www.twoagepress.org (and can be downloaded). Chapter 6, previously published by The Trinity Foundation as the March/April 2001 issue of *The Trinity Review*, is also posted on its website (www.trinityfoundation.org), with additional documents and responses at the close of the essay.

See the Theological Research Exchange Network (at www.tren.com) for copies of conference papers; the website of Robert Lotzer, a minister in the Orthodox Presbyterian Church, listing several papers relevant to the Shepherd controversy, at http://www.covopc.org/Shepherd_Contents.html; and the Presbyterian Church in America Historical Center's, "Historic Documents of American Presbterianism: The Justification Controversy," www.pcanet.org/history/documents/shepherd/justification.html.

# TABLE OF CONTENTS

**PREFACE** ................................................................. 1

**INTRODUCTION** ...................................................... 9

**CHAPTER 1** ............................................................ 29
Opposing Systems of Doctrine: An Overview

**CHAPTER 2** ............................................................ 57
A (New) Systematic Theology for Our Times

**CHAPTER 3** ............................................................ 93
Paul, the Law, and Contemporary Theology:
The Undoing of the Protestant Reformation

**CHAPTER 4** .......................................................... 123
Covenant Theology: A Post-Reformation accretion?

**CHAPTER 5** .......................................................... 137
John Piper on the Christian Life: An Examination of
His Controversial View of 'Faith Alone' in *Future Grace*

**A TRILOGY – Chapters 6 through 8**

**CHAPTER 6** .......................................................... 157
The Changing of the Guard: Westminster Theological
Semnary in Philadelphia

**CHAPTER 7** .......................................................... 205
The Impact of Norman Shepherd's Teaching in
Westminster Theological Seminary

**CHAPTER 8** ...................................................................... 235
Covenant and Imputation: The Federal System of Doctrine

\* \* \*

**APPENDIX A** ...................................................................... 279
Richard Gaffin's Teaching on Justification and the
Covenants: A Summary and Critique

**APPENDIX B** ...................................................................... 287
Review of Michael Horton's *Covenant and Eschatology*

**APPENDIX C** ...................................................................... 295
Review of Willem van Asselt's *The Federal Theology of Johannes Cocceius*

**APPENDIX D** ...................................................................... 305
Fighting the Good Fight: A Bout with John Frame

\* \* \*

**SUPPLEMENTAL BIBLIOGRAPHY** .............................................. 313

**AUTHOR INDEX** ................................................................. 319

# PREFACE

Reformed theology at the opening of the twenty-first century is characterized by two leading features; the one is theological ecleticism, the other perspectivalism (as a method of doing theology). This twofold characteristic of "Reformed" theology – what is actually a misleading label – mirrors the extreme relativism of our culture and times. Today's (enlightenment) slogan might well read: Construct your own theology! This is the age of the "isms," ecleticism and perspectivalism being only two of a great number. Practically speaking, what we discover in our day in the churches and in the culture is widespread accommodationism, consumerism (marketing), and globalizationism. Here the motto is: Do what you have to do to sell your product! Church historian David F. Wells (in his masterful trilogy assessing the state of evangelicalism) and Presbyterian theologian John Leith (in several insightful works on church and society) have written pungent exposés of the plight of Protestantism. It is not a pretty picture. But it is accurate, and it is balanced.

Nowhere is this more telling than in present-day misinterpretations of the Gospel – specifically, what concerns the very heart of the Gospel, the biblical doctrine of justification by faith. For several decades now I have championed historic Reformed teaching. Having obtained three theological degrees from Westminster Theological Seminary (Philadelphia), I write out of the conviction that Old School Westminster offers the most consistent and penetrating grasp of the system of doctrine contained in the

Scriptures, including (old) Westminster's apologetic defense of the Reformed faith and critique of contrary systems of thought arising over the centuries of Christian interpretation. But my studies at Westminster were conducted in a period of great change and upheaval at the seminary. All of this came to particular focus in the evaluation of the views of Norman Shepherd, successor to John Murray in the department of systematic theology, what ultimately led to his dismissal from the faculty.[1] The contemporary dispute in evangelical-Reformed theology over the doctrine of justification by faith (including the apostle Paul's understanding of the Mosaic law) is wide-ranging. The issues being debated at Westminster at present are part of a much larger debate in biblical and theological interpretation across a diverse spectrum of Christian tradition and modern-day "innovation." What the revisionists share in common is their disdain for the traditional Protestant "Law"/"Gospel" antithesis, an element vital to the system of historic Protestant-Reformed orthodoxy.

This book, sequel to my *Covenant Theology in Reformed Perspective*, is written in the hopes that an understanding of the dispute at Westminster will provide some insight into the origination and spread of false teaching in once-orthodox centers of learning. In this particular case, as in most, there is the exploitation of false notions and misformulations, some of which are deeply imbedded within the theological tradition. Such misconceptions can be the seeds for heresy, the fruit of further development and maturation of erroneous teaching (sometimes appearing in later generations). Alongside the doctrinal substance of the current dispute are the machinations of once-respected teachers in the Reformed churches. The effect of all of this is to render confusion and uncertainty in the minds of those uninformed or less informed. This state of bewilderment, combined with the eclecticism and individualism of our age, helps to explain the present lethargy, the lack of will to stand for the truth of the Gospel. Added to this is modern-day depreciation – if not outright rejection – of the creeds and confessions of the Protestant churches. These are, indeed, perilous and difficult times.

In its early, formative years Westminster Theological Seminary filled a unique niche in international Calvinism. That no longer is the case.[2] The tie between the confessional standards of English and America Calvinism (the *Westminster Confession of Faith* and *Catechisms*) and Westminster Seminary is now broken. The story of Westminster's capitulation to prevailing theological misconceptions is neither pleasant, nor edifying. Yet there are lessons to be learned. The story is one of deception and intrigue on the part of its perpetrators, courage and determination on the part of the opposition. The following provides only glimpses into the history of the controversy. The full account remains to be written. Before introducing my readers to the contents of this book, a few comments on the present state of affairs is in order.

The Presbytery of Philadelphia of the Orthodox Presbyterian Church is at present bitterly divided over the teachings of Elder John Kinnaird, teachings embodying the views of Norman Shepherd.[3] These views need to be placed in their proper theological and ecclesiastical context, one that brings the teachings of Richard Gaffin, Westminster's current Charles Krahe Professor of Biblical and Systematic Theology and senior systematician, to the forefront.[4] It is Gaffin who has – to a very large extent – orchestrated the affairs of the seminary and of the OPC. It was a rude awakening for many when the 2003 General Assembly upheld Kinnaird's appeal, exonerating him of false doctrine. (It has been reported that in his admonition to the delegates of the Assembly Gaffin cautioned that a vote against Kinnaird's teaching was a vote against his own. To be sure, concerning the controverted issues in this dispute, the teaching of Kinnaird and Gaffin is the same.)

The decision of the Assembly has unleashed severe criticism and outcry within the OPC and the wider Reformed community. Clearly, the OPC is reaping the fruits of Gaffin's labors in his denomination and seminary over these last three decades, and the effects of this decision will be felt for years to come. One further word of clarification: The dispute at Westminster Seminary does not center upon the difference between the theological formulations of John Murray and Meredith Kline (though some are wishing to make that the issue). One would hope that Murray's theology of the covenants (being the exception to mainstream Reformed teaching) would not be made the new standard for the OPC. Were such to occur, the OPC would only perpetuate the error of Murray for generations to come. In several respects Murray's interpretation is an aberration, a retrogression in the history of Reformed interpretation. With respect to the Shepherd-Gaffin-Kinnaird formulation the case for heresy is unmistakable. Mention should also be made of the Reformed Church in the United States, which has addressed the Shepherd teaching in an overture before its 2003 Synod, declaring that teaching to be heretical. The matter has been taken under study, with recommendation to come before the 2004 Synod. For this, the RCUS is to be commended. She is an example for those who love and preach the Gospel. May she prove to be a catalyst for needed reformation in our times.[5]

Chapters in this collection of writings contain some overlap and repetition. Many were originally written for a different audience in mind. It should also be stated that intense, ongoing debate renders my critique of Westminster Seminary (East and West) a work in progress. We do not yet know where the final lines will be drawn. Further acquaintance with my prior book issued by Wipf and Stock, to whom I am most grateful as my publisher, is essential for a fuller understanding of the disputed issues in this chapter of the history of Reformed doctrine. For the most part I have endeavored here to reach a broader, yet informed, lay readership. Some minor stylistic changes have been made in compiling these essays, including updates on bibliographical references. Special thanks to Jim Tedrick of Wipf and Stock Publishers for his competence and assistance, and to Steve Rives for his skill and expertise in formatting the manuscript for publication.

**NOTES**

[1] The germination of Westminster's revisionist theology can be traced back to the mid to late 1960s, when Shepherd and Gaffin were pursuing advanced theological studies and beginning their teaching careers at Westminster. Both were absorbed in the work of G. C. Berkouwer and Herman Ridderbos, the two guiding lights in Westminster's development of biblical theology (New School variety). In the course of this development the theological fruits of John Murray and Geerhardus Vos were planted in foreign soil, yielding a hybrid of neo-Reformed thinking. Neither Murray nor Vos rightfully belong in this field. An uncorrupted harvest of their writings will (re)establish them as guardians of historic Reformed orthodoxy (the peculiarities of Murray's covenant theology aside). See the addendum to my "Introduction."

Special mention – with mixed emotions – should be made of the fact that Mr. Shepherd initially took me under his wings at the beginning of my doctoral study. I am most grateful for the time and attention he gave me, but deeply regret that he and I were unable to agree on what were some of the fundamental doctrines of the Reformed faith. At the time of his dismissal Shepherd quipped: "Mark, you saved the seminary!" Hardly the case. If that were to happen, it will be the Lord's work. For the record, I care very deeply about Westminster – that is why I am speaking out.

[2] Longtime student of church history, Professor Clair Davis once observed that the theological integrity of confessional institutions –

specifically, fidelity to orthodox doctrine – generally lasts a period of fifty years. That certainly proved to be the case at Westminster, where Davis has taught for 37 years. Regrettably, he has helped history repeat itself. Various sections in the chapters which follow chronicle the Shepherd-Gaffin dispute.

[3] In the course of the conflict over Kinnaird's teaching at Bethany OPC, Bethany's pastor, the Reverend Dr. Clinton Foraker, rightly and wisely renounced the jurisdiction of the Presbytery of Philadelphia, of which he was a member. See his account (dated August 12, 2003), posted on the Warfield List: http://groups.yahoo.com/group/bbwarfield/message/15901. The Kinnaird Trial is posted at www.trinityfoundation.org.

[4] In the early phase of the Westminster controversy the Reverend Dr. Charles Krahe, in whose name the systematics chair had been endowed, stood against the Shepherd theology and successfully worked on the Board of Trustees to remove him from the faculty in 1982. He regards himself as too old to enter the current fray, believing that it is the responsibility of the present faculty, board, and administration to resolve the ongoing dispute (as stated to me in a personal telephone conversation on January 6, 2003). Upon the departure of Sinclair Ferguson from Westminster's faculty in 1998, the endowment was withdrawn. It has been reestablished, this time permanently. At present, it is occupied by Gaffin.

Rather surprising is Sinclair Ferguson's return to Westminster (the Dallas campus) in the Fall of 2003, after a brief stint as senior pastor at St. George's Tron Church (Glasgow, Scotland). He returns to promote the new teaching at Westminster as a full-time member of the faculty. (Plans for his return were two years in the works.)

[5] Both of these cases are reported in *The Counsel of Chalcedon* 1 (June 2003) 22-23. (Online at www.chalcedon.org/counsel/.) D. G. Hart and John Muether in *Fighting the Good Fight: A Brief History of the Orthodox Presbyterian Church* (Philadelphia: The Committee on Christian Education and the Committee for the Historian of the Orthodox Presbyterian Church, 1995) demonstrate the close ties between the OPC and Old School Presbyterianism. In Eric J. Miller's partially sympathetic book review (*TrinJ* 18 NS [1997] 122-124) the

# Preface

theological position of the OPC is portrayed as a relic of the past, out of touch with modern developments. If, as Mark Noll has remarked, the OPC is "the pea beneath the mattress," then Hart and Muether, in Miller's estimation, are "the guardians of the pea" (123). But times are indeed changing in the OPC. New theological developments, including increasing cooperation with broad evangelicalism, something which Hart and Muether rightly deplore, are rapidly impacting the denomination from the inside out. Miller again cites Noll (and Cassandra Niemczyk in *The Varieties of American Evangelicalism*): "instead of shouting from outside the walls of the OPC headquarters, 'the voices more open to cooperation with American evangelicals now come from the denomination's officials'" (124). Given the radical nature of some of these changes, Miller's conclusion is all the more significant. He commends the Hart-Muether history of the OPC as offering a "unique point of view," a view shared by too few. I would only add – as a footnote to account of Hart and Muether – that the future of the OPC very much hangs in the balance. As I noted elsewhere (see Chapter 6), this history omits any mention of the Shepherd controversy. Being a denominational publication, were the authors prevented from addressing this critical chapter in the history of the OPC?

# INTRODUCTION

The crucial issue in the controversy addressed in this book is not a matter of semantics. But the dispute does center upon the legitimacy and appropriateness of one or two theological terms having deep roots in Christian theology. Largely due to misuse, not all Reformed theologians have been comfortable with the term "merit" – with reference to human obedience. The other term commonly misunderstood (or rather misapplied) is "grace." Needless to say, this term is pervasive in the theological literature, as it is in the Scriptures. Before commenting further about these two theological terms and their importance in the articulation of the Gospel of grace, a brief summary of Calvinistic formulation on justification and the covenants is necessary.

On the following points there is consensus within catholic Reformed orthodoxy, that is, international Calvinism. (1) The event of the Fall marks a critical divide in the history of humankind – between an original state of communion with God in perfection and holiness and a subsequent state of estrangement on account of sin and transgression. The Fall introduced the (total) depravity of human nature and the complete inability of the sinner in his/her own strength to please God in a manner worthy of life and fellowship with a just and holy God. (2) The prohibition against eating of the tree of the knowledge of good and evil gave specific focus to the demand for and necessity of complete, unreserved obedience to the will of God set forth in his law (what is known to humankind by means of natural and special revelation). The significance of this prohibition must be understood against the backdrop of the contest between God and the Serpent, who sought to frustrate God's good purposes at the very creation of Adam and Eve, our first parents who were made in the image of the heavenly host (with precedence given to Adam as God's image-bearer). (3) The law of God in creation required of Adam – as federal head of the human race – full and perfect obedience. Reward of life everlasting was contingent upon Adam's success in guarding the sanctuary of God, overcoming the wiles of the Devil, and exercising full trust in and allegiance to the sovereign Lord of heaven and earth. The principle of inheritance was that of works – "works" being antithetical to "grace." (4) After Adam's transgression, God in his great mercy and love was pleased to establish the Covenant of Grace with Adam and his (spiritual) seed, which covenant would be realized for the elect in the future life, death, and resurrection of Jesus Christ, the Second Adam. Implicit in this interpretation of the history of redemption is what came to be known as the twofold covenants, the Covenant of Works in creation and the Covenant of Grace in salvation. (5) Adam's original justification before God would have been sustained on grounds of obedience, that is, by the works of the law, whereas after the Fall Adam's justification is secured on grounds of the meritorious righteousness of Christ imputed to sinners through the sole instrumentality of saving faith. There is no question or difference of opinion within Reformed orthodoxy concerning the merit of Christ's life and death (encompassing both his active and passive obedience to the law of God first revealed to Adam before the Fall). (6) All of these points are summarized in the classic Protestant distinction between the "Law" and the "Gospel." The relationship between these two is one of antithesis. It is not a relationship of "tension" or apparent discontinuity, but of radical contrast. Reformed theology has been united and uncompromising on these points of doctrine.

Where the picture begins to blur is with respect to the use of the term "merit" in connection with the required obedience of the First Adam in the original Covenant of Works. Misconception and theological inconsistency have characterized Reformed interpretation over most of its history. The dilemma that it has created for itself was something inherited from medieval scholasticism, specifically, application of the false, speculative dichotomy between nature and grace. This ingredient in the history of doctrine aside, many interpreters simply reasoned that the term "merit" – when applied to creatures made in God's image – suggests equality between the Creator and the creature, one that places the servant in a bargaining-position with God. Ascribing merit to human works has fostered in the minds of many the false notion of human autonomy. This reading of the theological term "merit," however, is entirely unwarranted. Denial of merit in the case of Adam undermines – to a greater or lesser degree – the doctrine of the merit of Christ's righteousness imputed to believers. What is required of biblical interpreters faithful to the teaching of Scripture is the excision of impurities resident within orthodox Reformed scholasticism, not their perpetuation. The grace of justification is the grace of the Lord Jesus Christ. It is *gospel grace*. Before the Fall, the benefit of divine grace is not operative. Simply put, there is no need for grace prior to Adam's breaking of the covenant. Grace is God's remedy for human sin and disobedience. The issue here in this modern-day dispute is that simple – nothing subtle or complex (though some have made it that).

There are those interpreters who deny human merit, yet recognize the "merit" of Christ's righteousness, the (legal) grounds of restored life and salvation. They point to the uniqueness of the Son of God, who exercised his obedience in accordance with his sinless human and divine natures. The righteousness of Christ is inherently meritorious, by virtue of his divinity. This truth, however, is wholly irrelevant with respect to the forensic implications of the covenant-bond, specifically, the legal demand for perfect and complete obedience. The uniqueness of Christ's person does not dissolve the legal parallel explicitly drawn by the apostle Paul in Romans 5. What stands as bedrock in Reformed covenant theology is the traditional Protestant contrast between the "Law" and the "Gospel." Whatever one makes of the use of the "merit" concept respecting the works of the law performed by the servant/son of God, the radical antithesis between two principles of inheritance – grace and law, faith and works – remains. An important aspect in the current debate concerns the interpretation of the Mosaic covenant as (in part) a reintroduction of the Covenant of Works in the history of redemption. Those who refute the traditional Reformed teaching concerning the twofold covenants and the traditional Protestant contrast between law and grace – both elements of doctrine being commonplace in Reformed federalism – likewise deny the presence of the works-principle in the Mosaic administration (a teaching stoutly affirmed in mainstream Reformed theology). Modern-day revisionists, once again, have shown their disdain for the forensic, legal conception respecting the creature's duty in the original covenant at creation. They cannot make sense of Adam's probation at the establishment of the Covenant of Creation, appropriately called the "Covenant of Works" (assuming they even acknowledge probationary testing at the outset of human history).

Application of the term "grace" to the original state of Adam, specifically, to the Covenant of Works, introduces confusion and misconception into the very system of Reformed doctrine, opening the way to further, radical reinterpretation of the covenants (the false teaching that has gained much ground in recent years). According to the teaching of the Bible, the gift of (saving) grace is an exclusively soteric benefit, a manifestation of the undeserved mercy and love of God extended to sinners. The term "grace" does not pertain to the pre-Fall economy. To argue otherwise is to counter the clear, consistent teaching of Scripture. There are only two kinds of grace in the Bible, *gospel grace* (grace extended to sinners undeserving of God's salvation) and *common grace* (the general beneficence of God that spans the time from the Fall to the end of the age, providing the historical context in which the Covenant of Grace operates in the history of redemption).

The opening chapter of this book begins with a summary of Calvinistic doctrine, utilizing an interdisciplinary approach that combines the fruits of biblical theology and confessional-dogmatics (Reformed systematics), and concludes by highlighting several recent attempts at reformulation – attempts that stand in opposition to classic Reformed interpretation. Particular focus is given to the subject of the relationship between the "Law" and the "Gospel." Chapter 2 provides an evaluation of the recent and notable handbook in Reformed dogmatics written by Robert Reymond, augmenting the doctrinal overview presented in the first chapter. Reymond's work is a mature statement of the theology of Westminster Calvinism/Old School Princeton (though in some instances he breaks from this tradition). Especially commendable – from the standpoint of this collection of writings – is Reymond's grasp of amillennial covenant theology, covenant theology in its most consistent form.[1] Reymond's handbook provides a good summary of the Reformed system of doctrine.

The controversial subject of Paul's interpretation of the Mosaic law is taken up in Chapter 3. Here the important matter of hermeneutical approach is the focus of discussion concerning the doctrine of the law of God, traditionally summarized in terms of its threefold classification and threefold usage. The next chapter is a paper I read at a seminar addressing the subject of Law and Gospel, held at the 2001 national meeting of the Evangelical Theological Society and sponsored by the Biblical Theology Study Group. On that occasion I was invited to represent the Reformed point of view. The other positions represented at the seminar were the Lutheran (Douglas Moo), the Progressive-Dispensationalist (Craig Blaising), and the New Perspective (Don Garlington).[2] Chapter 5 is a republication of my critique of John Piper's book, *Future Grace*, one that has contributed to the reformulation of Piper's views in his subsequent writing, *Counted Righteous in Christ*, a work I assess later in this book. Piper's *Future Grace* accents the contingency of faith as a working obedience, one that relies upon the faithfulness of God for final salvation (the outworking of "future grace"). The implications of this teaching for the biblical doctrine of justification by faith alone are devastating. My critique of Piper was initially requested by a pastor-friend and longtime supporter of my work. The book has disturbed pastors, students, and scholars alike.

Chapter 6 is a republication of my summary history and assessment of theological developments at Westminster Seminary laid out in *The Changing of the Guard*. Special attention is given to Norman Shepherd's book, *The Call of Grace*, evaluated in the context of the longstanding Westminster controversy.[3] Shepherd draws out the implications of his new teaching regarding election, justification, and the divine covenants for "Reformed" evangelism, as he sees it. My critique has been widely read and debated, and continues to stand at the center of ongoing discussion. I am indebted to John Robbins for publishing this exposé and for sparking renewed study of the Shepherd controversy.[4] Chapter 7 analyzes further the impact of Shepherd's teaching in Westminster Seminary by addressing the distinctive formulations of Shepherd's former colleague and strongest advocate, Richard Gaffin, coauthor of Westminster's new theology.[5] A subject that has preoccupied Gaffin's attention through much of his teaching career is the Pauline doctrine of union with Christ – read through the eyes of John Calvin, as (mis)interpreted by Gaffin. This reading of doctrine leads Gaffin to subordinate all the many and discrete soteric benefits granted to the believer to the one act of "union with Christ," with the result that all causal distinctions among the many benefits are minimized or obscured. At the same time, Gaffin maintains that union with Christ – including each and every benefit in the "application of salvation" (the *ordo salutis*) – is qualified by the semi-eschatological "already/not yet" dialectic. Justification, for example, is understood to possess both present and future aspects. In contradictory fashion, Gaffin contends that the believer united with Christ is already justified, but not yet justified with respect to final salvation. Once again, the biblical doctrine of justification by faith – justification as the act of God fixed at the moment of spiritual regeneration – is compromised. The closing chapter[6] takes up the latest round of debate centering upon Piper's *Counted Righteous in Christ*[7] and the essay of Tim Trumper in the Fall 2002 issue of *The Westminster Theological Journal*. Comparison is made between traditional covenant theology and the theology of Piper and New School Westminster. Taken together, the Piper-Gaffin response may properly be viewed as "Custer's last stand," the occasion for Piper and Gaffin to stake out their final position on controverted issues. Four appendixes shed additional light on the status of Reformed covenant theology at the beginning of the third millennium of Christian interpretation.

Before drawing this introduction to a close, a further word must be said about Trumper's essay, which stands as the most important statement of the seminary faculty since the writing of position papers for and against Shepherd in the mid-70s and early 80s. Though bearing the input of other faculty members, it is largely the work of Gaffin. It could not have been written without Gaffin's direct oversight as Westminster's senior systematician.[8] In Trum-per's doctoral work, "An Historical Study of the Doctrine of Adoption in the Calvinistic Tradition,"[9] special credit is given to Gaffin for the substance of Trumper's analysis and interpretation of the history of Reformed doctrine (including the classification "constructive Calvinists," among whom Gaffin and Trumper number themselves). Trumper considers the question of continuity and discontinuity (both theological and methodological) in the Reformed tradition. On the interplay between theology and method Trumper equivocates. What is clear, however, is that the "constructive Calvinists," unlike the "orthodox Calvinists," find some grounds for the criticism offered by "revisionist Calvinists," the likes of Karl Barth and Thomas Torrance. What is notable, Trumper tells his readers, is scholastic orthodoxy's "pre-occupation with the original status of the adopted in Eden."[10] What is more notable, in my estimation, is the fact that Trumper gives short shrift to Calvin's inchoate doctrine of the Covenant of Works, and he makes no mention of the traditional Protestant law/gospel contrast in his dissertation. Indirectly, he refutes it. (That refutation is made explicit in the *WTJ* article.)

Echoing the opinion of Sinclair Ferguson, Trumper accuses the Westminster divines for logical schematization of doctrine. Further, he accuses the traditionalists – the "orthodox Calvinists" – of fostering mere regurgitation of doctrine. In so doing, they "have been unable either to recognise or acknowledge [sic] the validity of the underlying issues."[11] Trumper contends: "Too often Westminster soteriology has been read more through the grid established by the retrospectively dominant perspective of later

Calvinists than through the more balanced statements of the Standards themselves. The preceding history of Calvinism has shown that despite the support of longevity the tradition of exposition that has developed over recent centuries ought not necessarily to be equated with the theology of the Assembly itself."[12] Trumper's study concludes by calling for "a fresh openness to those insights of Barth, which, upon reflection and/or modification, may be deemed biblical."[13] We can expect to read more of this line of argument in research emanating from Westminster's new Center for the Study of the Westminster Confession of Faith.[14]

The Reformed church today faces the greatest battle in its history – the purity of the Gospel itself is at stake in this raging controversy. The lines have now been clearly drawn. What now follows is an analysis, statement, and defense of historic Reformed covenant theology against the criticisms of modern-day revisionists, notably, that of New School Westminster.

**ENDNOTES**

[1] For a recent, popular treatment of covenant eschatology, see Kim Riddlebarger, *A Case for Amillennialism: Understanding the End Times* (Grand Rapids: Baker, 2003). G. K. Beale provides an exhaustive commentary on the Book of Revelation from the amillennial perspective in *The Book of Revelation: A Commentary on the Greek Text* (The New International Greek Testament Commentary; Grand Rapids: Eerdmans, 1999).

The lead article of the Spring 2003 issue of *The Westminster Theological Journal* by John R. Franke (Biblical Theological Seminary), entitled "Reformed Theology: Toward a Postmodern Reformed Dogmatics," is startling and troubling. Though aware of the problem of relativism, the author calls for a nonfoundationalist approach to interpretation, in which all theological reflection is tentative in nature (open-ended). According to Franke, this is what it means to say that *Reformed* theology is always in process of being reformed. Nothing is absolutely certain and established in the mind of the church. Hence, there can be no "dogma," for what the church confesses is always subject to revision. Franke's position entails the leveling of all theological discourse to a common religious experience, one which minimizes God's special providence and spiritual illumination, whereby the faith, once-for-delivered to the saints, is preserved down through the ages of church history (in varying degrees of fidelity to the teachings of Scripture). Franke's view undermines the perspicuity of Scripture. Though in many respects provocative, Franke's thesis is fundamentally flawed and misformulated. Curiously, Franke regards Robert Reymond's recent work in systematics to be – in the words of Robert Letham's book review (*WTJ* 62 [2000] 314-319) – "biblicistic and sectarian in its thrust" (p. 3). Franke sees Reymond's work as nothing more than an update of Louis Berkhof's classic handbook in systematics. The full reference to Franke's article is *WTJ* 65 (2003) 1-26.

Far more accurate is the assessment of Richard A. Muller in his "Preface" to Louis Berkhof's *Systematic Theology* (new combined edition; Grand Rapids: Eerdmans, 1996): "It remains the best modern English-language introduction to doctrinal theology of the Reformed tradition" (viii). Compare further, the work Franke coauthored with Stanley Grenz, *Beyond Foundationalism: Shaping The-*

*ology in a Postmodern Context* (Louisville: Westminster John Knox, 2001). Grenz is a leading, contemporary proponent of a radical revision of Protestant theological discourse. In *The Gagging of God: Christianity Confronts Pluralism* (Grand Rapids: Zondervan, 1996) D. A. Carson writes: "With the best will in the world, I cannot see how Grenz's approach to Scripture can be called 'evangelical' in any useful sense" (481). Similar to Grenz's argument against traditional theology is that held by former Westminster Seminary professor John Frame in his advocacy of "theological multiperspectivalism." Frame's formulations and analysis are hopelessly garbled (see Appendix D).

2 During the course of this seminar, Garlington acknowledged the imputed righteousness of Christ, an alien righteousness, the ground of the believer's salvation. He noted that rejection of this element was a major error in the work of N. T. Wright, one of the leading framers of the New Perspective. If Garlington does hold fast (and consistently) to what he has confessed, he can no longer be numbered among those advocating the New Perspective. And needless to say, this conviction must lead him to reformulate the position advanced in his writings to date. Surprisingly, Moo and Blaising expressed their reservations concerning the "active obedience" as a component of the righteousness imputed to faith. According to them, the "one act of righteousness" has reference to the Crosswork of Christ (his sufferings or "passive obedience"). Moo's stated position on this occasion stands in conflict with his exposition of Rom 8:4 in *The Epistle to the Romans* (NICNT; Grand Rapids, Eerdmans, 1996). Happily (though somewhat inconsistently), the traditional Protestant "Law"/"Gospel" contrast was affirmed by all the presenters. A twofold question, however, remains: What role does this theological construct occupy in the system of evangelical-Protestant doctrine? How does it impact biblical theology and systematics?

3 For additional critique of Norman Shepherd's book, *The Call of Grace: How the Covenant Illuminates Salvation and Evangelism* (Phillipsburg: Presbyterian and Reformed, 2000), consult the review by Cornelis Venema in the *Mid-America Journal of Theology* 13 (2002) 232-248. Much of Venema's critique of Shepherd echoes

my analysis presented in *The Changing of the Guard* and, in briefer version, in my book review published in *TrinJ* 22NS (2001) 131-136.

Shepherd has more recently summarized his thinking in "Justification by Faith Alone," *Reformation and Revival Journal: A Quarterly for Church Leadership* 11 (2002) 75-90. This issue of the journal contains several articles on the doctrine of justification as it is now being debated among contemporary "evangelicals." Compare also the several essays in *The New Southern Presbyterian Review* 1 (2002) opposing the Shepherd theology. The largely antiquarian Banner of Truth Trust ventures out in challenging contemporary reinterpretations of the Protestant-Reformed doctrine of justification by faith in the August/September 2003 issue of *The Banner of Truth*. Clarity and decisiveness on the controverted issues in this modern-day dispute are compromised, however, by favorable appeal to the views of John Piper, views virtually identical to that of Piper's mentor, Daniel Fuller. It must be emphasized that the doctrine of the imputation of Christ's righteousness is but one element (however weighty) in the system of Reformed teaching. See Chapter 8.

[4] John Robbin's acquaintance with the dispute over the doctrine of justification by faith led him to contact Westminster's President, Samuel Logan, requesting relevant documents. His request was denied. For additional history, see O. Palmer Robertson's *The Current Justification Controversy* (Unicoi, TN: The Trinity Foundation, 2003); John Robbins's *A Companion to The Current Justification Controversy* (Unicoi, TN: The Trinity Foundation, 2003); and, "Historic Documents of American Presbyterianism: The Justification Controversy" (PCA Historical Center: www.pcanet.org/history/documents/shepherd/justification.html).

As a correction to Robbin's understanding of the seminary dispute, Cornelius Van Til stood "outside the loop." Based on my conversations with Van Til, he was not fully apprised of Shepherd's theology until late in the history of the debate – at a time when old age deprived Van Til of his characteristic acumen and balanced judgment. (What we see on the part of certain faculty members is the exploitation of Van Til's good name for deviant, misleading purposes.) See Robbin's account in *A Companion to The Current*

*Justification Controversy;* an abbreviated version appears in *The Trinity Review* 222 (July/August 2003). That there is no compatibility between the covenant theology of Van Til and Shepherd is made abundantly clear in Van Til's many writings. (See my *Covenant Theology in Reformed Perspective.*)

5 This paper was read at the 2001 national meeting of the Evangelical Theological Society in Colorado Springs, Colorado. Some supporters of Gaffin say that he is (substantively) different from Shepherd. Where does Gaffin say that? This is mere wishful thinking – the evidence proves otherwise. Westminster Seminary remains resolute and unflinching in its position (see the "Addendum" below). Westminster Seminary in California, like Mid-America Reformed Seminary, remains divided over the Shepherd theology.

6 Originally "Covenant and Imputation: The Federal System of Doctrine" was presented at the Eastern regional meeting of the ETS in Lancaster, Pennsylvania (April 4, 2003).

7 In his glowing endorsement of Piper's book, Gaffin regards this study as providing "what is most urgently needed in the face of this charge [against Protestant doctrine]: a clear and convincing *exegetical* case for the gospel truth affirmed in its title. The broader church is deeply indebted to John Piper for what it has been given to him to produce in the midst of the already overly full demands of a busy pastorate" (*Counted Righteous in Christ: Should We Abandon the Imputation of Christ's Righteousness?* [Wheaton, IL: Crossway Books, 2002] iv). Gaffin has also given hearty endorsement to Shepherd's *The Call of Grace*. Yet another popular treatment of this theology is found in T. M. Moore, *I Will be Your God: How God's Covenant Enriches Our Lives* (Phillipsburg: Presbyterian and Reformed, 2002). Reformed educator Luder Whitlock finds this study to be "a most engaging and insightful explanation of the covenant" (back cover). Let's be clear on this: Piper's theology has no place for the classic Protestant law/gospel antithesis. It is simply not to be found in his thinking.

8 The final composition of this published essay may well have prompted Trumper's resignation from the faculty. Whose article is

it? Who all collaborated in its writing? For more reasons than one, we need to hear from Trumper himself – certainly by way of further examination of views published under his name.

[9] Ph.D. dissertation, University of Edinburgh, 2001. Trumper's command of language and the style of writing here are inferior to what appears in his 2002 *WTJ* article. This circumstance gives further credence to the supposition that Gaffin had a direct hand in the final composition of the article.

[10] *Ibid.* 35. For a reading of Barth that is itself representative of the thinking of many evangelicals today, see R. Albert Mohler, "Evangelical Theology and Karl Barth: Representative Models of Response" (Ph.D. dissertation, Southern Baptist Theological Seminary, 1989).

[11] "Historical Study of the Doctrine of Adoption" 459.

[12] *Ibid.* 471.

[13] *Ibid.* 472.

[14] Given developments within the immediate seminary confines – one marked by contention and acrimony – and within the wider ecclesiastical arena, Trumper resigned from the faculty during the academic year 2002, in order to return to his native Wales. (Allegations of moral indiscretion have been made within the seminary against Trumper. After four communications President Samuel Logan has informed me that the seminary had promised Trumper not to divulge publicly the reasons for his resignation. This broken promise has now created a legal liability for the seminary.) Trumper's colleague on the Dallas campus, systematician David McWilliams, has likewise resigned. (He is returning to his former pastoral in Lakeland, Florida.) Whatever differences there may be in the theology of Trumper and McWilliams, their departure appears to have been prompted – at least in part – by theological considerations, favorable or unfavorable to the Shepherd-Gaffin theology. This reading is based upon personal conversations with both individuals. Turmoil and upheaval have plagued Westminster

Seminary ever since the days of the Shepherd controversy. Logan's leadership has proven disastrous. He has tried his level best to silence the opposition (of which I am the leading voice). The criticisms will not go away. Westminster Seminary must take responsibility for her actions. Her theology and conduct are subject to public scrutiny.

## ADDENDUM

Timothy J. R. Trumper in "Westminster Systematics: Yesterday, Today, and Tomorrow," appearing in *The Bulletin of Westminster Theological Seminary* 42/1 (Winter 2002), defends the new direction taken by the current seminary faculty, particularly those working in the Department of Systematics. He attempts to answer Westminster's critics by identifying a "paradigm shift" established by John Murray in the earliest days of the seminary through his application of insights drawn from Geerhardus Vos' work in the field of biblical theology. (By way of historical note, Vos died in relative obscurity, though he stands in the Reformed tradition as one of the great theological giants of the twentieth-century.) Richard Gaffin's subsequent work at Westminster in biblico-theological exegesis and interpretation, notes Trumper, calls into question two characteristics of traditional Reformed exposition: (1) the dogma concerning "the centrality of *ordo salutis* in Paul's thought," and (2) "the impression, created by [the traditional dogmatic] model, that the constituent elements in the application of salvation are different phases linked together sequentially as in a chain." These new (more accurately, borrowed) insights and modifications in theological formulation on the part of the Westminster systematicians, observes Trumper,

> coincided with the lessons emerging from an ongoing renaissance in Calvin studies. The findings of Calvin scholarship have demonstrated that the Murray/Gaffin emphases on redemptive history and union with Christ, far from indicating a departure from the Reformed tradition, were anticipated by its theologian par excellence. This reflection of Calvin's approach has laid the basis for a mediating stance vis-a-vis the "Calvin versus the Calvinists" debate. As constructive Calvinists, Mur-ray, Gaffin, and their disciples have maintained the orthodox Calvinistic claim that the theology of the Westminster Confes-sion of Faith (WCF) is continuous with Calvin, but question aspects of its form (contrary to the Calvinistic revisionist position of Barth and the Torrances). Accordingly, systematics at Westminster encourages students to study both Scripture and the Westminster Standards, but, in doing so, to read the WCF through Scrip-

ture and not simply, as has to often been the case in orthodox Calvinism, the Scripture through the WCF.

By way of rejoinder, Trumper is entirely mistaken in labeling the Barth-Torrance school as Calvinistic. Revisionist, yes. Calvinistic, no. Cornelius Van Til, Westminster's leading apologist and defender of historic Reformed orthodoxy, cogently argued that Barthianism and Christianity give expression to two entirely different theologies, two different religions. Barthianism is properly portrayed as one more variation of Modernism, what had become dominant in twentieth-century theology. (At the beginning of the twenty-first century, the new form is Post-Modernism.) The "ongoing renaissance in Calvin studies," of which Trumper speaks, is sharply divided between two camps, the Reformed and the revisionist. Regrettably, the Westminster faculty is caught up in the mix of these two. From the standpoint of the history of covenant theology, Gaffin and his colleagues are of the opinion that the Van Til-Kline-Karlberg school is simply too dogmatic in its posture (and too obscurantist). They conclude that the Reformed apologetico-theological critiques of divergent systems of thought are, in the hands of such representatives, drawn too sharply, too simplistically, too black and white – with no allowance for the gray areas (so they read, for example, Van Til's *Christianity and Barthianism*). Needless to say, Westminster now finds itself in very good company with modern-day "evangelicalism" on such matters.

Another grievous error surfacing in Trumper's theology is his return to the old form/content dichotomy, one that always ends up muddying the waters and inhibiting clear-headed, theological analysis. Does Trumper really think that modifying the form (the structure) of the theological system does not jeopardize content (the substance)? In the current theological dispute centering upon the work of Norman Shepherd and Richard Gaffin, does repudiation of the twofold doctrine of the covenants – the structure underlying the history of redemptive revelation, defined in terms of the Covenant of Works and the Covenant of Grace – not effect doctrinal interpretation? Can we concede with Trumper that modification of the one does not impact the other? Can we properly conclude that the doctrine of union with Christ as espoused by Gaffin and Trumper –

wherein the logical and/or temporal sequence in the *ordo salutis* is dissolved, leaving a homogenized "already/not yet" event-complex respecting both the accomplishment and the application of redemption – is faithful to Calvin's teaching and to Scripture?

It is curious that the only objection Trumper raises against Herman Ridderbos' seminal work (which he praises) is that it fails to take up the subject of missions as a vital aspect of Paul's theology of grace. This leaves in question a number of doctrines in Ridderbos' exposition previously viewed as matters of concern (compare Gaffin's earlier critique of Ridderbos' *Paul* in "Paul as Theologian: A Review Article," in *The Westminster Theological Journal* 30[1968] 204-232). In brief, the link drawn by Trumper between Murray and Gaffin is false and deceptive. Doubtless, many would be helped in their study of the doctrines of the covenants, justification, and election (*vis a vis* Westminster's repudiation of traditional Reformed teaching) by reading some of the many papers and critiques of Shepherd's theology that have been written, notably during the days of the controversy on Westminster's campus prior to Shepherd's dismissal from the faculty. The problem is that virtually all of these documents are not readily accessible. Added to this is the fact that the administration will not freely furnish material upon request – not without close scrutiny, and certainly not to those who have not proven themselves sympathetic to the position taken by the seminary faculty. (Westminster's library archives house much pertinent material, including Raymond Dillard's personal file relating to this dispute.) Perhaps the best summary review of the debate – including an account of the involvement of numerous pastors and scholars from different parts of the country and the world – is found in O. Palmer Robertson, *The Current Justification Controversy* (St. Louis, 1983; Unicoi, TN: The Trinity Foundation, 2003).

A second development – or forage – of the Westminster faculty is in the area of biblical hermeneutics, including the issue of "authorial diversity" in the canons of the Old and New Testaments. Trumper comments:

> We acknowledge that both redemptive history and authorial diversity complicate doctrinal synthesis. Yet the system, namely

> the coherence of the oneness of God, Scripture, and the gospel, is not in doubt. It is precisely our confidence that there is this oneness that underlies our efforts to bring out of Scripture the doctrinal interconnectedness it contains. Because we are both sympathetic and critical (in that order!) *vis a vis* the Westminster tradition, we refuse to follow the scholastic imposition on Scripture of an alien logical tightness that led many over the centuries to turn away from the theology of the WCF. Therefore, in defending the content of Westminster theology, our systematics seeks belatedly to recast its form. We recognize that an apologetic for Westminster Calvinism that merely replicates the form is inadequate to recapture for our community the atmosphere of Scripture [in terms of the "humanness" of the biblical writings and the redemptive-historical cast of the biblical message]. Nor can it effectively safeguard Scriptural content from rejection by those either within or outside the Westminster tradition. That is why we teach the system in the way that we do.

This opens up another wide range of questions and issues lurking beneath the surface. What needs to be pointed out here is the fact that traditional Reformed dogmatics is, once again, castigated for introducing "an alien logical tightness" into its formulation of the doctrine of Scripture. Trumper tells his readers that this propensity for logical schematization and coherence – what is characteristic of Protestant orthodox scholasticism as a whole – has driven many away from Calvin. (With respect to the doctrine of Scripture Calvin the humanist is placed in tension with the orthodox scholastic Calvinists, that is, biblical humanists versus "wooden" inerrantists and harmonizers.) The New Westminster school forces us to answer the twofold question: Who are the legitimate heirs of Calvin? And more importantly, who are the faithful interpreters of Scripture? What is at stake in this controversy is the faith of our fathers.

# Chapter 1

# Opposing Systems of Doctrine: An Overview

Reformed theology is a system of doctrine reflecting the system of doctrine contained in Scripture, Old and New Testaments. Among the several Protestant formulations of biblical teaching, Reformed theology offers the most consistent restatement of doctrine. Historically speaking, what distinguishes this brand of theology from others is the interplay between two interpretative approaches, the biblical-theological and the dogmatic (the systematic, confessional strand). Throughout the history of God's covenants with humankind, from the creation of the world to the establishment of the new covenant (and the close of the NT canon), God has revealed himself by means of special, verbal revelation – alongside general revelation, which always and everywhere bears witness to God as Creator and sovereign Lord. Scripture is not only a historical document; it is the uniquely authoritative, inerrant, written revelation of God's saving purpose. History and theology are inextricably bound together in the Bible. What, more precisely, is meant by the theological term "system?" Is the notion of "system" alien to the biblical text, or is it reflective of the unity and comprehensiveness of its teaching as the Word of God? What is the relationship between the history of God's acts in redemption and inscripturated revelation (what is the divine interpretation of God's acts in history)? The Reformed answer to these questions, as already indicated, lies in the interplay between two, vital theological approaches to biblical interpretation, biblical theology and systematics. Exegesis is informed by both of these hermeneutical methodologies. (Biblical theology focuses upon the historical and progressive unfolding of redemptive revelation.) Elsewhere I have discussed this subject in some detail.[1]

The purpose of the opening chapter of this book is not to traverse that same ground, but rather to summarize biblical teaching with respect to the subject of the relationship between the two Testaments (and the relationship between the Law and the Gospel) and leading challenges to the Reformed system of doctrine within the conservative Reformed camp. With respect to that doctrine which serves as the lynchpin of Christian orthodoxy, namely, justification by faith alone (*sola fide*), there are four principal contestants in the history of theological interpretation. They are: (1) Arminianism, (2) antinomianism, (3) neonomianism, and (4) Barthianism (or neoorthodoxy). Included among these four, broadly speaking, are the teachings of classic dispensationalism,[2] theonomy (or Christian Reconstructionism), and the New Perspective on Paul and the law. The lines between these four systems of doctrinal interpretation are not rigid; there is significant overlap and mingling of theological elements among these various schools of thought. What they share in common is objection to the Reformation doctrine of justification by grace (apart from the works of the law), as that relates to the entire epoch of redemption from the Fall to the Consummation – what pertains to the continuity of God's saving purpose in the history of salvation. Central to these several, diverse formulations is the interpretation of the covenants of God in the Bible and the revelation of God's justifying grace in redemptive history. The first section of this chapter summarizes the teaching of classic Reformed theology; the second looks at deviations from historic Reformed teaching.

## 1. The Story of Redemption

The contemporary approach to biblical interpretation known as "narrative theology" attempts to recapture the historical component of the ongoing revelation of God's story of redemption in the Scriptures. For centuries the system of Christian doctrine has been formulated in accordance with the scholastic (*loci*) method, what is called the "commonplaces" of doctrine, such as the doctrine of God (theology proper), humanity before and after the Fall (anthropology/harmatology), Christ (christology), the Holy Spirit (pneumatology), and the church (ecclesiology). This body of teaching restates the doctrinal content of the Bible in its essential unity, sometimes at the expense of historical diversity. The degree to which scholastic theology recalls the history of redemption varies among individual dogmaticians, and from one theological tradition to another, from one period in the history of Christian interpretation to another. Reformed theology is distinguished by its effort to delineate the truth of Scripture explicitly in terms of the progressive, unfolding history of God's covenants.

Adam's creation in the image of God brought him immediately into a covenant relationship with the Lord God, Creator and sovereign Lord. Prior to Adam's appearance on the scene, the angels were brought into existence as personal, intelligent creatures – created in covenant relationship with God. They were made perfect in righteousness, holiness, and knowledge, yet capable of willful transgression. Initially, the angelic host was placed on probation. Depending on the outcome of that test in heaven, a test requiring full and uncompromising submission to the will of God, the obedient angels would stand in the integrity of their proven righteousness, whereas Lucifer, the Prince of Darkness, and his legion of disobedient angels would become castaways. Being created a little lower than the (good) angels, now confirmed in righteousness through their successful completion of probation, Adam was also placed on probation, with the happy prospect of confirmation in righteousness upon his faithful covenant-keeping. With respect to these two probationary tests at the opening of the history (angelic and human), what distinguishes the covenant relationship between the Adam and his Creator is the principle of federal representation. Adam was constituted representative head of the entire race of earthlings.

Whenever we have a situation of probation, the covenant is one of works, not grace. The covenant is what Reformed theology has accurately labeled a "covenant of works". Indeed, the term "grace" is not applicable to the created, earthly order in its original state of perfection and beauty. At this initial point, sin had not yet entered the earthly scene; there was no blemish or deformation in the world of humanity. "Grace" only and always contemplates human demerit. Grace is the undeserved favor of God to sinners.[3] (In the eternal wisdom and purpose of God saving grace was not extended to fallen angels.) Adam's "one act of righteousness" had in view his compliance with the (legal) demand of the covenant, highlighted in the prohibition against eating from the tree of the knowledge of good and evil. Adam was to guard the sanctity of the Garden against the encroachments of the Serpent. What was holy ground had become unholy through the transgression of Adam and his helpmeet, Eve. The head of the human race had succumbed to the wiles of the Devil, and immediately tasted death for all (spiritual separation from God). In his great mercy and love God acted to save Adam and the seed of the woman belonging to Christ, outwardly manifested in the bestowal of clothing to cover the physical nakedness of Adam and Eve. God's promise of salvation followed immediately upon the heels of Adam's disobedience; it marks the beginning of the Covenant of Grace, extending from the fall of Adam to the consummation of history. The divine act of clothing anticipates the sacrifice of God's only-begotten Son. From this point onwards, the justification of the ungodly is grounded exclusively upon the meritorious obedience of Jesus Christ, the Second Adam, who would fulfill all righteousness – even to the point of death on a cross. It is this "one act of righteousness," the alien righteousness of Christ, that is imputed to all who believe (before and after Christ's coming into the world to make full and final atonement for sin). Justification is by grace through faith, apart from the meritorious works of the law (what was required under the first Covenant of Works). Adam's confirmation in righteousness would have brought closure to his time of probation. That now has been secured through the work of Christ. Deliverance from the curse of the law would be accomplished (once-for-all) in the fullness of time by Christ's completion of the probationary task assigned to him in the Counsel of Redemption, that eternal pact between the three Persons of the Godhead before time began. This mission of God's Anointed One, Jesus Christ, and its successful completion is recorded in the four Gospels – Matthew, Mark, Luke, and John.

The effects of the Fall were twofold, legal and moral. Firstly, all humanity stands guilty before God by virtue of Adam's representative sin. Secondly, human nature has become depraved, a condition preventing any individual human being from pleasing God, or even desiring to please him. Except by the grace of God, each and every sinner would remain in his/her state of guilt and disobedience. Redemption becomes an actuality, not a possibility, through the atoning sacrifice of the Son of God on behalf of the sins of the people (the true seed of Christ, the elect of God). There is no salvation apart from the shed blood of Christ. The redemption of the elect prior to the coming of Christ into the world is experienced in anticipation of the future death and resurrection of Israel's Messiah. Before the establishment of the old covenant under Moses, which came in glory, the promise of redemption was already realized in the lives of the saints who preceded him. Abraham, the father of all the faithful, enjoyed seeing Christ, even as had those numbered among the godly reaching back to the time of Adam and Eve's expulsion from the Garden. The spiritual seed of the woman had been guaranteed by the promise of God, whereas the seed of the Serpent had merely been granted an extension of life – and limited worldly dominion – prior to the final Day of Judgment. In the case of humankind, the postponement of physical death was itself a manifestation of God's bestowal of common grace upon all creatures of the dust. Those who enter into the fullness of life in Christ are the beneficiaries of God's special, saving grace. In the terms used by the apostle Paul, Adam was created a "natural body," the redeemed of the Lord are created a "spiritual (glorified) body," fully realized at the end of the age. The present, eschatological life in Christ is merely the initial down-payment of what is to come.

Eschatology is the study of things to come. The beginning of this study takes place in the paradisal Garden of Eden. Humanity's creation in the image of God bears a decidedly eschatological orientation; it looks forward to God's Sabbath-blessing of consummation and glorification. Prior to that Day, Adam and his race were given a specific task to perform, the subjugation of all things under the rule and reign of God the King in the faithful exercise and stewardship of humanity's gifts and earth's resources.

But before that could be realized in eschatological fullness, Adam had first to pass the test of probation, as discussed above. Failure to keep covenant with God would have meant the termination of all life and blessing, consignment under God's eternal wrath and displeasure. The introduction of common grace into the world provided an extension to human life, making possible the gradual differentiation between the elect and the reprobate across the span of human history leading up to the end of the age, the Second Coming. The original cultural mandate has now been modified to suit the contours of a fallen world. Humankind would now labor under harsh and unpleasant circumstances, in the context of a recalcitrant earth prepared to receive bodies of death and corruption, the wages of sin. The culture of this world – what is the collaborative effort of the godly and the ungodly – is sustained by God's common grace until the close of history, at which time all cultural monuments and accomplishments will cease to endure. The inauguration of the new heavens and earth comes about solely by means of God's supernatural, cataclysmic intervention at the return of Christ. No human hands contribute to the building of this consummate House of God. Such is the plan and wisdom of God in the order of things ordained in eternity past. The "sanctified culture" of the saints of God across the millennia of history will be ushered into the eternal kingdom of the Lamb. What, then, is the enduring culture? It is nothing else than the sanctified people of God, distilled through the vicissitudes and passage of time by means of God's redemptive grace and special providence. She is the Bride prepared and adorned to meet her Bridegroom. These gathered saints are also described as the Temple of God, the place where the Spirit abides eternally. These are just some of the rich metaphors descriptive of the New Man, the body of Christ, the glorified saints.

In OT times, God, who is patient and longsuffering, was preparing the way for the coming of the Savior of the world. In the "world that then was" (the period from the Fall to the Deluge) the word of the Lord came through prophets like Noah, men who "walked with God" as recipients of God's special revelation. The covenant with Noah before the great flood was typological of the covenant established in Christ (what is the final installment of the Covenant of Grace). The ark itself was symbolic of Jesus Christ, savior from the everlasting flood of destruction. (The covenant established with Noah and all humanity after the flood was of a very different order from the predeluvian covenant. Here the grace extended to humankind was common, not special or saving. God promised to preserve the world as humanity's temporal habitat until the dissolution of the earth by fire at the close of the age.) This presently is the "world that now is" – the period from the Flood to the Second Coming.

God's grand program of redemption makes its most visible expression in early redemptive history in the election of Abraham, the father of a multitude of nations called into the spiritual kingdom of life and light. The covenant between God and Abraham is twofold in signification: (1) there is the promise of God to satisfy divine justice on behalf of sinners by means of the sacrifice God himself would provide; and (2) there is the institution of circumcision, sign and seal of the Covenant of Grace, the outward means of the administration of God's kingdom on earth. The Abrahamic promise includes the grant of land in Canaan. Under the old economy of redemption the land of Palestine serves as the temporal, typical form of the eternal, heavenly kingdom of God. After the time of bondage, the Israelites are brought out of Egypt by God's strong arm. This signal event of redemption in OT times also serves a symbolico-typological purpose in the history of God's covenants. "Out of Egypt have I called by people," declares the Lord. Israel's national experience is anticipatory of the everlasting deliverance to be wrought by the coming Messiah. The drama of redemption in the former days of the old, Mosaic economy takes on a peculiar cast: The people of Israel embody the purpose and plan of God yet to be realized in the fullness of times. As "servant of the Lord" Israel is representative of the true and final Servant of the Lord, Jesus Christ. Rightly interpreted, the Old Testament is thoroughly typological (that is, christological).[4] The teachings of the Law and the Prophets concern Christ, both his person and his work. Lastly, by way of summation, the period of time between Moses and Christ serves as a parenthesis in the historical unfolding of the Covenant of Grace.

With the giving of the law Israel was constituted a nation of priests and kings. Canaan became the new Eden, the sanctuary of God, the holy place where the Lord of heaven would reveal himself. He would reside in the midst of his chosen people. The nation of Israel was a theocracy similar to the first theocracy established at creation with the royal family of Adam. The entrance of sin into the world necessitated the establishment of the state as an institution bearing arms for the purpose of the safety and welfare of the citizens of the world and for the maintenance of justice in her midst. (The state is a manifestation of God's common grace.) Among the nations of the world Israel was signaled out as God's elect son, typically speaking, not because she was better or stronger than other nations, but solely because of God's grace. It was wholly a matter of undeserved favor. To be sure, this election of corporate Israel as a people is distinct from individual election unto salvation. Here we are obliged to distinguish between corporate, national election, on the one hand, and individual, decretive election, on the other.

What is most characteristic in the covenant mediated by Moses is the introduction of the works-inheritance principle on the earthly, physical level. Once resident in Canaan, theocratic Israel would prosper on grounds of her own compliance with the law of God. The principle of blessing in the land is that of works, not grace (hence, the vital and essential Reformed-Protestant distinction between the "Law" and the "Gospel," between "works" and "faith"). Under the Mosaic administration of the Covenant of Grace the law-principle is added to the Abrahamic promise. The question arises: Does the law of Moses jeopardize the promise previously granted to Abraham and his seed? Not at all, since the principle of works-inheritance pertains exclusively to temporal life and prosperity in the land of Canaan. The giving of the law, like so much in the old economy, is typological. With respect to its pedagogical purpose (the so-called "second use" of the law of God) the Mosaic law points sinners to Christ for salvation. Only Christ can satisfy the legal demand associated with the first Covenant of Works in the Garden of Eden, which covenant is reinstated in the Mosaic economy (with necessary modification suited to the post-Fall epoch and to God's revelation and plan of redemption in the period leading up to the appearance of Christ, born of a woman, born under the law).[5]

Christ's advent has been variously described as the "climax of the covenants," the "midpoint" of salvation-history.[6] What is of chief importance in our present survey of the biblical story is that the coming of Christ ushers in a glorious new age, one that is marked by the institution of the new covenant in the period between the two advents (what is termed the semi-eschatological age of the Spirit). The epistles of the New Testament explicate the theological ramifications and ethical implications of this great eschatological event. (Paul's letter to the Romans is the fullest exposition of the Gospel.[7]) The New Testament canon closes with John's Apocalypse, the visionary description of the interadventual period leading up to the consummation of history. In a breathtaking, panoramic view of the end times the apostle John employs the rich and diverse imagery and symbolism of Old Testament revelation, chiefly in terms of Temple-worship. The reader is given to understand the heavenly context of the present, spiritual warfare on earth. The battle is ultimately between heavenly powers, principles, and principalities (compare Paul's teaching in Eph 6). The suffering of the saints is one that bears the marks of Christ's suffering. While Christ's life of obedience ("active" and "passive") – what is the fulfillment of all righteousness in accordance with the law of God and the penal sanctions for covenant-transgression for the sake of God's elect – makes full atonement for sin and achieves the complete reconciliation between God and sinners, the sufferings and the testimony of the sanctified saints, those who keep covenant with God by grace through faith, witness to the sufferings of Christ and the gospel of a life lived under the cross. (The suffering of the saints is the suffering of Christ, now transcendent in Glory and interceding on behalf of God's elect. Christ's death on the cross, apart from the sufferings of the saints, has made full satisfaction for sin. See Col 1.) John's Apocalypse prophetically records the final vindication of the saints of God at the Eschaton, when sin and suffering are removed altogether.

## 2. Theological Controversy:
### Representative points of view

The biblical narrative conveys historical and theological significance. Indeed, the two strands cannot be divorced from one another. Redemptive revelation includes both the record of God's acts in history and his own interpretation of those acts – hence the importance of the two theological disciplines, biblical theology (the history of special revelation) and dogmatics (the collection of affirmations/summations/restatements of the faith once-for-all delivered to the saints). Confessional summaries of the Christian faith are extensions of the pattern of truth already enunciated in the pages of Scripture. The creeds and confessions are more or less faithful to the Word of God. (As secondary norms of faith and practice, the confessional documents are not free from error. They require clarification and reformulation that only comes with time and ongoing reflection – including contention for the faith.[8] The primary norm is the inerrant, uniquely authoritative, written revelation of God contained in the Old and New Testaments. We must not elevate the confessional norms, as important as they are, to scriptural status.) We proclaim God's truth in accordance with his own Word, which is self-interpreting.

To be sure, the Bible does not provide the church a systematic handbook in the manner of scholastic theology (via the *loci* method). The very question whether or not the Bible contains a "system" of doctrine continues to perplex many Christian interpreters. Some prefer to accent the biblical story and its accompanying imagery (oftentimes at the expense of systematic exposition, which is increasingly questioned by a host of contemporary theologians[9]). The debate is surely one of interpretation at its most basic level. What does the Bible teach concerning itself, God, humanity, as well as many other subjects? How do we "access" this teaching? What is the proper method of biblical interpretation? How do we exegete the text of Scripture?[10] Despite all disclaimers, every interpreter does employ a "system" of doctrine that shapes his/her exegesis of the Bible. Some systems are more comprehensive, coherent, and consistent than others. All Christian interpretation, however, is subject to ongoing analysis and refinement – and so will remain until the Eschaton. Furthermore, each interpreter stands within a particular ecclesiastical and theological tradition. No one works in isolation from a specific branch of Christianity, however "free-thinking" one presumes to be. Every interpreter of the Bible labors from a specific historical, cultural, and philosophico-theological context. The question is: Which "system" is more faithful to the teaching of Scripture? How can one be certain of the truths of Scripture? Simply put: It is the Spirit of God who works illumination and conviction of the Word. The believer's apprehension of divine truth is God's work.

Given the summary of the biblical story provided above, our attention is now directed to several critical doctrines in the interpretation of the Bible, doctrines essential to the system of teaching set forth in the Bible. Whether we consider the history of redemptive revelation (what is domain of biblical theology) or the totality of divine revelation, general and special (what is the domain of systematic theology), the covenants of God are highly prominent in the biblical text. Significantly, the doctrine of the covenants – in its many and varied formulations – has become a commonplace in virtually every school of contemporary theology, evangelical or modernist. What chiefly separates one school of thought from another, however, is adherence to the historic, orthodox Protestant teaching concerning the "Law" and the "Gospel." Other related doctrines in dispute include divine sovereignty and human free will (soteriology), the eschatological design of creation (protology), and the nature and extent of the atonement (christology). The doctrinal differences between the various schools of biblical interpretation are systemic; they concern the foundations of a given theological system.[11] Central to the current debate among conservative biblical interpreters is the doctrine of justification by faith alone (*sola fide*), including the apostle Paul's understanding of the Mosaic law.[12]

Viewing the discussion as a whole, one can be easily overwhelmed by the different shades of meaning and the many nuances of thought. What concerns us is the major cleavage within the "Reformed" tradition (broadly speaking) between orthodox and neoorthodox interpretation. The modern-day debate centers upon the classic Protestant antithesis between the Law and the Gospel. Does the Bible provide warrant for the theological contrast between two ways or means of justification, one by works (legal obedience) and the other by grace (specifically, one that necessitates the imputation of Christ's "alien" righteousness for justification of sinners before a holy God)? Among the confessional documents of the Protestant Reformation of the sixteenth and seventeenth centuries, a general consensus of teaching is found concerning the doctrine of justification by faith. Critical elements in the Calvinistic formulation of this doctrine include the twofold covenants (the Covenant of Works and the Covenant of Grace), probation, and imputation.[13]

On the one hand, does God ever relate to his image-bearer(s) in terms of legal obedience? Does Scripture teach that the works of the law are the (legal) grounds for the creature's justification/vindication? Does God reward servants of the covenant (the sons of God) with blessing and life, contingent upon full and perfect obedience to the law of God at the close of probationary testing? (The implementation of the principle of works-inheritance is restricted to the time of probation. According to Reformed theology, the eschatological design of creation is incompatible with an indefinite period of contingency for those created in the image of God[14]). Or, on the other hand, are all God's blessings bestowed as gifts of free, unmerited grace? Is the very notion of "meritorious reward" foreign to the theology of the Bible? Is Christ's life of vicarious obedience the exclusive meritorious ground of salvation for sinners or merely the exemplary model for Christian imitation and discipleship? Study of the history of Reformed doctrine indicates that the scholastic federalists were neither clear nor consistent in their formulations concerning the reward granted to covenant-keepers in the initial order of creation.[15] Some of these difficulties in theological exposition relate to doctrines lying at the very heart of the Gospel, including the doctrines of election, covenant, and justification.

The dilemma posed by these questions can best be illustrated in the otherwise fine summary of Reformed teaching provided by Louis Hodges in his book *Reformed Theology Today*. The author claims that early covenant theology, imbibing contractual notions of covenant widespread in the socio-political age of the sixteenth and seventeenth centuries, manifested "a legalistic strain as men attempted to fulfill the conditions in order to receive God's grace."[16] The notion of the "Covenant of Works," contends Hodges, "seriously overlooks its gracious character." He explains: "God always deals with man in grace, giving what He requires; man never earns God's favor."[17] Regarding the Mosaic covenant, Hodges speaks of "the essential graciousness of the Law with its various imperatives. . . . The obedience mandated was not a covenant of works whereby men could earn salvation by works; rather it was a manifestation of faith in the promise."[18] In dispensational fashion Hodges erroneously reasons that the new covenant is new (and better) due to the empowering work of the Holy Spirit now operative in the hearts of new covenant believers. "[T]he inability of man to fulfill the obligations of the old covenant is answered by the transforming work of the Spirit in the heart of the believer by which he is enabled to obey the commands of God. The legal content (torah) expressing God's requirements is now internalized so that obedience can be offered from the heart."[19]

Hodges' objection to the notion of meritorious reward also leads him to express reservation concerning the Reformed doctrine of the Covenant of Redemption, preferring to speak of "the inter-trinitarian economy of salvation," terminology that "emphasiz[es] the sovereign grace behind Christ's coming rather than a contractual obligation."[20] At the same time Hodges upholds the active obedience of Christ which "won that right [to eternal life] for His people. . . . Thus the righteousness of Christ and the reward earned by His obedience are imputed to His people." He further explains that Christ had "also fulfilled the demands of the Law of God, suffering the penalty and paying the debt owed by His people."[21] Hodges offers these additional comments:

> The atonement, therefore, means that a salvation is provided in which man's penalty is paid in full and a life of perfect obedience to God's Law is put to his account.[22]
>
> Justification is accordingly a judicial act (or declarative act) of God whereby He declares that by virtue of the imputed righteousness of Christ, all the demands of the Law upon a particular sinner are satisfied. By this act the one joined with Christ has the full forgiveness of sin (past, present, future) and is judged not on the basis of his own life, but upon the perfect life of Jesus Christ. Since the final verdict has been passed concerning the believer's acquittal, and God will not reverse His decision, the doctrine affords to the Christian the strongest possible comfort and assurance.[23]
>
> Man's standing before God's Law is not a matter of "legal fiction" but one of the most sober realities in Scripture. The doctrines of sin, the atonement, and subjective soteriology presuppose the reality and importance of man's legal standing.[24]

We ask: What are these demands of the "Law" requiring full and perfect obedience? What in Hodges' thinking is meant by a "legal" standing before God (as opposed to gracious)? On the one hand, Hodges clearly affirms the traditional Protestant "Law"/"Gospel" antithesis; on the other, his rejection of the merit concept with regard to the original Covenant of Works jeopardizes the biblical doctrine of atonement and reconciliation based on the imputation of Christ's righteousness to sinners saved by grace alone. Critical in this discussion is Paul's teaching on the two Adams in the fifth chapter of Romans. What is required – not optional – is consistency of thought and expression.

Equally problematic are the theological formulations of John Murray on justification and the covenants.[25] Crucial to the modern-day controversy is the exegesis of one of the principle OT texts, Leviticus 18:5. There is little room here for debate over whether or not the apostle Paul contrasts – as antithetical principles of inheritance – grace and law, faith and works. Throughout Scripture, Leviticus 18:5 is summoned as evidence of the works-principle. Murray is quite alert to the importance of the fundamental contrast between these two principles of inheritance. So much so, that while arguing that Leviticus 18:5 in its original context enunciates (in his opinion) the faith-principle – what Paul calls "the obedience of faith" – Murray finds himself obliged to conclude that Paul extracts this principle of obedience from its gracious context. Murray ends up speaking of "law in general," the bare principle of law, or law in abstraction. Though there is some precedence for Murray's exegetical interpretation of this OT text in the Puritan-Reformed tradition, this reading is strained and unnatural. Mainstream Reformed theology teaches otherwise.[26]

A variation of Murray's line of argument is found in Clarence Stam, *The Covenant of Love: Exploring Our Relationship with God*, a popular treatment of the brand of covenant theology that is rapidly gaining ground in Reformed circles today. Stam begins by observing: "The Bible tells us that the covenant is a matter of God's great love.

He is not obligated to enter into a relationship with us. But he has done so from the time of creation."[27] Already we are off on a misleading foot in tracing out God's covenant purposes in history. Could God have chosen not to enter into covenant with Adam as image-bearer of God? Stam adopts the wholly speculative and erroneous notion which views God's covenant with Adam as an act of divine condescension – over and above what is seen to be a prior, natural order at creation. Here the covenant relationship is understood as an added, higher blessing – grace is viewed as superimposed upon nature (what the medieval scholastics identified as the *donum superadditum*, the supernatural gift of grace). What needs to be clearly acknowledged is the fact that Adam was constituted the federal (covenant) head of all humankind right at the outset of creation. He was placed on probation, enjoying the future prospect of confirmation in righteousness and (eventual) glorification at the consummation of history on grounds of perfect, personal obedience. We are mistaken in contemplating Adam as standing in an initial, noncovenantal state of nature. To do so is pure speculation, pure abstraction. Such theologizing is foreign to Scripture.

The tendency in recent formulations of the covenants between God and his people over the course of biblical history (beginning at creation), is to dissolve or nullify the discontinuity plainly taught in Scripture. Stam defines covenant generically in terms of God's covenant faithfulness and promise. He writes:

> The people of Israel could count on God's covenant faithfulness. This was not an automatic guarantee which did away with the requirement of Israel's positive response. But the point is again that this faithfulness rests not upon human actions but on God's own promise.[28]

Stam has in view God's covenant-making with humankind, whether before or after the Fall. He emphasizes continuity among all the divine covenants throughout all ages of biblical history. What, more precisely, is the nature of God's covenant promise? Stam explains:

> The covenant is not a temporary arrangement; it is everlasting. . . . The covenant is made to last by God's power and through his faithfulness. It is everlasting because God is eternal. It remains, because God is faithful. It is remarkable how often and how clearly the Bible makes this assertion.[29]

The question here arises: Why did the first covenant, broken by Adam at creation, necessitate the making of a different covenant (traditionally called the "Covenant of Grace")? With regard to the peculiar covenant of law (the covenant established with Israel at Sinai through Moses as mediator), why did Israel's breaking of this particular covenant necessitate the making of the new and better covenant in Christ's blood?[30] Simply put, Stam denies the doctrine of the merit of Adam's righteousness, had Adam rendered full and perfect obedience to God in that first covenant in Eden. Stam reasons:

> The suggestion that man in paradise by perfect, personal obedience would merit eternal life is unsubstantiated and quite problematic. . . . Man's fall into sin is not a matter of his failing to do the required works; it is, rather, a matter of rebellion and unfaithfulness, a *breaking of the covenant* which God in his goodness had made with man.[31]

> In reality, things are much simpler. Placing Adam in paradise, the LORD did not put him on trial. . . . [God] pointed to the unmerited blessings of this covenant

> which Adam was already receiving: abundance and life.[32]

> [Adam] could not climb to greater heights than those on which he was already placed (Ps 8). Only by loving God would Adam's life be preserved, continued, and blessed.[33]

Setting aside the question regarding the appropriateness of the theological term "merit" for the moment – a term frequently misconceived and maligned – the weightier question is this: Was the reward of the covenant based upon Adam's successful completion of probation? Was it grounded upon his "one act" of obedience? Was it based upon his perfect, personal obedience? Denial of the essential Law/Gospel antithesis as taught in traditional Protestant-Reformed theology has immediate repercussions throughout the system of doctrine. Stam allows no room for the doctrine of probation, either in the case of the First or the Second Adam. Similarly, there is no explication of the biblical doctrine of imputation of sin or Christ's satisfaction of the righteous demands of God's covenant in his work of atonement and reconciliation. Lastly, Stam's interpretation inhibits a proper understanding of biblical eschatology. Contrary to his thinking, Adam at the outset did not yet enjoy the full blessings of eschatological life in covenant with God. There was to be movement from glory, to glory (fuller and richer).

Each of these representative authors – Louis Hodges, John Murray, and Clarence Stam – has failed to do justice to the biblical text to different degrees and with varying consequences for the system of Reformed doctrine. Least orthodox of these three is the view of Stam. We must recognize that there is not only progression in doctrine over the course of the history of the church, but there is also retrogression. The challenge before the Christian church today is to retrieve the truth of Scripture in its fullness, specifically, the truth of the Gospel of sovereign, electing grace – that is, *gospel grace*. Heresy is an ever-present danger. We are reminded of the words of Samuel John Stone in the one of the church's great hymns, "The Church's One Foundation":

> Though with a scornful wonder men see her sore opprest,
> By schisms rent asunder, by heresies distrest;
> Yet saints their watch are keeping, their cry goes up, "How long?"
> And soon the night of weeping shall be the morn of song.

## ENDNOTES

[1] See my discussion of the historical progress of Christian theology in "Doctrinal Development in Scripture and Tradition: A Reformed Assessment of the Church's Theological Task," *CTJ* 30 (1995) 401-418; republished in *Covenant Theology in Reformed Perspective: Collected Essays and Book Reviews in Historical, Biblical, and Systematic Theology* (Eugene,OR: Wipf and Stock, 2000) 341-355.

[2] I am restricting the term "dispensationalism" to its characteristic teaching, wherein the Mosaic law (the Sinaitic covenant) is seen as God's offer of salvation to the ancient Israelites on the meritorious basis of law-keeping. This test marks one specific dispensation among several dispensations spread across the history of redemption. (In its best formulation, dispensationalism contends that this offer of God is merely hypothetical, in light of the fact that no sinner can actually fulfill the requirement of perfect obedience.) The dispensational schematization of the history of redemption – considered as a whole – differs significantly from the teaching of Reformed covenant theology, notably in the former's interpretation of Israel and the church. It is this element of doctrine that stands as the critical divide in ongoing discussions between today's "progressive dispensationalists" and exponents of historic Reformed theology. See my "Israel and the Eschaton: A Review Article," *WTJ* 52 (1990) 117-130; republished in *Covenant Theology in Reformed Perspective* 309-323.

A semi-dispensational argument for the unique indwelling of the Holy Spirit among new covenant believers is presented by James M. Hamilton, Jr., in "God with Men in the Torah," *WTJ* 65 (2003) 113-133; and in "Old Testament Believers and the Indwelling Spirit: A Survey of the Spectrum of Opinion," *TrinJ* 24 NS (2003) 37-54. Hamilton's misreading of Scripture is based upon a defective christo-pneumatology, one which is at odds with traditional Reformed soteriology. Likewise, D. G. Hart, relying on the work of Sinclair Ferguson, abandons the Reformed position for the dispensational understanding of the varying role of the Holy Spirit in the application of redemption under the old and new covenant epochs. See his *Recovering Mother Kirk* (Grand Rapids: Baker, 2003) 96.

³ To introduce the notion of grace here in connection with the first order of creation is entirely without biblical justification. This misapplication of theological terminology has the potential of making havoc of the system of doctrine set forth in Scripture (what has proven to be the case in much of recent theological exposition). The Westminster divines, though guilty of this obfuscation, were nevertheless correct in identifying the twofold covenants, the Covenant of Works and the Covenant of Grace – what B. B. Warfield has identified as the "architectonic principle" of Reformed, biblico-dogmatic theology. (Teaching on the twofold covenants is a necessary extrapolation of the traditional Protestant Law/Gospel antithesis in the Reformed system of doctrine.)

⁴ See my essay "The Significance of Israel in Biblical Typology," *JETS* 31 (1988) 257-269; republished in *Covenant Theology in Reformed Perspective* 193-207.

⁵ In *Covenant Theology in Reformed Perspective* I have analyzed Reformed teaching concerning the Mosaic covenant from the standpoint of the history of doctrine, biblical theology, and systematics. Raymond B. Dillard and Tremper Longman III in *An Introduction to the Old Testament* (Grand Rapids: Zondervan, 1994) reduce the Law/Gospel relationship to one of tension, not opposition (contrary to the unanimous teaching of Protestant orthodoxy): "As much as theologians may seek to establish the priority of law over grace or grace over law, the book of Judges will not settle this question. What Judges gives the reader is not a systematic theology, but rather the history of a relationship. Judges leaves us with a paradox: God's relationship with Israel is at once both conditional and unconditional. He will not remove his favor, but Israel must live in obedience, and faith to inherit the promise" (p. 127). The authors explain further: "This very paradox, the tension between God's promises and his justice, remains unrelieved throughout the Deuteronomic History. It is in fact the tension that drives the entire narrative forward. . . . This tension between God's electing love and his holy justice is resolved at the Cross: there one who embodied faithful Israel – one who had himself been all that God had intended for Israel to be, God's chosen one, his own Son – bears the penalty of divine judgment for sin" (pp. 146-147).

⁶ Compare N. T. Wright, *The Climax of the Covenant: Christ and the Law in Pauline Theology* (Minneapolis: Fortress, 1993); Herman Ribberbos, *Paul: An Outline of His Theology* (Grand Rapids: Eerdmans, 1975); and Oscar Cullmann, *Salvation in History* (London: SCM, 1967). Ted M. Dorman attempts to apply the insights of Cullmann to the doctrine of justification by faith in "Holy Spirit, Hermeneutics and Theology: Toward an Evangelical/Catholic Consensus," *JETS* 41 (1998) 427-438. Dorman anticipates many of the same points made by Richard Gaffin of Westminster Seminary (see Chapter 7).

⁷ See my essay entitled "Paul's Letter to the Romans in the *New International Commentary on the New Testament* and in Contemporary Reformed Thought," *EvQ* 71 (1999) 3-24, republished in *Covenant Theology in Reformed Perspective* 227-245.

⁸ The Calvinistic branch of the Christian church properly understands itself as "reformed and reforming according to the Word of God." See the generally helpful introductions by M. Eugene Osterhaven, *The Faith of the Church: A Reformed Perspective on its Historical Development* (Grand Rapids: Eerdmans, 1982) and John H. Leith, *Introduction to the Reformed Tradition: A Way of Being the Christian Community* (Atlanta: John Knox, 1977). Compare also the essay by Alister E. McGrath, "The Importance of Tradition for Modern Evangelicalism," in *Doing Theology for the People of God: Studies in Honor of J. I. Packer* (ed. D.Lewis and A. McGrath; Downers Grove, IL: InterVarsity, 1996) 159-173.

⁹ Consult Gary Dorrien, *The Remaking of Evangelical Theology* (Louisville: Westminster John Knox, 1998); two works by Stanley J. Grenz, *Revisioning Evangelical Theology* (Downers Grove: InterVarsity, 1993) and *Renewing the Center* (Grand Rapids: Baker, 2000); and Robert E. Webber, *The Younger Evangelicals: Facing the Challenges of the New World* (Grand Rapids: Baker, 2002). Each of these authors calls for a radical reformulation of Christian theology and hermeneutical methodology. Consult further the exchange in *Evangelical Theology in Transition: Theologians in dialogue with Donald Bloesch* (E. M. Colyer, ed; Downers Grove: InterVarsity, 1999). For one example of revisionist Reformed dog-

matics, see Gordon J. Spykman's *Reformational Theology: A New Paradigm for Doing Dogmatics* (Grand Rapids: Eerdmans, 1992).

[10] See, for example, the useful volume by Grant R. Osbourn *The Hermeneutical Spiral: A Comprehensive Introduction to Biblical Interpretation* (Downers Grove: InterVarsity, 1991).

[11] B. B. Warfield's discussion in *The Plan of Salvation: A Study of the Basic and Essential Differences Between Various Interpretations of the Christian Religion* (revised edition; Grand Rapids: Eerdmans, 1970) remains a classic.

[12] See endnote 7 above.

[13] See Chapter 8.

[14] Consult Meredith G. Kline, *Images of the Spirit* (Grand Rapids: Baker, 1980), and his *God, Heaven, and Har Meggedon: A Covenant Theology Primer* (Overland Park, KS: Two Age, forthcoming).

[15] See my essay "The Original State of Adam: Tensions in Reformed Theology," *EvQ* 59 (1987) 291-309; republished in *Covenant Theology in Reformed Perspective* 95-110.

[16] Louis Igou Hodges, *Reformed Theology Today* (Columbus, GA: Brentwood Christian Press, 1995) 38.

[17] *Ibid.* 40

[18] *Ibid.* 42.

[19] *Ibid.* 43. See endnote 2 above.

[20] *Ibid.* 46.

[21] *Ibid.* 73.

[22] *Ibid.* 74.

²³ *Ibid.* 89.

²⁴ *Ibid.* 198, n. 54. Compare the similar thinking of J. Mark Beach in "The Doctrine of the *Pactum Salutis* in the Covenant Theology of Herman Witsius," *Mid-America Journal of Theology* 13 (2002) 101-142; Roland S. Ward in "Some Thoughts on Covenant Theology and on Justification [Part 1]," *The Presbyterian Banner* (March 2002) 11-12; Part 2 in the April 2002 issue, 10-11; and most recently, in Roland S. Ward, *God and Adam: Reformed Theology and the Creation Covenant,* published by the author (Wantirna, Australia: New Melbourne, 2003). Ward attributes current interest in the Reformed doctrine of the Covenant of Works largely to the influence of Westminster Seminary (East and West) and the heated controversy originating within the Philadelphia faculty back in the mid-1970s. Though he is not altogether happy with Norman Shepherd's formulation, Ward does not regard it as all that serious or heretical. (As it turns out, his opinion is largely based upon that of Richard Gaffin, with whom he has been in dialogue.) Contrary to Ward's assertion, neither he nor Gaffin stands in the line of Herman Bavinck and Geerhardus Vos with respect to the issues in this dispute. Ward's own analysis of Reformed teaching is shallow and hastily drawn. Rather than bringing clarity, the author blurs the picture and fails to address the substantive issues in this wide-ranging dispute in contemporary theology. Ward leaves out of account those Reformed interpreters down through centuries of covenant theology who have applied the "merit" concept in their exposition of the doctrine of the Covenant of Works.

²⁵ See endnote 7 above.

²⁶ On this exegetico-theological issue individuals like Moisés Silva and Tom Schreiner have been all over the map (and still remain uncertain where they stand). Most recently, see Moisés Silva's "Abraham, Faith, and Works: Paul's Use of Scripture in Galatians 3:6-14," *WTJ* 63 (2001) 251-67; and Thomas Schreiner's otherwise exceptionally fine study, *Paul: Apostle of God's Glory in Christ: A Pauline Theology* (Downers Grove: InterVarsity, 2001). Others, like Scott Hafemann, remain resolute in their defense of the Piper-Fuller theology. Peter Lillback, a protegé of Norman Shepherd and Rich-

ard Gaffin, in *The Binding of God* has essentially read a Barthian dogma into Calvin's theology. His linking of Calvin's teaching to that of medieval voluntarism is sheer fabrication. Were he correct, Luther and Calvin would not be the Protestant reformers we in the Reformation tradition have always understood them to be. They would merely be standing within the stream of (Roman) catholic doctrine. This is exactly what we are hearing from many contemporary "evangelicals" nowadays. The thinking of Ted Dorman is illustrative; see his discussion in "The Joint Declaration on the Doctrine of Justification: Retrospect and Prospects," *JETS* 44 (2001) 421-434. Compare Scott McKnight, "From Wheaton to Rome: Why Evangelicals become Roman Catholic," *JETS* 45 (2002) 451-472.

[27] Clarence Stam, *The Covenant of Love: Exploring Our Relationship with God* (Winnipeg: Premier, 1999) 8.

[28] *The Covenant of Love* 19.

[29] *Ibid*. 21.

[30] Stam remarks: "A covenant is meant as a lasting bond which may not be broken. When covenants are routinely broken, the very fabric of society is becoming unraveled and chaos is imminent" (*ibid*. 26). Two observations here: (1) covenants in the Bible are arrangements that can be broken, and oftentimes are broken; (2) care must be taken to avoid the false views of the theonomists, views based on the faulty application/interpretation of biblico-covenantal law to the state as a secular (common grace) institution. Compare my discussion in "Covenant and Common Grace: A Review Article" (*WTJ* 50 [1988] 323-37); republished in *Covenant Theology in Reformed Perspective* 297-307) with that of Jan van Vliet in "From Condition to State: Critical Reflections on Cornelius Van Til's Doctrine of Common Grace" (*WTJ* 61 [1999] 73-100). See also his "Decretal Theology and the Development of Covenant Thought: An Assessment of Cornelis Graafland's Thesis with a Particular View to Federal Architects William Ames and Johannes Cocceius," *WTJ* 63 (2001) 393-420. See also Appendix C.

R. Scott Clark and Joel Beeke offer an able defense of the Reformed doctrine of the Covenant of Works in "Ursinus, Oxford, and the Westminster Divines," *The Westminster Confession into the 21st Century: Essays in Remembrance of the 350th Anniversary of the Publication of the Westminster Confession of Faith* (eds. J. Ligon Duncan and Duncan Rankin; Greenville, SC: Reformed Academic Press, forthcoming).

[31] *The Covenant of Love* 48-49.

[32] *Ibid.* 50.

[33] *Ibid.* 52.

# Chapter 2

# A (New) Systematic Theology for Our Times:
# A Review Article*

It is always an occasion for celebration when the Reformed world is treated to a comprehensive statement of what the church – reformed according to the Scriptures – confesses. The work under review, *A New Systematic Theology of the Christian Faith* by author Robert L. Reymond, is the culmination of nearly three decades of instruction at two institutions, Covenant Theological Seminary in the early years and Knox Theological Seminary in the latter. It is unquestionably a helpful addition to Reformed dogmatics, a valuable compendium of Calvinistic teaching.[1] At the same time, however, the appropriateness of the title of the work under review can be fairly questioned. Does this work truly set forth a *new* systematics? If so, what is really new about the method or the content? As for originality, there are only isolated places in the text where the author breaks from tradition. Essentially, this handbook in dogmatics relies heavily upon the exegetical and theological formulations of others, notably that of Charles Hodge, B. B. Warfield, Louis Berkhof, and John Murray. What Reymond offers his readers is a repristination of Old School Presbyterianism (nineteenth to mid-twentieth century): for this reason it is difficult for this reviewer to regard Reymond's work as saying something truly new for Reformed Christianity at the turn of the millennium. Nevertheless, the study does have its place and it does helpfully interact with the current scene.

With reference to the theological encyclopedia, the present volume is properly classified as a study in confessional dogmatics. Reymond's outline and discussion highlight the *Westminster Confession of Faith* and *Catechisms*, and the purpose of this handbook is to defend and explicate that system of doctrine for the present generation. In light of this it is surprising that Reymond does not address the matter of confessionalism, what is itself an important and vital component of Christian (that is, church) doctrine. And closely related to confessionalism is the discipline of historical theology. It would have been helpful to the reader if Reymond had focused greater attention upon the historical nature of the theological enterprise, and elucidated his own work more fully in terms of that historical-ecclesiastical stream to which he belongs. Of course, no comprehensive dogmatics (such as that produced by Reymond) can be expected to provide all the required exegetical work. It is in the nature of a dogmatics to summarize the fruits of a particular exegetical-theological tradition. Nonetheless, this consideration makes the historical element all the more important in dogmatic exposition. No Christian theologian can work independently of churchly doctrine; every interpreter of the Bible approaches his/her task from a specific theological vantage point. In the case of Reymond, there is no doubt where he stands. The reader of *A New Systematic Theology* will readily discern that its author is an exponent of Reformed Puritanism, a doctrinal system summarily, yet comprehensively, set forth in the Westminster standards.[2] For the most part, Reymond sees it as his task to defend that system of doctrine against modern attacks. In establishing his case the author might also have given further attention to the topic of hermeneutics.³ Needless to say, in contemporary theology issues of hermeneutical methodology have come under intense, critical scrutiny. Other competing theologies (and methodologies) on the contemporary scene – such as neoorthodoxy, contextualization, liberation theology, and feminism – receive little or no attention in this compendium. Their inclusion would have been highly instructive in a restatement and defense of the historic Christian faith.⁴

The purpose of this review is to engage in a critically constructive analysis of Reymond's *magnum opus*. My questions and comments hopefully will generate further discussion and debate. (Space restraints necessitate that my remarks be selective and suggestive.) Reymond's special interests over the course of his teaching career have been principally two: Reformed epistemology and the person and work of Jesus Christ. What detracts from an otherwise insightful exposition of Reformed theology, however, is the author's extreme supralapsarianism. (More on this below.)

### 1. Theological Prolegomena: The stance of faith

For an understanding of the author's theological convictions and orientation, we must turn to the "Preface." There we are told that Reymond writes from a "Reformed perspective," but that he has not "slavishly followed the established pattern of 'orthodox' or 'Reformed' thought when it did not commend itself to me because of its failure to conform in some way to what I perceive to be the teaching of Holy Scripture."⁵ Rightly, the Word of God is regarded by the author to be the final rule of faith and life; the creedal statements of the Reformed churches, by implication, are secondary norms. As a confessional dogmatician, Reymond takes up the theological task as an unabashed presuppositionalist, applying the reformational principle of the analogy of Scripture (whereby Scripture is understood to be its own best interpreter). But there is more to biblical presuppositionalism than this, as subsequent discussion will indicate. The author's "Reformed perspective" is further described as follows: "the distinctive nature, richness, and beauty of the Reformed faith [is] the teaching of Holy Scripture, and [is] interpreted, expounded, and exhibited in John Calvin's *Institutes of the Christian Religion* and the great national Reformed confessions, particularly the Westminster Confession of Faith and the Westminster Assembly's Catechism, Larger and Shorter."[6] This, in sum, is "the established pattern" of Reformed orthodoxy.[7] Each chapter and section of the dogmatics opens with a citation from the Westminster standards. Clearly, the reader is to understand that Reymond is not a free thinker, but rather one who stands squarely in the tradition of post-Reformation, Puritan-Reformed orthodoxy (that is, Westminster Calvinism).

What is the justification for theological study? Who needs theology? Theologian and social critic David Wells in his three-volume jeremiad castigates modern-day evangelicalism for its doctrinal shallowness and moral indecisiveness.[8] Significantly, Reymond's prolegomenon addresses both the necessity and warrant for theology as an *intellectual* (as well as moral) discipline. In the words of Anselm, Christian faith is a faith that seeks understanding. Reymond begins by addressing the nature and necessity of divine revelation. Humankind as created by God was to become a race of peoples enjoying covenant fellowship and communion with God as Creator and Lord. Adam and Eve, our first parents, were God's image-bearers. All nature revealed the power and goodness of God, but general revelation could not be rightly interpreted apart from special, supernatural revelation. Subsequent to the Fall, personal renewal (regeneration and illumination) by the Spirit of God became necessary for true knowledge of God and humanity.

Concerning the Word incarnated and the Word inscripturated Reymond explains that, contrary to the teaching of neoorthodoxy,

> It is still biblical to insist that Jesus Christ is the incarnate Word of God, the supreme revelation of God, and not a vague "event" that occurs in a nonverbal personal encounter. And it is still appropriate to teach that the Bible is the written (propositional) Word of God, divinely inspired and therefore infallible. And the Holy Spirit both inspired the Bible and creates saving faith in the redeemed, illuminating them with respect both to the nature of Scripture itself and to Scripture's message to them.[9]

Human language as a gift of God is the appropriate vehicle of God's Word-revelation, even though God *accommodates himself to human capacity.* Modernist language philosophy wrongly regards the infinite distance between God (the unknowable One) and the finite creature as implying the inability of human language to serve as a vehicle of divine communication. God's revelation, according to this viewpoint, is *supratemporal,* beyond all rational comprehension. (There is no place in this philosophy for "propositional truth" as that contained in the sacred writings. Accordingly, the Bible is understood to be merely an account of the human community's religious experience of the Ineffible.) Reymond correctly points out the weaknesses in this modernist philosophical attempt to undermine the Bible's inspiration and authority. However, Reymond's conception of the eternality of the Word of God leads him to view the Bible mistakenly as a collection of "timeless truths." He writes: "despite the 'occasional' or *ad hoc* character of its many literary parts, the Scripture's doctrine of Scripture binds us to view its teachings as timeless truths intended 'for our instruction, reproof, correction, and training in righteousness.'"[10] Neither the ana-logical character of human knowledge of God nor the historico--covenantal nature of divine revelation is given its proper due. With respect to the latter, the author fails to draw together adequately the various biblico-theological and systematic threads.

Just how does Reymond understand the relation between knowledge in the mind of God and knowledge in the mind of man? Is there an identity of content? Reymond lays out the three alternative positions, namely, that the relationship is univocal, equivocal, or analogical, and then opts for the first of these three. There is, Reymond maintains, an *identity of content,* although human knowledge is not as exhaustive as God's.[11] Here Reymond takes vigorous exception to the views of the twentieth-century's greatest Reformed apologist and presuppositionalist, Cornelius Van Til, who espoused the analogical understanding of human knowledge. Reymond attempts to undercut Van Til's teaching by referring to the views of John Frame, one of Van Til's students who "attempted to extricate [his] revered mentor from the serious difficulty in which he has ensnared himself."[12] But Reymond rightly proceeds to speak of the problem in Frame's own theological method, what is called multiperspectivalism. This methodology causes Frame to misread Scripture and the Reformed tradition, including the writings of Van Til. At the foundation of Van Til's thought is acknowledgment of the Creator/creature distinction, one which underscores the infinite distance between God and humanity. Although the knowledge that God imparts to humanity is true and genuine, such knowledge is never identical with God's. Nor is any aspect of humanity's being identical with God's. God is wholly other than his creation. Reformed epistemology must reckon with the analogical character of human understanding – man thinks God's thoughts after him.[13]

As a student of Van Til, I recall well his insistence upon the paradoxical nature of *all* biblical doctrine (the term he used was "hyperdox"). Truth as it exists in the mind of God is beyond finite, human understanding: God's truth is inexhaustive, something the creature can never fully (that is, exhaustively) comprehend. Contrary to Reymond's reasoning, to know truth (or some truths) *as God knows it* would imply that the creature was equal with God. Divine mystery is resolved only in the exhaustively rational mind of God. Reymond's analysis entails the faulty equation of biblical "paradox" with genuinely contradictory teaching. The two are not the same: to the finite mind divine truth merely gives the *appearance of contradiction*. It is the nature of faith to take God at his word. But Reymond urges students of the Bible to "be solicitous to interpret the Scriptures in a noncontradictory way," and commends to them the practice of biblical harmonization.[14] (This recommendation is quite different from the reformational principle of comparing Scripture with Scripture.)

The largest portion of Reymond's prolegomena is devoted to setting out the evangelical and Reformed doctrine of the Word as the infallible, inerrant revelation of God. According to Reformed orthodoxy, the authority of the Scriptures is self-attesting. In this *locus*, as elsewhere, Reymond favors a collage of biblical passages, rather than detailed exegetical argument. Concerning the process of canonization, Reymond correctly favors the position of Herman Ridderbos. "In sum," observes Reymond, "the formation of the twenty-seven-book New Testament canon, after all is said and done, appears ultimately to have been the work, not of men, not even of the church, but of God's Spirit alone."[15] In an appendix he adds: "the Christian must and will rest confidently in the assumption that God led His church in those first four that God led His church in those first four centuries to recognize what He had intended should be included in the New Testament canon."[16]

## 2. Theology: God and humanity

John Calvin in his *Institutes of the Christian Religion* states that knowledge of God is inseparable from man's knowledge of himself.[17] From this same conviction Reymond in his "Introduction to the Doctrine of God" offers his personal reasons for belief in God against the backdrop of the classical theistic proofs (which he rejects). He explains that "my faith as a Christian in the Christian God and the self-attesting Christ of the New Testament is the result of the regenerating work of the Spirit of God which he wrought in my heart by and with the objective, revealed truth of the self-evidencing, self-validating Word of God."[18] In this compact statement of faith the author summarizes the Calvinistic doctrine of the Word and the Spirit as divine interpreter. It serves as a fitting link between the opening prolegomena and the theological exposition that ensues. Although the existence and divinity of the true God are known by all men and women, saving knowledge after the Fall is imparted only to the elect. That knowledge is dependent upon God's special, supernatural revelation, which in divine providence God was pleased to preserve in the pages of the inscripturated Word, itself the product of human authors inspired by the Holy Spirit. (Unlike any other literature the sacred writings are both human and divine.) God's revelation has been made known in nature and in Scripture. True knowledge of God is, accordingly, dependent upon general and special revelation. Reymond's assertion that Christian faith (that is, church doctrine) is the product of the self-attesting Christ speaking through the Scriptures and of the illumination of the Holy Spirit fails to reckon with the fallible, human component in the interpretive process. If the apprehension of Christian faith is simply the result of God's working in the human heart, why do genuine believers differ in their interpretation of the Bible? Why do not all believers share the *same* doctrinal understanding? (And why the plethora of Protestant denominations?) The answer lies in the interplay between Scripture and tradition in the act of interpretation. Theology finds expression in the community of faith, resulting in dogmatic statements which bind a particular confessing body to the teachings of Scripture as interpreted by its ministers (more broadly, the ruling bodies). These statements of faith function as subordinate standards within the life of the church(es); they comprise a collection of writings that, unlike the Word of God, are always open to revision and correction. Ultimately, God the Spirit is the final interpreter of his Word. We are reminded once again that the church of Christ is to be reformed and ever reforming in light of the teachings of Scripture.

Reymond begins his exposition of theology proper by considering two aspects of God's self-revelation, his name and his nature. The church confesses the triune God of the Bible to be the only true God, the creator, redeemer, and sustainer. Christians commonly identify God as "spirit," John 4:24 serving as the classic prooftext. According to Reymond, "when we say that God is "spirit," we are only using theological shorthand for saying that God is personal and noncorporeal – two of his other attributes."[19] On the matter of God's eternality, Reymond takes exception to the Augustinian position. He contends that this attribute of God must not be viewed in terms of "timelessness." Returning to the question of knowledge as it exists in the mind of God, Reymond queries whether there is any "consciousness of successive duration in his mind." Denial of such, argues Reymond, results in "much theological mischief."[20] The danger, as I see it, lies in attempting to probe the divine mind from the standpoint of finite human reason. God's supratemporal existence ("timelessness") is *sui generis*. This divine attribute does not prevent or impede God's rule over and governance of his creatures in history, nor does it imply that God is somehow incapable of entering into the "real" world of space and time. Contrary to Reymond's contention, God's existence transcends time. What weighs heavily in Reymond's discussion is his insistence upon a univocal relation between divine and human knowledge (including the epistemological aspect concerning *how* one knows).

The first indication of the triunity of God in the OT, states Reymond, is found in Genesis 1:26. The reader is not apprised of other interpretations of this divine pronouncement ("Let us make man"). Preferable is the view that the (angelic) sons of God are summoned in the creation of man after God's image, an image likewise borne by the angelic host. The Spirit of God (theophanic Presence) brooding over the unformed earth is also identified in Scripture with the Son in whom all things were created.[21] The economic distinctions within the Godhead, the unique operations of the three Persons in creation history and in redemption, become increasingly apparent with the progressive unfolding of the history of salvation. With respect to the opening chapter of Paul's letter to the Romans (vss. 3,4), Reymond is persuaded that the apostle contrasts the eternal, divine Sonship of Christ with his humanity. Hence "Spirit" in this passage is understood to refer to Christ's divine nature. However, redemptive-historical interpretation of this text, as Reymond notes, sees a contrast between Christ's prior state of humiliation (his incarnation) and his subsequent exaltation in eschatological glory (his resurrection and ascension into heaven). The consensus of Reformed opinion now appears to favor the latter view. Other important texts relating to Christ's role in creation and redemption include the opening chapters of John's Gospel (vvs. 1-5), Colossians (vvs. 15-20), and Hebrews (vss. 2,3). It would have been helpful if Reymond interacted more fully with the exegesis presented by those in the salvation-historical school of interpretation on these and other biblical texts.[22]

Reymond rejects the trinitarian formulation advanced by the ancient church fathers at Nicea, notably, the assertion that the Son was "begotten out of the Father." He maintains that "these Fathers taught that the Son derives his essential being or existence as God from the Father (see their 'out of the being of the Father') through an 'always continuing and yet ever complete' act of begetting on the Father's part. In sum, the Father alone has being from himself; the Son eternally derives his being from the Father."[23] Although Reymond turns to Calvin and to Gerald Bray (a modern-day interpreter of Calvin) for support, the case against Nicea has not been fully established. Better is Warfield's reading cited by Reymond. To be sure, defining precisely the distinguishing properties of the Father, Son, and Spirit is difficult. Reymond concedes:

> I do not intend to deny that the three Persons of the Godhead do have distinguishing, incommunicable properties which are real, eternal, and necessary. Indeed, without them there would be no Trinity. The distinguishing property of the Father is paternity *(paternitas)* from which flow "economical" activities in which the Son and Spirit do not share; the Son's is filiation *(filiatio)* from which flow "economical" activities in which the Father and Spirit do not share; and the Holy Spirit's is spiration *(spiratio)* from which flow "economical" activities in which the Father and the Son do not share, all descriptions which can be justified by Scripture.[24]

Reymond's argument is unclear and inconsistent. I doubt that twentieth-century theologians have attained the philosophico-linguistic tools lacking in the early church. Ancient and modern attempts to explain what it means that the Son, in the words of the *Westminster Confession*, is "eternally begotten of the Father" (whereby the unique property of the second Person of the Trinity is filiation) and that the Spirit "eternally proceeds from the Father and Son" (whereby the unique property of the third Person is spiration) are justified and necessary. There is no evidence that the Westminster divines intended to distance themselves from the formulations of Nicea. If the confessions of the evangelical and Reformed churches can be improved upon, Reymond has not convincingly shown the way.

In the section on the decrees of God, including both election and reprobation, Reymond's chief disputant is Clark Pinnock. Calvinism does not contradictorily teach that whereas God determines (that is, foreordains) all things that come to pass in history, man freely chooses to act of his own will. Man (male and female) as a creature of God, God's image-bearer, is not autonomous – the human will is exercised only in the context of the sovereign, all-determinative will and purpose of God. In regards to the evil performed by humanity and angels Reymond correctly refutes the notion of "bare permission" on God's part. God foreordains whatsoever comes to pass. "Divine *permission* and human *freedom* simply do not resolve the difficulties which Pinnock presumes that they do."[25] Reymond speculates that if Adam had sustained the probationary test, all humankind

> would have needed gratefully to look to Adam, still living among us, as our "Savior" from sin and death and as "our righteousness." God would then have been required eternally to share his glory with the creature, and his own beloved Son would have been denied the mediatorial role which led to his messianic lordship over men and to his Father's glory which followed (see Phil 2:6-11).[26]

Reymond reasons that God decreed Adam's fall into sin in order to magnify the surpassing grace revealed in Jesus Christ. Adam's transgression, on this view, becomes merely the means to an end. Two comments are offered by way of response. Firstly, does not this formulation detract from the integrity of Adam's original knowledge, righteousness, and holiness? The implication is given that Adam was somehow dependent upon the (mediatorial) strength and merit of Christ's righteousness in order to accomplish the "one act of righteousness" (Rom 5). It is simply wrong to suggest that Adam functioned as a savior from sin. Salvation from sin was not in any sense applicable to the original state of Adam. Secondly, Reymond fails to discern the mediatorial role of the Son in creation. The Son's mediation was not an aspect of his incarnation exclusively. In the eternal counsel of God, the so-called "Covenant of Redemption" between the Father and the Son, Christ's messianic office was (is) founded upon the Father's determination to save the elect.

The Reformed world of scholarship has become increasingly divided over the interpretation of the days of creation. Reymond unhesitatingly favors the teaching found in the Westminster standards concerning the literal six days ("in the space of six days"). The question arises whether Reymond would advocate strict adherence to these confessional statements as the means of securing peace and unity in the Reformed communions? If so, what does this say of his endorsement of the reformational principle of *sola scriptura*? Is he prepared to allow diversity of opinion on matters that do not undermine the system of doctrine nor jeopardize the fundamentals of the faith? Reymond boldly asserts: "I can discern no reason, either from Scripture or from the human sciences, for departing from the view that the days of Genesis were ordinary twenty-four-hour days."[27] While Reymond is free to express (and teach) his opinion, can he and the six-day creationists extend the same freedom to those who think otherwise? On the question of the age of the universe Reymond shows greater reserve. Although he and I favor "a relative young earth and a relative short history of man to date," neither of us is dogmatic on the issue.[28]

Concerning God's design of the universe, Reymond views redemption as the purpose for creation. John Murray, on the other hand, sees redemption as God's purpose for the *postlapsarian* world. Murray's position, in my judgment, distinguishes more carefully between the historical epochs of creation and redemption, each having its own particular purpose and design.[29] (One aim of recreation is to bring the original goal of creation, namely, eschatological consummation, to fulfillment by means of the reconciling work of Jesus Christ.) The doctrine of the decree(s) of God must not obscure the historical diversity associated with God's planning for the sake of its ultimate unity. Unfortunately, differences among Reformed dogmaticians on these issues resulted in the unnecessary division between infra- and supralapsarians.[30]

Moving on to what is viewed in the Westminster standards as God's special work of providence, namely, the Covenant of Works between God and Adam prior to the Fall, the reader is introduced to some of the problems and complexities in scholastic Reformed orthodoxy. At the time the Westminster divines worked on their confession and catechisms, a new Protestant scholasticism was emerging. Some of the scholastic definitions and terminology recovered from a former period in the history of Christian doctrine were helpful, others were not. Great care must be exercised in the study of Reformed dogmatics, perhaps nowhere more so than in its doctrine of the covenants. For example, reintroduction of the Thomistic nature/grace scheme unknowingly undermined teaching pertaining to the covenantal relationship between God and humankind at creation. Contrary to Reymond's assertion, the natural state of Adam was not distinct from the covenantal – human obligation to obey God was natural as it was covenantal. There were not two stages or orders of creation, one natural and the other covenantal. The dichotomy between an initial state of nature and a subsequent covenantal order is unbiblical; it is wholly speculative in origin.[31] Equally unacceptable is the notion that the Covenant of Works, though broken, remains perpetually in effect after the Fall. Contrary to Reymond, the legal principle ("do this and live") is no longer operative, not even hypothetically. The original Covenant of Works has forever been abrogated. Under the Covenant of Grace, which extends from the Fall to the Consummation, the legal principle was reinstituted on the earthly, *temporal* level during the period from Moses to Christ, the time when the Israelites were subject to the stipulations and sanctions of the legal covenant made at Sinai. Prosperity and blessing in the land of Canaan was contingent upon Israel's own obedience to the law of Moses. Wherever there is covenant based on works, there is simultaneously a period of probationary testing. Such was the case at the beginning with Adam in the Garden of Eden, later under the Mosaic economy, and finally in conjunction with the messianic task of Christ, the second Adam.[32]

These criticisms aside, Reymond defends traditional Reformed teaching on the covenants against its detractors, particularly revisionists like Norman Shepherd and Daniel Fuller. He agrees with those who maintain that Adam's successful completion of the probationary assignment would have meant that he *merited* the covenantal reward of confirmation in righteousness and, ultimately, entrance into eschatological glory at the consummation of history. The theological term "grace" pertains *exclusively* to the redemptive era, in that it speaks of the saving beneficence of God extended to sinners (in spite of their *demerit*). Hence the term "grace" is not applicable to the preredemptive epoch of creation history. The reward promised to Adam for faithful obedience to God was a matter of justice, not grace. (The discussion in this section should lead Reymond to reconsider his interpretation of Adam's probationary task and the mediatorial role of the Son in creation noted earlier.) Reymond's discussion of the divine covenants has a direct and immediate bearing upon the biblical doctrine of justification by faith ("apart from the works of the law"), the subject of another *locus* in Christian dogmatics.

### 3. Soteriology: The doctrine of Christ and his Spirit

This section opens with a discussion of the "plan of salvation." Here one finds a strictly logical presentation of God's decree(s), the occasion for probing into "the rational mind" of God. Starting from the end and proceeding to the means necessary for its accomplishment, Reymond claims that "The rational [human] mind recognizes that only in this way is each element of the plan purposive and contributory to the coherence of the entire plan."[33] Here again, Reymond's supralapsarianianism says more than is warranted from the text of Scripture (on the basis of exegesis and what the author calls "legitimate 'sanctified' deductions").

What is uniquely distinctive in Reformed theology is the doctrine of the covenants. With respect to the progressive unfolding of biblical revelation the divine covenants provide the structural framework for the history of creation and redemption. The redemptive epoch is the subject of Reymond's chapter on "The Unity of the Covenant of Grace." While summarizing the Reformed (federalist) position, Reymond offers a critical analysis of the teachings of dispensationalism, which he fairly examines in terms of both its earlier and its later exponents. To be sure, contemporary dispensationalism manifests a wide range of thinking. The so-called "progressive dispensationalists" of recent years have adopted many features of Reformed covenant thinking, the chief exceptions being (1) its understanding of the relation between Israel and the church, and (2) its strict adherence to premillennial eschatology. Another aspect of this debate is the question concerning the nature and content of saving faith in the Old and New Testaments. Reymond observes: "It is difficult to conceive of two evangelical perspectives on Old Testament faith differing more radically." He concludes: "these two theological systems are mutually exclusive." In dispensationalism there are "*at least two* different plans of salvation in Scripture."[34] Reymond identifies these doctrinal peculiarities as the "soteriological discontinuities and difficulties of the dispensational system."[35] In his elaboration of covenant theology Reymond at the same time appears oblivious to what is mainstream Reformed interpretation of the Mosaic Covenant. It was largely through the teaching of John Murray that contemporary Reformed orthodoxy was diverted from the classic position. Little did Murray realize that (independently of his work) the revolution which was to take place in historical and biblical studies at the close of the twentieth century – especially the contentious debate over Paul's understanding of the Mosaic law – would radically transform the theological landscape less than five hundred years after the Protestant Reformation.[36] (So significant is this development that the future of evangelicalism itself remains uncertain.)

The next place in the theological system where these issues converge is the teaching on substitutionary atonement. Reformed theology maintains that Christ, born under the law, fulfilled all righteousness for the sake of God's elect. By means of his active obedience Christ satisfied the legal demands of the original Covenant of Works, and by means of his passive obedience he exhausted its penalty and curse. Supralapsarian speculation leads Reymond to question the doctrine of the *consequent* absolute necessity of Christ's atonement. Problematic here is Reymond's understanding of God's aseity and the eternal decrees as they exist in the mind of God. Reymond fails to recognize that God was not obliged to save the elect any more than he was obliged to create the world. The decree(s) to create and to redeem is external to God's essential being. After treating the topic of the accomplishment of redemption on the basis Christ's atoning sacrifice, attention turns to the application of redemption by the Holy Spirit, who in the economy of redemption is the Spirit of Christ. Reymond upholds the Calvinistic interpretation over against the unstable and inconsistent position of Moise Amyraldus (the view that came to be known as "Amyraldianism"). According to Amyraldus, Christ's atoning death was universal in extent (that is, unlimited), while the Spirit's efficacious application of salvation was restricted to the elect alone. Consistent Calvinism teaches the doctrine of Christ's limited atonement and its effectual application by the Holy Spirit to those chosen in Christ .[37]

Reymond follows the traditional *ordo salutis* (order of salvation). In recent years questions have been raised concerning this formulation. Reymond observes that "the divine application of salvation is not 'one simple and indivisible act' but rather comprises a 'series of acts and processes' [and follows] a very definite order."[38] The several benefits, though distinct, are nevertheless inseparable – the believer united to Christ in his death and resurrection does not possess one without possessing all of these saving benefits.[39] Agreeing that union with Christ has two foci (one in eternity and one in time), Reymond maintains that the former refers to *being* in Christ from all eternity and the latter to *becoming* actually ingrafted into Christ. Reymond's distinction between "being" and "becoming" is confusing. Murray's view, with which Reymond differs, does greater justice to the historical dimension of union with Christ, without in any way detracting from the truth of God's eternal predestination of those elected in Christ.[40] The doctrine of justification by faith is formulated along precise Calvinistic lines, emphasizing the sole instrumentality of faith in the appropriation of Christ's perfect righteousness, the (alien) righteousness imputed to the believer. Good works, though necessary as evidence of justifying faith, are what have been prepared in advance by God for believers; they exemplify the power of the gospel to transform the believer into a new creation. The imputed righteousness of Christ, however, ever remains the exclusive basis of salvation. Final justification, that is, judgment according to works (but not on the *ground* of works), is God's vindication and approbation of the saints who walk in true righteousness and holiness.[41] Recent assaults upon the confessional Reformed teaching have arisen in some very unexpected places and among some of the most distinguished voices in Reformed theology. Reymond rightly opposes a statement drawn up in the 1990s, entitled "Evangelicals and Catholics Together: The Christian Mission in the Third Millennium."[42] Reymond also takes vigorous exception to the argument of John Gerstner claiming that Aquinas held a Protestant understanding of the doctrine of justification.[43] Disappointingly, however, Reymond only makes passing reference to the highly important debate among contemporary biblical theologians and exegetes regarding Paul's interpretation of the Mosaic law. Surely this controversy deserves more analysis and critique than is offered in *A New Systematic Theology*.[44]

The remainder of this section takes up the subject of sanctification. Although the sinner redeemed by God's grace has been delivered from the curse of the law, he is called to be perfect just as his Father in heaven is perfect. (In Reformed theology the "third use of the law" has reference to the commandments of God which are normative for godly living.) The ethics of the kingdom of Christ are laid out in the canonical documents of the New Covenant. Reymond regards the Decalogue, what is presented in the Bible as a summary of the Mosaic law, to be an ethical code for Christian living. Of particular importance to Reymond is the (Puritan) doctrine of the sabbath, as enunciated in the *Westminster Confession of Faith* and *Catechisms*. However, one must not lose sight of the fact that since the time of the Reformation onwards, the doctrine of the sabbath has proven to be one of the major points of contention among Reformed interpreters.[45] Whereas the reality of the Christian's struggle with sin remains uncontested, differences of opinion arise in the interpretation of this ongoing spiritual battle. Departing from the Augustinian position on Romans 7, what has been the dominant view among Reformed exegetes, Reymond construes Romans 7:14-25 as a description of the apostle's struggle with sin when he was yet unconverted. (Reymond devotes an entire appendix to this Pauline text.) With respect to the filling of the Spirit Reymond correctly states: "The Spirit's filling activity follows upon the Spirit's sealing work, is ongoing in the life of the Christian, and is involved in and is an aspect of the Christian's progressive sanctification." He adds: "To be filled with the Spirit is to be indwelt by the word of Christ; to be indwelt by the word of Christ is to be filled with the Spirit."[46] God who sovereignly initiates the work of salvation in the life of the believer will see it to completion. Salvation both begins and ends with God. Bringing to a close Reymond's discussion of the application of salvation by the Spirit of Christ to God's elect, the author reiterates the judgment of John Murray and J. I. Packer that adoption (that is, sonship) is the "apex of redemptive grace and privilege."[47] What greater blessing can one experience or conceive than the enjoyment of being a son of the Most High, a member of God's family having the privilege of intimate fellowship and communion with God. These are only some of the many gems that

Reymond has gleaned from the treasury of Reformed soteriology.

## 4. Ecclesiology: The Church reformed and reforming

Some would argue that the real test of the church's doctrine lies in the ecclesiastical ordering of the life (and faith) of God's covenant people. Agreeably, this stands as a biblical objective or standard by which to measure the health of the church. In the presbyterian and Reformed communions the local church is governed by elders who are committed to rule God's household according to the doctrines and principles of the faith delivered once-for-all to the saints. But sin, in both its individual and corporate dimensions, impedes the perfect attainment of this goal. Even so, the church must ever strive after (perfect) holiness and righteousness. In the Reformed tradition the marks of the true church include the preaching of the Word and the proper administration of the sacraments. Important also – some would say essential – for the spiritual wellbeing of the household of faith is ecclesiastical discipline.

The people of God, called the church, are those who by God's sovereign good pleasure are called out of the world to bear God's name among the nations. Beginning in the Garden of Eden after the Fall, God established his Covenant of Grace with faithful sons and daughters, those confessing his name and walking in his commandments. This covenant was not restricted to the elect seed (those chosen from all eternity to be the heirs of everlasting life), though the *proper purpose* of redemptive covenant is sovereign election and grace. "The church of God in Old Testament times," observes Reymond, "was not equivalent to the nation of Israel *per se*, for there were always some – and sometimes many, if not most – within that nation who were never more than the physical seed of Abraham."[48] After surveying the history of the church in the Old and New Testaments, Reymond concentrates on the church after Pentecost, the New Covenant people of God.[49] (The spiritual core is the seed of election.)

Worship in the Reformed tradition is conducted in accordance with the "regulative principle." God's people worship their Creator and Redeemer not according to their own desires or inclinations, but according to the dictates of Scripture. The elements of worship (namely, singing, the reading of the Scriptures, prayer, the presentation of offerings, the exposition of the Word) are set forth in the pages of the New Testament; nothing more and nothing less is appropriate or legitimate in corporate, public worship on the Lord's Day. Reformed churches, however, have not been able to agree fully on the *application* of this principle. Among the divisive issues is the use of instrumental accompaniment and "special music" by choir or vocalists. Some congregations observe exclusive psalm-singing. More recently, debates have arisen over "contemporary worship," including the legitimacy of drama, dance, and Scripture songs in place of (or alongside of) the traditional hymns of the church. Controversy also surrounds the use of "church-growth" methodologies in worship, missions and evangelism, a controversy, which reflects in part differences between Old School and New School Presbyterianism in the nineteenth century. According to the regulative principle, explains Reymond, "true worship may include only those matters which God has either expressly commanded in Scripture or which may be deduced from Scripture by good and necessary consequence."[50] Reymond urges that worship be "biblical, spiritual, simple, weighty, and reverent."[51] Even though his application of the Reformed principle of worship is somewhat wooden, Reymond's discussion is highly instructive for evangelical and Reformed churches at the close of the twentieth century. I maintain that there is room for (cultural) diversity as reflected in music and in liturgical forms and practices, be they "formal" or "informal."

With regard to the doctrinal and confessional life of the church Reymond rightly contends that "the church must reflect deeply on the truth of God's Word and frame what it finds there in symbols and confessions in order better to engender in its members a clear conception of their faith and to convey to outsiders a definite understanding of its doctrines."[52] This responsibility cannot be emphasized enough. One of the pressing needs among the Reformed churches today is a modern creedal statement formulated in the context of present-day challenges and controversies.[53] Evangelical Reformed Christianity will not survive this new millennium unless it takes seriously its obligation to know, love, and revere God's Word. (Were this to take place, doubtless, many of the lesser problems facing the church would dissipate.) Central to the church's fulfillment of the Great Commission is the establishment of learning centers as part of the educational ministry and missionary outreach of the church throughout the world.[54] Here lies the biblical formula for genuine church growth. Reymond sadly notes: "Even the evangelical church shows signs of losing confidence in the convincing and converting power of the gospel message. . . . The winning message, it seems, is the one that helps people to solve their temporal problems, improves their self-esteem and makes them feel good about themselves."[55] Preaching to the heart and to the mind remains the God-ordained method of building the kingdom of Christ. By his sovereign and powerful working through the preaching of the Word and the faithful administration of the sacraments God is establishing his everlasting kingdom of life and righteousness.

The basis of admission into the church of Christ is a credible, sincere profession of faith in Jesus Christ as Savior and Lord. While catechetical instruction is both advisable and necessary (in order for those converted to the faith to make a *credible* profession of faith), growth in Christian doctrine and life takes place over a lifetime. The presbyterian directory or book of church order describes the government of the church from the lowest judicatory to the highest (from session to presbytery to general assembly). In this system of church government the bond which unites individual churches is twofold: (1) a shared confession of faith; and (2) the book of order. Apostolicity, one of the attributes of the true church, brings into view the requirement for doctrinal purity among the churches.[56] The chief responsibility of the elders is the spiritual nurture and protection of Christ's flock. Church discipline, exercised in truth and in love, is a matter of moral suasion, not physical coercion.

The second ecclesiastical office in presbyterianism is that of the deacons, those appointed to attend to the temporal needs of the congregation (thus freeing the elders to devote their time and energies to spiritual oversight). Here also, Reformed congregations have manifested divergent understandings of the church's diaconal responsibilities. Properly conceived, "the work of Christian benevolence [has] reference to all the church's needy."[57] Reymond views this duty of the congregation in caring for the needy within her own walls, however, as merely one of priority. Included in the ministry of the diaconate, he argues, is care for the needy in the community and in the world at large. This all-too-common (mis)understanding confuses the cultic and cultural institutions as established by God after the Fall. Church and state are two distinct and separate realms. By common grace, Christians and nonChristians work and live together; in their civic affairs they are governed by rules and policies laid down by the ministers of the state. One of the responsibilities of civil servants is the protection and care for the poor, the distressed, and the needy within the commonwealth. Beyond this, God has made special provision for the saints by ordaining the office of the deacon as part of the institutional governance of the church. What is required of Christians is the prayerful and responsible allocation of time and talent, finances and other resources, to these cultic and cultural tasks respectively. The church of Christ is not a social organization serving the needs of the secular community; its task is wholly different from that of the state. The church is the communion of the saints gathered for worship and service; its task is to declare God's message of mercy and grace to those who are perishing. Apart from faith in Christ, sinners remain under God's wrath and condemnation.

Until recent years the ecclesiastical offices of elder and deacon had been restricted to men. That policy is now rapidly changing in both evangelical and Reformed communions. There are many ramifications of this debate for the Christian church. For instance, Reymond's understanding of the teaching of Scripture precludes women from having any voice whatsoever in public worship. Presumably, his view would exclude women from ushering, praying, reading Scripture, or rendering musical solos. And what about women serving on committees of the session or assisting in the diaconal work? While Reymond encourages women "to engage in the intellectual discipline of theological study," can that education be put to good use in the church and in the seminary? Much hard thinking is yet to be done in this area. Reymond points out: "the world of the Old Testament was a patriarchal world. Originally its patriarchy was a perfect patriarchy, reflecting the federal headship of the male in the pre-Fall Edenic condition." The fact that the Fall had introduced injustices and abuses in the male/female relationship (both in the marriage institution and in society as a whole) explains why God was willing in OT times "to recognize and adapt himself to a *sinful* patriarchal culture."[58] Such recognition, however, makes it all the more necessary for the New Covenant people of God – those who enjoy the status of full sonship and who are the recipients of the complete revelation of God in the Scriptures of the Old and New Testaments – to dismantle those barriers which prevent women from exercising their God-given talents and abilities.

## 5. Eschatology: The consummation of history

"This area of theology," writes Reymond, "is the capstone of systematic theology, with every other locus of theology finding its resolution in it."[59] As a spokesman for covenant amillennialism, the author anticipates Christ's second advent to be "the next important messianic event on the horizon."[60] It is this event, also called the Day of the Lord, which signals the final judgment, the separation of the wheat from the tares. Are all evangelicals agreed on the import of these two eschatological events, the return of Christ and the last judgment? Sadly, the answer is no. But as Reymond accurately states, "the doctrines of the final judgment and of hell for the impenitent and the unbeliever are among the *cardinal* doctrines of the Christian faith."[61] The controversial views of Pinnock are again featured in Reymond's critique of (radical) evangelical theology and defense of historic Christian teaching on the end times.

Prior to that great and awesome Day, there is the present, interadventual conflict between Israel of the flesh and the true Israel of God. This conflict is but one aspect of the spiritual battle fought in the earthly and the heavenly realms, a warfare involving the entire cosmos. While the hardening of the Jews at the outset of the Christian era means blessing for the Gentiles, the apostle Paul anticipates the complete accomplishment of God's redemptive purpose. Through the preaching of the gospel to both Jew and Gentile, God is calling the full number of the elect to faith and repentance. Together, believing Jews and Gentiles comprise the Israel of God. "The instrumentality of the church's proclamation of the gospel," explains Reymond (in opposition to the teachings of premillennialism), "meets all the details of [Romans] 11:26 as well as or better than the instrumentality of Christ's second coming."[62] To offer any other word of hope to unbelieving Jews would amount to the preaching of another gospel. Israel's former, ethnic identity as the chosen people of God has no significance with respect to the heavenly reward to be enjoyed by all those who are elect in Christ. The earthly land of Canaan is no longer the site of God's (theocratic) dwelling; the temple of Jerusalem has been destroyed, never again to serve as the sacred place of worship; the altar of sacrifice has been replaced by the heavenly throne upon which the victorious Lamb of God is seated in power and glory. "It is indeed a strange twist of thinking, if not outright disloyalty to the gospel," observes Reymond, "for the Christian to aid or abet the Jew in the retention of these Jewish distinctives which provide him the ground for his hope of salvation, the holding on to which only solidifies him in his unbelief."[63] Failure to recognize these teachings of biblical eschatology betrays a fundamental misreading of the Old Covenant. Indeed, "[realized] eschatology is the capstone of systematic theology." It is that which draws together all the strands of redemptive revelation. Hopefully, renewed appreciation of amillennial covenant theology will be one of the many rewards of reading and digesting *A New Systematic Theology of the Christian Faith*.

**ENDNOTES**

*Robert L. Reymond, *A New Systematic Theology of the Christian Faith* (Nashville: Thomas Nelson, 1998). (This review essay first appeared in *Foundations: A Journal of Evangelical Theology* 45 [2001] 23-41.)

[1] Two recent works in Reformed systematics which incorporate the distinctive contributions of biblical theology (with different degrees of success) are Gordon J. Spykman, *Reformational Theology: A New Paradigm for Doing Dogmatics* (Grand Rapids: Eerdmans, 1992), and Richard Lints, *The Fabric of Theology: A Prolegomenon to Evangelical Theology* (Grand Rapids, 1993). For a broad perspective on developments in contemporary evangelicalism, see Gary Dorrien, *The Remaking of Evangelical Theology* (Louisville: Westminster John Knox, 1998). Dorrien favors the revisionist school represented by such writers as Stanley Grenz and Clark Pinnock.

[2] Compare Mark W. Karlberg, "Doctrinal Development in Scripture and Tradition: A Reformed Assessment of the Church's Theological Task," *CTJ* 30 (1995) 401-418; republished in *Covenant Theology in Reformed Perspective* 341-355. On problems relating to creedal subscription, see *The Practice of Confessional Subscription*, ed. David W. Hall (New York: University Press of America, 1995).

[3] Consult especially, Grant R. Osborne, *The Hermeneutical Spiral: A Comprehensive Introduction to Biblical Interpretation* (Downers Grove: InterVarsity, 1991).

[4] For a succinct overview of various contemporary theologies see the study by Donald K. McKim, *The Bible in Theology and Preaching: How Preachers Use Scripture* (Nashville, Abingdon, 1985).

[5] *A New Systematic Theology* xxi.

[6] *Ibid.* xxxiv.

⁷ See the provocative work of John H. Leith, *The Reformed Imperative: What the Church Has to Say That No One Else Can Say* (Philadelphia: Westminster, 1988).

⁸ David F. Wells, *No Place for Truth: Or Whatever Happened to Evangelical Theology?* (Grand Rapids, Eerdmans, 1993); *God in the Wasteland: The Reality of Truth in a World of Fading Dreams* (Grand Rapids: Eerdmans, 1994); *Losing Our Virtue: Why the Church Must Recover Its Moral Vision* (Grand Rapids: Eerdmans, 1998). John H. Leith in *From Generation to Generation: The Renewal of the Church According of the Church According to Its Own Theology and Practice* (Louisville: Westminster/John Knox 1990) offers an analysis of the contemporary church that differs from, yet compliments, Wells'.

⁹ *A New Systematic Theology* 17.

¹⁰ *Ibid.* 52, original italicized.

¹¹ *Ibid.* 102.

¹² *Ibid.* 102, n.19.

¹³ For my critique of Frame's (multi-)perspectivalism, see "On the Theological Correlation of Divine and Human Language: A Review Article," *JETS* 32 (1989) 99-105; and for my critique of Frame on Van Til, see "John Frame and the Recasting of Van Tilian Apologetics: A Review Article," *Mid-America Journal of Theology* 9 (1993) 279-296. Regarding the discipline of systematics, Van Til maintains that Reformed theology "is not a system of theology in accordance with a logical methodology borrowed from Aristotle or from Kant. On the other hand, it is not chaos. Biblical truth is systematic; that is, it is orderly. Its various doctrines are not deductions from a common central theological principle, but they stand in orderly relation to one another. The one is meaningless without the other. They supplement one another. Together, they form what may properly be called a system of truth; that is, the content of Scripture is an analogical system of truth" *(The Theology of James Daane* [Philadelphia: Presbyterian and Reformed, 1959] 123).

[14] Reymond writes: "Certainly there are biblical concepts that we cannot fully understand. . . . Such concepts are *mysteries* to us, but they are not contradictions in terms." In a footnote he adds: "If someday [God] tells us how he did these things, then of course we will be able to understand them" (*A New Systematic Theology* 107, n. 31).

[15] *Ibid.* 68.

[16] *Ibid.* 1112.

[17] John Calvin, *Institutes of the Christian Religion*, ed. John T. McNeill; Philadelphia: Westminster, 1960) 1.1.

[18] *A New Systematic Theology* 152.

[19] *Ibid.* 162; compare 166-67. Reymond perpetuates an ancient tradition of exegesis. Dissenting from this interpretation, I contend that the Johannine text speaks contrastingly of two ways of worship observed by the people of God: under the Mosaic economy worship focused upon the holy, theocratic site in Jerusalem, whereas under the New Covenant worship is unrestricted. The contrast is redemptive-historical and eschatological. "Spirit" has reference to the (Spiritual) presence of God in the midst of his people (there is some overlap here with the letter/Spirit contrast as that pertains to the two covenants, the Mosaic and the New; see especially the argument set forth in the Letter to the Hebrews). In his Gospel, John is particularly fond of comparing OT shadows with NT realities. Jn 4:24 is one instance of it.

[20] *Ibid.* 173, 174.

[21] See the illuminating work of Meredith G. Kline, *Images of the Spirit* (Baker Biblical Monograph; Grand Rapids, Baker, 1980). Elsewhere Kline writes: "In pre-Consummation earth history the heavenly Glory-Presence has appeared occasionally in localized symbolic fashion in the form of the theophanic Glory-cloud. This earthly projection is identified in the Bible as the Spirit, and accordingly the heavenly reality, while a trinitarian manifestation, is more par-

ticularly identified with the Spirit." He continues: "There is then an eternally continuing Glory-embodiment of God's Spirit-Presence in creation, shaping creation and constituting it a temple. The primal creation event that brought this Glory-Spirit epiphany into existence (Gen 1:1) may be called the endoxation of the Spirit. It is comparable to the incarnation of the Son. Incarnate Son and endoxate Spirit are both living embodiments of the God of Glory" ("The Exaltation of Christ," *Kerux* 12/3 [December 1997] 12).

[22] Geerharus Vos, the pioneer of twentieth-century Reformed biblical theology, was also a notable dogmatician. Standing in that same tradition today is Meredith G. Kline, whose literary output has been significant. See my "Reformed Theology as the Theology of the Covenants: The Contributions of Meredith G. Kline to Reformed Systematics," in *Creator, Redeemer, Consummator: A Festschrift for Meredith G. Kline* (eds. H. Griffith and J. R. Muether; Greenville, SC: Reformed Academic Press, 2000); republished in *Covenant Theology in Reformed Perspective* 357-377.

[23] *A New Systematic Theology* 325.

[24] *Ibid.* 336.

[25] *Ibid.* 355. Compare Paul K. Jewett, *Election and Predestination* (Grand Rapids: Eerdmans, 1985), and my review of this book in *WTJ* 48 (1986) 388-91. See also the "Declaration of Faith Regarding Predestination," written on the occasion of the 50th anniversary of the Reformed Church in Japan, published in *Theological Forum* 26 (1998) 27-42; the same issue carries Richard A. Muller's positive evaluation, "Declaring the Faith Today: The Reformed Church in Japan on Predestination" (43-46).

[26] *A New Systematic Theology* 377; compare 414.

[27] *Ibid.* 392.

[28] *Ibid.* 396. Compare the discussion in *Three Views on Creation and Evolution* (eds. J. P. Moreland and J. M. Reymonds; Grand Rapids: Zondervan, 1999).

29 *Ibid.* 397-403.

30 See especially Van Til's *The Theology of James Daane*. Concerning true knowledge of God after the Fall, both Murray and Reymond oppose a natural theology standing independently of God's supernatural revelation. Reymond's appeal, however, to the christomonistic formulation of T. H. L. Parker in this discussion is unfortunate. Surely Reymond does not advocate neoorthodoxy, but his extreme supralapsarianism does blur the biblical distinction between creation and redemption, and between common grace and special grace. Kim Riddlebarger in "The Lion of Princeton: Benjamin Breckinridge Warfield on Apologetics, Theological Method and Polemics" (Ph.D. dissertation, Fuller Theological Seminary, 1997) argues unpersuasively that Warfield's natural theology is biblical and presuppositionalist; his case rests on Warfield's belief in the absolute necessity of the regenerative work of the Spirit for understanding God's revelation in nature and in Scripture. "Despite the unfortunate and ill-deserved confusion that surrounds his methodology," writes Riddlebarger, "B. B. Warfield must be placed among the most significant American apologists of the period" (p. 132). Lacking in this work is substantive interaction with the theological argument and apologetic of Van Til, as well as other exponents of this school of thought.

31 Better is Reymond's statement that "The covenant of works reflects the fact that the most fundamental obligation of man the creature to God his Creator always has been, is now, and always will be obedience to the will of the Creator. As *covenant* creature (and therefore always as either covenant *keeper* or covenant *breaker*), man is always ultimately related to God on a *legal* (covenantal) basis" (*A New Systematic Theology* 439). Consult further Mark W. Karlberg, "The Original State of Adam: Tensions in Reformed Theology," *EvQ* 59 (1987) 291-309; republished in *Covenant Theology in Reformed Perspective* 95-110.

32 The angels, like our first parents, were initially placed on probation; those who with Satan rebelled against God were cast out from the Presence of God. There is an ethical dimension to creaturely knowledge of God. Failure to guard the holy temple of God

in the Garden of Eden culminated in Adam's expulsion from the earthly sanctuary, just as the evil angels were previously cast out from the heavenly sanctuary. Compare my "Israel Under Probation: An Evaluation of Frank Thielman's *Paul and the Law*," paper read at the regional meeting of the Evangelical Theological Society in Valley Forge, PA (April 4, 1995), available at www.tren.com; and "The Significance of Israel in Biblical Typology," *JETS* 31 (1988) 257-69, republished in *Covenant Theology in Reformed Perspective* 193-207.

33 *A New Systematic Theology* 492.

34 *Ibid.* 509.

35 *Ibid.* 544. Compare the helpful collection of essays in *Continuity and Discontinuity: Perspectives on the Relationship Between the Old and New Testaments,* ed. J. S. Feinberg (Westchester, IL: Crossway Books, 1988), and in *Dispensationalism, Israel and the Church: The Search for Definition,* eds. C. A. Blaising and D. L. Bock (Grand Rapids, Zondervan, 1992). I have reviewed the former volume in my "Israel and the Eschaton: A Review Article," *WTJ* 54 (1992) 135-152; republished in *Covenant Theology in Reformed Perspective* 309-323.

36 See Mark W. Karlberg, "The Search for an Evangelical Consensus on Paul and the Law," *JETS* 40 (1997) 563-79; and my "Paul's Letter to the Romans in the *New International Commentary on the New Testament* and in Contemporary Reformed Thought," *EvQ* 71 (1999) 3-24. Both of these essays are republished in *Covenant Theology in Reformed Perspective* 209-226 and 227-245. Consult also P. T. O'Brien, "Justification in Paul and Some Crucial Issues of the Last Two Decades," *Right with God: Justification in the Bible and the World,* ed. D. A. Carson (Grand Rapids: Baker, 1992) 69-95. Edmund P. Clowney in "The Biblical Doctrine of Justification by Faith," *Right with God* (17-50) cites the study paper "Westminster Statement on Justification" (May, 1980) drawn up by the faculty of Westminster Seminary addressing issues in the seminary's doctrinal controversy on justification, a controversy that has divided both faculty and constituency since the mid-1970s. On the broader

context of these debates, see the collection of essays in *Presbyterion* 8/1 (1982) and Reymond's summary analysis in *A New Systematic Theology* 431-22.

[37] Compare B. B. Warfield's superb treatment in *The Plan of Salvation: A Study of the Basic and Essential Differences Between Various Interpretations of the Christian Religion* (Revised edition; Grand Rapids: Eerdmans, 1970). See also my review of G. Michael Thomas' recent study, *The Extent of the Atonement: A Dilemma for Reformed Theology from Calvin to the Consensus* in TrinJ 20 NS (1999) 116-119; republished in *Covenant Theology in Reformed Perspective* 147-150.

[38] *A New Systematic Theology* 704. Compare Anthony A. Hoekema's treatment in *Saved by Grace* (Grand Rapids: Eerdmans, 1989).

[39] Reymond questions Murray's analysis of the *ordo*, specifically, his contention that union with Christ is foundational to the entire process, wherein regeneration is seen as the result of God's initial act in effectually calling sinners to Christ (*A New Systematic Theology* 716).

[40] Reymond adds the clarifying comment: "the Scriptures will not permit us to believe that, because God elected certain people in Christ from all eternity, they have therefore always enjoyed the fullness of his favor in history and that for them there is no transition from wrath to grace in history. . . . It is only when they are brought to faith in Christ by their effectual calling that the elect *actually* become partakers of Christ and of the salvific blessings of his cross work" (*ibid.* 737).

[41] Reymond espouses the common, but problematic, view that rewards in heaven result in gradation among believers: *A New Systematic Theology* 750-52, 1020-22.

[42] I would add that the sequel, "The Gift of Salvation," does not fare any better. See the remarks by W. Robert Godfrey in "A Discussion on Justification," *The Outlook* 49/2 (February 1999) 5-7.

[43] *A New Systematic Theology* 746, n. 54.

[44] Consult Philip Eveson, *The Great Exchange: Justification by Faith Alone in the Light of Recent Thought* (Bromley: Day One, 1996), and the "Interview with Peter Jensen" in *Modern Reformation* 8/2 (March/April 1999) 19-23.

[45] See the useful collection of essays in *From Sabbath to Lord's Day: A Biblical, Historical, and Theological Investigation*, ed. D. A. Carson (Grand Rapids: Zondervan, 1982).

[46] *A New Systematic Theology* 765, 766.

[47] *Ibid.* 761.

[48] *Ibid.* 806.

[49] See further, J. A. Heyns, *The Church*, trans. D. R. Briggs (Pretoria: N. G. Kerkboekhandel Transvaal, 1980), and Edmund P. Clowney, *The Church* (Contours of Christian Theology; Downers Grove: InterVarsity, 1995).

[50] *A New Systematic Theology* 870.

[51] *Ibid.* 872. Consult *Leading in Worship: A Sourcebook for Presbyterian Students and Ministers Drawing Upon the Biblical and Historic Forms of the Reformed Tradition*, ed. T. L. Johnson (Oak Ridge, TN: The Covenant Foundation, 1996), and Hughes Oliphant Old, *Worship That is Reformed According to Scripture* (Guides to the Reformed Tradition; Atlanta: John Knox, 1984). See also my "Music in Worship: An Historical Sketch and Theological Appraisal," *The Outlook* 49/9 (October 1999) 3-6. For thoughts on the misuse of patriotic song in the ecclesiastical setting, see my "Patriotic Music in Worship," *The Outlook* 53/6 (July/August 2003) 4-5.

[52] *A New Systematic Theology* 878.

[53] See endnote 2 above.

[54] Reymond places special weight on seminary training; see my discussion in "Current Theological Trends in Reformed Seminaries: The Dilemma in Ministerial Education," paper read at the Eastern regional meeting of the Evangelical Theological Society in Lancaster, PA (April 3, 1998; available at www.tren.com).

[55] *A New Systematic Theology* 882.

[56] Concerning the minister of the gospel, Reymond writes: "He is ever to bear in mind that his authority as a minister is subordinate to the authority of Scripture. . . . he must not take offense when his auditors examine the Scriptures, as did the Bereans (Acts 17:11), to see if what he is preaching is true" (*ibid.* 917).

[57] *Ibid.* 892.

[58] *Ibid.* 938.

[59] *Ibid.* 980. Consult further the amillennial studies by Anthony A. Hoekema, *The Bible and the Future* (Grand Rapids: Eerdmans, 1979), and G. K. Beale, *The Book of Revelation: A Commentary on the Greek Text* (The New International Greek Testament Commentary; Grand Rapids: Eerdmans, 1999).

[60] *A New Systematic Theology* 1023.

[61] *Ibid.* 1084.

[62] *Ibid.* 1029.

[63] *Ibid.* 1031.

# Chapter 3

# Paul, the Law, and Contemporary Theology: The Undoing of the Protestant Reformation*

Especially since the late 1970s and the publication of the views of British theologians E. P. Sanders and J. D. G. Dunn on the subject of the Pauline interpretation of the Mosaic law, a virtual revolution in the "Protestant" understanding of the NT doctrine of justification by faith – justification apart from the works of the law – has been taking place. It is a revolution that has changed the entire landscape of contemporary biblical and theological studies. The New Perspective on Paul and the law begins not with the reassessment of early Palestinian Judaism advanced by Sanders, but rather with the anti-juridical bias adopted by the Barthians and other eclectic groups of biblical interpreters. One need not be a "total Barthian" to imbibe from his theological cistern. Specifically, one need not hold to Barth's philosophico-theological construct of ordinary history (*historie*), subject to the rigors of the modern scientific method, and salvation-history (*heilsgeschichte*, or "holy history," what belongs to the realm of Faith) to join the chorus of voices castigating Protestant scholasticism for alleged rationalistic, speculative reconstructions in the interpretation of the Bible.

## 1. Theological Introduction:
## The issue of method in interpretation

At the heart of the Christian faith is the proclamation of the free justification of sinners by grace through faith. According the apostle Paul, the divine act of justification is foundational in the revelation of God's saving action in the death and resurrection of Jesus Christ (see especially Paul's letter to the Romans). For Barth the question whether Jesus actually rose from the dead is a question to be answered by the (secular) historian; what is significant for the theologian is the meaning early Christians attached to the sufferings, death, and "resurrection" of Christ. In other words, what matters to Barth is how the Christ-event impacts the lives of Jesus' followers and, beyond that, all humankind (here is the universalistic reach of Barth's thinking). The good news of the gospel, according to Barth, is an affirmation of Faith, one not subject to scientific, historical investigation. From this point of view Christianity is but one expression of the universal aspiration of humankind searching for ultimate truth, however that be defined in this postmodern, postChristian world. What John Calvin called the "sense of divinity" implanted by God in the human heart is, for Barth, reflected in both religious and non-religious ways of human self-understanding. (The ecumenical view – with its universalistic overtones – has been more fully and more consistently developed by Barth's disciples.)

Although evangelicalism may readily part company with the universalism implicit in Barth's teaching, the emphasis Barth placed upon the sovereign grace of God in creation and recreation ("redemption") has been echoed time and again in contemporary theology at the close of the twentieth century, into the twenty-first. This teaching, however, is simply the reverse side of Barth's polemic against "legal(istic)" interpretations of covenant, atonement, and justification allegedly taught by the Protestant scholastics, Lutheran and Reformed. At the heart of this dispute is the acceptance or rejection of the traditional Protestant law/gospel contrast.[1] What factors contribute to this revolution in contemporary biblical and theological interpretation, a revolution which has even impacted modern-day "evangelicalism" across a very wide spectrum? To that question we now turn our attention.

If not an outright renunciation of the discipline, systematic theology has in recent years received a very low estimate among modern interpreters. Since the Bible itself does not provide readers a comprehensive, logico-systematic presentation of divine revelation – the likes of Francis Turretine's or Louis Berkhof's textbook in theology – we are cautioned against imposing a detailed ("scholastic") schematization or systematization upon the Scriptures. The truth of the matter is, however, that the Bible does contain the rudiments of systematico-theological reflection, best seen in Paul's letter to the Romans. Interpreters in succeeding centuries of church history are building upon the Christian tradition handed down to those who are of the household of faith. Unquestionably, there is a system of truth (as well as a method of interpretation) inherent in the teachings of the Old and New Testaments.

Happily, there are some signs of renewed interest and commitment to the systematico-theological discipline. Illustrative of this current change in perspective is the study entitled *Between Two Horizons: Spanning New Testament Studies and Systematic Theology*.[2] The editors of this volume explain:

> One reason [for this publication] is that the great commentary series have become increasingly detailed and

methodologically complex, and many individual volumes are now so exhaustive that they are virtually inaccessible to all but the most well trained. . . . Nearly all the major commentaries leave the reader firmly within the horizon of the ancient author's world, and offer little or no academically disciplined guidance concerning the contemporary *theological* significance of the work in question.³

It is their observation that "Many biblical interpreters today are possessed by habits of mind and by hermeneutical practices that either disallow the need for building a bridge from biblical to theological studies or undermine (unself-consciously?) the necessary engineering. Clearly, a new set of dispositions and habits needs to be cultivated."⁴ This is an encouraging development in contemporary theology.

The task before the Christian church is always confessional and dogmatic in nature. The church seeks to profess that which is either expressly or implicitly taught in the Bible by means of summary statements of faith which vary in degree of detail and complexity (compare, for example, the difference between the *Westminster Confession of Faith* and the companion *Larger* and *Shorter Catechisms*). Confessional theology arises out of a particular community of faith, one having a history of biblical interpretation behind it (beginning with that found in the canonical documents of the Old and New Testaments). These secondary norms are ever subject to correction and revision in light of the church's understanding of the teachings of the Bible over the course of centuries of polemical debate. Theology is forged in the fires of controversy.

All is not well, however, in the project under review. Robert W. Wall, contributing essayist in *Beyond Two Horizons*, mistakenly argues against the Protestant reformers that "Scripture is not self-interpreting, but is rather rendered coherent and relevant by faithful interpreters whose interpretations are constrained by this Rule [what he identifies as the church's Rule of Faith, that summary of ecumenical, orthodox teaching crafted by the early church fathers during the first five centuries following Pentecost]."[5] Wall proceeds to speak of the "richly variegated confession" of the church universal, wherein one finds that each denominational rule conforms, more or less, to "the core beliefs and deeper logic of the catholic Rule of Faith."[6] Wall does recognize a certain leveling or relativizing of doctrine in his reading of church doctrine, and so offers a word of caution: "This kind of relativism can be abused, of course, if performed in an uncritical fashion, so that every interpretation is tolerated as equally cogent and important for Christian formation."[7] The variety of "theological perspectivalism" advocated by Wall, in principle, renders the Bible free from dogmatic exposition. On this view, a wedge is driven between the biblical documents of the Old and New Testaments and church's theological interpretation, what some mistakenly describe as "doctrine" versus "theology." Without confusing primary and secondary norms in the life and faith of the church, to the extent that the teachings of the church are true to the teachings of the Bible those teachings are to be believed and obeyed. There is a theological tie between Scripture and Christian interpretation. Where the church's dogma conflicts with the teaching of the Bible, it is to be challenged and reformulated.[8]

Resolution of the centuries-long controversy between Arminians and Calvinists, for example, is not obtained in the melding of two "perspectives," the attempt to take the best in both positions. The Reformed doctrine of divine sovereignty is the result of careful exegetical-theological exposition of Scripture attained in the context of ongoing polemical debate. At the root of the differences between Calvinist and Arminian interpretations of the doctrine of the sovereignty of God are divergent assumptions or presuppositions (arguably drawn from Scripture) concerning the nature and consequences of sin, including the question regarding human ability after the Adam's fall.[9] Agreeably, one's presuppositions must be drawn from inscripturated revelation. But that itself is a matter of interpretation. Whatever else must be said in defense of a proper, valid biblical hermeneutic, divine illumination – crucial in the interpretation of the Bible – is wholly the work of the Spirit of God. Only the Spirit can work unity in faith and witness within the community of believers.

Turning again to Wall's essay, the author maintains:

> The intended meaning of a biblical text is not the property of its author but of the church to whom Scripture belongs. . . . The normative meaning of a text sought by biblical interpretation is not that fixed in the author's mind for all time; nor is it found in the constantly shifting locations of various interpreters. Rather, Scripture is canonical precisely because believers recognize its power to convey *God's* intended meaning and transforming grace to all its faithful readers. . . . The simultaneity of the biblical canon conveys a sense that the hermeneutics of its authors did not place a wedge between what their Scripture meant and what it now means; this critical construction is simply foreign to the hermeneutics of the biblical literature itself.[10]

As in the interpretation of John Frame, meaning is thought to reside in the application of the text of Scripture. Frame insists: "Meaning is application."[11] Here one finds a shift from the established view of Protestant Orthodoxy to the revisionary view of contemporary ("evangelical") theology, wherein truth is experientially discerned. Accordingly, meaning is thought to lie not in the text of Scripture itself, but rather in its application. Knowledge of God, the world, and oneself flows out of the faith-community's shared experience and witness to the God who speaks and acts on behalf of his redeemed people.

There are several aspects to biblical interpretation, namely, the exegetical, the theological, and the historical. Where does the process of interpretation begin? Do philosophico-theological presuppositions have a rightful place in the discipline of biblical exegesis (assuming they are biblically rooted), or are interpreters to begin with a *tabula rasa* (a blank tablet in the mind)? The answer is that the hermeneutical process is a circle. It requires all three components: grammatical-historical exegesis, biblico-theological/systematico-theological analysis, and churchly doctrine (confessional dogmatics). These three are interrelated and necessary, though exegesis possesses an intrinsic priority as the foundation of the entire theological enterprise. We thus enter the hermeneutical circle at any point, with the realization that the principle known in Reformed theology as *sola scriptural* governs the entire exercise in biblical interpretation. Summarily stated, meaning resides in the text of Scripture, not in the church's understanding/application of the Bible to faith and life. One of the characteristics of the Word of God is its perspicuity. With respect to the essential doctrines of the faith Scripture is clear and understandable.

In the final analysis it is the Spirit of God who is our teacher. He is the one who illumines our understanding and impresses upon our hearts and minds the truth of his Word. Theological consensus is ultimately (and singularly) the providential work of God in the history of the Christian church. Trevor Hart, another contributor to *Beyond Two Horizons*, erroneously contends that the internal testimony of the Holy Spirit must be understood as God's present communication with his people by Word and Spirit. He explains:

> The Spirit is God in his relatedness to us in the event of meaning through which he addresses us. He is the 'presence' who finally renders the text 'authoritative' for faith. The church turns to the text seeking an event in which, as the text is interpreted, it will speak authoritatively for the community. *This event happens.*[12]

In the Protestant-Reformed tradition Scripture is seen as self-sufficient, self-validating, and self-interpreting. John Calvin's teaching on the Word and the Spirit best captures the Reformational understanding of the "formal principle" (the Scripture principle). Against subjectivistic readings of the Bible, the clearer passages of Scripture interpret the more obscure texts. This too is a hermeneutical principle of the Protestant Reformation.

## 2. The Law as Means of Justification

The above discussion is preparatory to our consideration of what is called the "material principle" of the Reformation – the doctrine of justification by faith (*sola fide*), the article of faith affirmed in the Lutheran and the Reformed traditions alike. What distinguishes these two theological traditions, however, is the Reformed doctrine of the covenants, what is vital for a proper understanding of Paul's teaching on the Mosaic law. Before turning to this crucial Reformed distinctive, we begin by summarizing the law of God in its traditional threefold classification and threefold usage.

### (a) Three kinds or classifications of the law: moral – civil – ceremonial

It was on Mount Sinai that the law was given to Israel as a constitutional, theocratic nation. The purpose of this law (and covenant) was to distinguish Israel from all other peoples of the earth. In this specific context the law served first and foremost a pedagogical function in the life of Israel (see the discussion below on the uses of the law). The law in its totality was the legal constitution for Israel as a theocracy, the only one of its kind in the entire epoch of redemptive history from the time of Adam's fall into sin to the consummation at the return of Christ. Israel's obedience to the law of God was the meritorious basis of (temporal) life in the land of promise.[13] Looming large on the pages of Scripture, Old and New Testaments, is the antithesis between two contrary principles of inheritance, grace for the eternal (spiritual) inheritance and law for the temporal (physical) inheritance throughout the course of the Mosaic economy of redemption. Israel's compliance with the commandments of God had in view the law in its totality, the Mosaic law as a covenant document, a comprehensive blueprint for blessing and prosperity in the land of Canaan.

Looking more closely at the particular stipulations given to Israel through Moses, mediator of the old covenant, we discern three kinds of law – moral, civil, and ceremonial. Abrogation of the old, Mosaic covenant upon the establishment of the new covenant in Christ in the fullness of time meant that obedience to the law of God (the ceremonial, the civil, and the moral laws) no longer is the meritorious ground of temporal blessing for God's covenant people. To be sure, in Christ the law of God is (re)established and upheld as the moral norm for Christian living, what Reformed theology correctly identified as the "third use" of the law (see discussion below). Under Moses the meritorious reward of the covenant made at Sinai was temporal prosperity in the land. The principle of inheritance was that of works, not grace. That is to say, the principle was that of merit, denoting the just requirements and recompense of the Lord of the covenant. (Compare the similar circumstance regarding Adam at the opening of human history and the angelic host. The good angels were confirmed in their blessed state of righteousness on grounds of their meritorious obedience. In each instance, probation was the way to confirmation in glory. Adam, however, failed the test. In her time of probation theocratic Israel relives, as it were, the story of Adam and his transgression of God's law in the Garden of Eden, the original thecratic site of life in covenant with God.)

It is often said that, whereas the civil and ceremonial laws terminated with the coming of Christ and the new covenant, the moral law is eternally binding. This understanding, however, obscures from view the fact that even the moral commandments given by God to Israel through Moses were part and parcel of that comprehensive, legal entity to which Israel's full compliance was necessary for her enjoyment of temporal life and prosperity in Canaan. Such is not the case with respect to spiritual life in Christ (whether under the old or the new economies of redemption). Compliance with the moral law is never the basis for reconciliation and redemption. (Christ alone has satisfied the legal requirement of the law of God on behalf of God's elect.) Furthermore, the moral laws established by God are subject to his sovereign purpose and determination. The prohibition against taking human life (under normal conditions applicable in all places, in all times, and among all peoples[14]) could be suspended, as in the case of Israel's holy war, what was prelude to Israel's possession of the (typological) land of promise. Think also of the command given to Abraham to sacrifice his own son (in spite of the fact that God would provide Abraham the sacrificial substitute in place of Isaac) or the vow taken by Jephthah respecting his only daughter.[15]

As for the civil code, consider these two examples. In Leviticus 19 we read:

> You are to keep my statutes. You shall not breed together two kinds of your cattle; you shall not sow your field with two kinds of seed, nor wear a garment upon you of two kinds of material mixed together (vs. 19).
>
> You shall not round off the side-growth of your heads, nor harm the edges of your beard (vs. 27).

Since the coming of Christ, these peculiar commands are no longer binding upon the Israelite theocracy (which has ceased to be). Were these arbitrary stipulations on God's part? That question is to be answered in the negative. They served a unique, typical purpose in distinguishing Israel from all the other nations of the world. The difference was between the "holy" and the "common."[16] (In the case of God's prohibition to Adam not to eat of the tree of the knowledge of good and evil this command of the Lord gave specific focus to the crisis that would ensue for our first parents in connection with the Serpent's temptation in the Garden. The mission of the first Adam, as federal head of the entire human race, was to guard the holy sanctuary of God against any and all challenges to God's absolute rule and authority. Adam was to "prove" that there is but one Lord, the God of the covenant.)

Thirdly, there are the ceremonial laws of Moses, which symbolize in different ways the necessity of sacrificial offering(s) for the atonement of sins. The book of Hebrews explores this aspect of old covenant revelation most fully among the inspired documents of the new covenant. John in his theologico-historical account, unique among the four gospels, contrasts the old covenant institutions and economy (what is shadow) with the superiority of the new covenant (what is eschatological reality). Thus, for example, when Jesus informs the Samaritan woman that the day is coming when the people of God will no longer worship at a centralized location (notably, in Jerusalem) but rather "in Spirit and in truth," he is contrasting typical worship in Israel with preconsummate, eschatological worship. Worship is now decentralized, freed from ethnic and ceremonial distinction. The new covenant people of God, refashioned in the image of Christ, are the Temple of the Spirit. (Of course, the same spiritual truth pertains to the elect of God under the old economy; merely the hulk of OT symbol and type falls away with the coming of Christ.)

### (b) Three uses of the law of God: civil – tutelary – normative

Here we find some overlap with the previous discussion, overlap suggesting that the traditional Protestant teaching concerning the classification and usage of the law of God may be somewhat artificial. (For this reason, some have jettisoned the traditional teaching altogether. To do so, however, is extreme and unwarranted.) For what purpose was the law of God given to his people?

An example from the American religious experiment in the sixteenth and seventeenth centuries (with ramifications down to the present) is informative, as well as illustrative of a common misunderstanding of Scripture. Unsuccessful in their attempts to christianize Old England and reform the established church, the Puritans settled in New England (and elsewhere in the American colonies) in the hopes of founding Christian communities, wherein the Bible would serve as their religious and social norm. Whether in Old or New England, the Puritans saw themselves as the "new Israel." Like theocratic Israel in the latter days of the OT prophets, these new Israelites were convinced that God had now entered into "controversy" with the English people in order to test her sole allegiance to him as sovereign Lord. The English (and Scottish) people took on a national covenant with the God of the Bible. The OT civil code was interpreted not merely as a guide in national affairs, specifically, in the formation of civil policy, but as the civil and social *norm*. The English Puritans reestablished the law of Moses in its civil usage (what properly pertained to the ancient Israelite theocracy exclusively). From the time of the cessation of the Mosaic theocracy to the modern period of western civilization, Christians have wrestled with the question of the applicability of the civil code of Moses to the nation as a whole. This historical example serves to highlight the question regarding the role of God's law explicitly revealed in the pages of the Bible to society at large. Does the ancient law of Moses retain its civil use? And if so, in precisely what ways? As a guide or as a norm?[17]

The first generation of Protestant reformers rightly identified the first use of the law of God in its function as a moral compass for every society (the law serving as a guide, not norm). God has clearly revealed his will to humankind. He has made know what man's duty to the Creator is. This law has been inscribed upon the hearts of all God's image-bearers, though now marred by human depravity and sin. Special revelation explicitly teaches the covenant community what is good and what is evil. Despite differences between special and general revelation, between theocratic and nontheocratic governance, the commandments of God are for the good of humankind at large. At the same time, the sovereign Lord providentially upholds (or brings to ruination) nations and kingdoms by effectuating his own mysterious will in the governance of all the affairs of this world. This is the civil use of the law of God. (On this subject the teachings of historic Reformed theology differ significantly from that of Christian reconstructionism.[18])

Secondly, there is the pedagogical or tutelary use of the law. The law of Moses with its requirement of obedience as the basis for divine reward and blessing – specifically, as meritorious grounds for temporal life and prosperity in the land of Canaan – serves to convict Israel of sin and of her inability to secure God's favor on grounds of works-righteousness. To be sure, the law was not given to Israel as a means of salvation. Such would conflict with the promise God granted to Abraham. Rather, the law of Moses was added to the Abrahamic promise. Reformed theology has wrestled long and hard with this datum of biblical revelation. How can one maintain – as we must – the crucial antithesis between contrary principles of inheritance (works vs. faith, law vs. grace), on the one hand, while upholding the continuity of God's redemptive purpose throughout the course of the unfolding Covenant of Grace in the entire epoch of redemptive history from the Fall to the Consummation, on the other? The (only correct) answer lies in the restriction of the works-inheritance principle to the temporal sphere of life in the ancient land of promise. Those who refute this interpretation of covenant theology insist – contrary to the witness of Scripture – that the Mosaic covenant, as part of the progressive manifestation of the single Covenant of Grace, contains no element of works (antithetical to grace). They erroneously contend that the covenant with Moses was exclusively an administration of sovereign grace and promise. Not only does this interpretation ignore the clear teaching of the Bible, it cannot explain Moses' exemption from entrance into the land of Canaan or Israel's deportation to Babylon. In both of these instances the elect fall prey to God's (temporal) wrath and displeasure. If Christ secured the earthly inheritance in the land of promise on Israel's behalf, as is implied in the interpretation under consideration, how then do we explain the temporal judgment inflicted upon the elect of God when that has occurred? Did Christ remove the curse or did he not? We maintain that on the typological level the principle of inheritance was that of law, not grace (= forgiveness on the basis of Christ's sacrificial atonement for sin). Had it been otherwise, the Israelites would have enjoyed perpetual bliss in the land of Canaan. Such was clearly not the case. In his encounter with the rich young ruler Jesus was not suggesting that the law of Moses taught works-righteousness as the means of salvation. On this particular occasion, Jesus was saying hypothetically: Were one to exemplify perfect obedience, that would indeed be meritorious of divine favor and reward (such is the justice of God). Jesus directed his exhortation to the self-righteous individual. In the postlapsarian epoch, the law with its demand for perfect obedience as grounds for reward only works wrath and condemnation against transgressors. In the history of redemption the purpose of the law of Moses was to frustrate Israel on the temporal level, and in so doing point her to the only Savior from sin and all its consequences. In Protestant-Reformed theology this elenchtic, tutelary use of God's law has been identified as the "proper purpose" of the law of Moses.

Thirdly, there is the normative (or regulative) function of the law. Some historians of doctrine erroneously contend that it was Calvin, not Luther, who gave full, unqualified recognition to this use of God's law in the sanctification of the saints.[19] We must be absolutely clear on this: Neither Calvin nor Luther would allow the good works of the believer – works evidential of true, saving faith – to stand with faith as the instrumental means of justification. Did they differ on the importance of obedience to God for the disciples of Christ, those regenerated by the Spirit of God? Did one emphasize this component of Christian living more than the other? There is ample indication in the writings of Luther and Calvin that they were in full agreement on the necessity of good works (though not as the grounds of the sinner's justification before God). There were differences in formulation, to be sure. Those differences were most apparent in the Calvinistic formulations of the divine covenants in the Bible. (Classic Lutheranism, following the teaching of Luther, has no doctrine of the covenants.) Whatever the differences in theological formulation between Lutheranism and Calvinism, both were equally emphatic on the importance and necessity for sanctification in the lives of the saints. Whether or not the terminology of the law's "third use" was employed, this doctrine was essentially the same. Among covenant theologians the question is posed in these terms: What are the conditions of the Covenant of Grace? Or is the Covenant of Grace unconditional? This debate within Calvinism is essentially semantic. In sum, Protestantism was unified in its teaching concerning the believer's justification and sanctification, twin benefits (among others) of union with Christ in his death and resurrection.

### 3. Doctrine as Theological System

In the opening section of this chapter we noted the recent movement in contemporary theology to reaffirm the importance of theological system as reflective of the teachings of the Bible, a system of doctrine which recognizes the interrelatedness of biblical teaching. Consistent application of this insight will require us to abandon the artificial distinction some have made between "doctrine" (what the Bible teaches) and "theology" (Christian interpretation subsequent to the close of the canonical writings). That distinction posits a false dichotomy between the two. To the extent that the teachings of the church are true to the teachings of Scripture they are to be believed and obeyed.

The formative era of Reformation theology was ushered in by Luther's studies in Romans and the Psalms – specifically, by his recovery of the biblical teaching on justification by faith alone. This was followed by the period of codification associated with the movement known as orthodox Protestant scholasticism, Lutheran and Reformed. Luther's teaching on justification and divine monergism (especially as articulated in his classic study, *The Bondage of the Will*) accented the sovereignty of God's electing grace in salvation. This twofold doctrine was further developed by Calvin explicitly in terms of the covenants of God in the economy of redemption (from the Fall to the Consummation). Most notably, it was in his commentaries that Calvin exploited the law/gospel distinction to the fullest, demonstrating the supreme importance he placed upon the crucial Protestant and biblical antithesis between the principle of works and the principle of faith. As the historical development of doctrine testifies, no two elements within the Reformed-Protestant system of doctrine are more pivotal than that respecting the justification of sinners before a holy and righteous God, sinners wholly incapable of performing spiritually good acts (including the exercise of saving faith) apart from the regenerative work of the Spirit of God, and sovereign, electing grace. In Calvinism, both of these elements of theology are explicated in terms of the unfolding Covenant of Grace. What follows here is a summary statement of the theology of the covenants, gleaned from five centuries of Reformed theological reflection.

Humankind was created in covenant relationship with God. Since the fall of Adam into sin creatures relate to God either as covenant-keepers (those who are redeemed in Christ) or covenant-breakers (those who are outside of Christ). All creatures made in the image of God know him truly, though not savingly. Saving knowledge comes through the regenerating, illuminating work of God's Spirit. The biblical hermeneutic known as presuppositionalism teaches students of the Word to think God's thoughts after him. We believe because God has revealed truths concerning himself, the world, and ourselves through special revelation. The regenerate mind freely and truly believes that God is and that he rewards those who seek him. The believer freely and willingly submits to the Scriptures as the inspired, inerrant, authoritative Word of God. (To be sure, sin and unbelief can impair the believer's apprehension of God's truth in Scripture.)

The Scriptures, Old and New Testaments, are the covenantal documents of the two economies of redemption, the Mosaic and the New. The canon of Scripture for the people of God is defined redemptive-historically, that is, in terms of the historical unfolding of the Covenant of Grace. With the coming of Christ and the establishment of the new covenant, the books of the New Testament are the unique canonical documents for the household of faith. (All the books of the Bible comprise the Christian church's scriptures, but only the New serves as the church's canon. Canon is defined by God's covenant-institution.) The speech and acts of God in creation and redemption (all that is extrinsic to God as he is in himself in his supremely exalted majesty and self-existence) are always covenantal. These outward, divine manifestations comprise the historical realization of the eternal, intratrinitarian counsel of God. The triune God consists of three distinct personalities – that of the Father, the Son, and the Spirit – personalities united within the single Godhead. Here lies the source of all unity and diversity in created existence. Because there is genuine unity and diversity within the Godhead, there is genuine unity and diversity within the created order.

The question arises: Is covenant relationship intrinsic to the Godhead? Does the covenant bond apply to God as he exists in himself as triune personality? Does covenant describe the eternal, ontological, intratrinitarian relationship of the three persons of the trinity? Or is the covenant relationship purely extrinsic to the self-existent being of God? In other words, is covenant a fundamentally historical reality (something outside God's own nature and being)? In twentieth-century Reformed thought there have been some theologians, like Geerhardus Vos, who have traced the covenant concept back into the Godhead itself.[20] Personhood, thereby, is descriptive of covenantal relationship, and vice versa. Covenant by definition means bond, relationship, commitment. In terms of the divine-human engagements recorded in the Scriptures, covenant is a relationship under sanctions, blessing for obedience and curse for disobedience.

Humankind's salvation – the redemption of God's elect – is achieved only by way of the covenantal faithfulness of God's Son, Jesus Christ, the only mediator between God and redeemed humanity. Christ is the fulfillment and consummation of all God's purposes in creation and re-creation. By his obedience and death, Christ actively and passively has made full satisfaction for sin (including satisfaction of the legal demands of the first covenant with Adam).[21] The kingdom granted to the Son by the Father in fulfillment of the Covenant of Works is not merely the present, spiritual rule of Christ in the hearts of believers, but the consummate, eternal kingdom, depicted in the Scriptures as the New Heavens and the New Earth, what awaits Christ's return at the close of history.

The Lord of the covenant is also the Lord of the Sabbath. Having created all things in six days (the interpretation of the "days" of creation is hotly disputed in contemporary Reformed orthodoxy), God rested. The same pattern pertains to humankind. Subsequent to Adam's successful completion of probation (had that been rendered), humankind over time would have fulfilled the so-called "cultural mandate," and then have entered its final rest in the consummated new heavens and new earth. The weekly Sabbath-rest, as sign of God's covenant, pointed to this grand day of eschatological fulfillment. The reward of eternal life – according to the terms of the original Covenant of Works – would have been secured through the obedience of the First Adam. That obedience would have been reckoned to the account of each and every human being that came into the world. After the Fall, it was the redemptive work of Christ that guaranteed the final outcome anticipated in the Edenic covenant. Recreation of redeemed humanity in the image of God's Son is wholly a work of sovereign, electing grace. (Observation of the Sabbath now belongs exclusively to the people of God, the fellowship of saints.)

In this present, semi-eschatological age, the church – the Spirit-filled people of God – is the assembly of the new covenant saints, the holy community set apart unto God. The fellowship of believers is a voluntary association upholding the doctrinal and ethical teachings set forth in the Bible. It is a religious association whose discipline is noncoercive. The eschatological design of creation finds explicit description in the pages of the Old and New Testaments. God's promise of salvation finds provisional, typological realization in the former economy of salvation, the Mosaic epoch of redemptive revelation. Rightly interpreted, typology is a subset of eschatology. The twofold covenants of God, the Covenant of Works in creation and the Covenant of Grace in redemption, serve as the vehicle for the administration of God's kingdom in this world.[22]

## 4. The Gospel of Justification by Faith in the History of Doctrine

Reformed preoccupation with the subject of Law and Gospel characterizes Reformed theological exposition down to present times. As we have accounted elsewhere, the twofold doctrine of the covenants, the Covenant of Works and the Covenant of Grace, appeared first in the late sixteenth century, rapidly becoming the staple of Reformed thought in the seventeenth century onwards.[23] Only in the late twentieth century has this teaching been subject to vigorous criticism by neoorthodox reinterpreters of doctrine, notably by those following in the footsteps of Karl Barth.

The biblical doctrine of justification by faith was largely lost in the early period of Christian doctrine – in the period of the ancient church down to the time of late-medieval scholasticism. Failure to identify two contrary principles of inheritance, law and gospel (merit and grace), contributed in large part to this deviation from biblical teaching. The theological concept of "merit," first introduced by Tertullian (a lawyer by training), was a legal, forensic term, as is the term "justification." Favor with God and life everlasting was seen as the meritorious reward for faithful obedience, as exemplified in the life of Jesus Christ. It was not until the time of Augustine that the biblical doctrines of election and justification began to come to light, notably in Augustine's teaching on the "letter" and the "Spirit." Augustine's insight helped pave the way for later Reformed-Protestant teaching on justification and the covenants.

Medieval nominalism made extensive use of the covenant concept. According to this school of thought, the promised reward of God would be obtained by means of the sincere efforts of sinners who did their very best. Salvation was conceived as a cooperative effort between God and the sinner (in covenant with God). This doctrine of divine acceptation was echoed in subsequent Reformed scholasticism. Reintroduction of the theological dichotomy between an original state of nature and a subsequent covenant arrangement (understood to be superimposed upon the order of nature, and the consequence of God's condescending grace) would prove to be a major setback for biblical interpretation.[24] This unwelcome development in Reformed federalism led to the devolution of doctrine – deviation from the biblical doctrine of the Covenant of Works as that was articulated by the first-generation covenant theologians. Fortunately, the scholastic formulation did not result in the dissolution of the classic Protestant Law/Gospel antithesis so essential to the Reformation doctrine concerning justification by faith alone. It did, nevertheless, create problems for those following in the tradition of scholastic Reformed federalism, problems that have not been fully resolved to this day in Protestant orthodoxy.[25]

The catalyst for the Reformed-Protestant understanding of the Law/Gospel contrast was the biblical teaching on the Mosaic covenant. Both Lutheran and Reformed interpreters of the Bible identified a legal principle operating within the Mosaic economy of redemption. At the same time, the Mosaic administration was viewed – notably within the Reformed tradition – as wholly consistent with the progressive unfolding of the Covenant of Grace, spanning the entire epoch of redemption. Significant differences in interpretation came to the surface in later English federalism, which adopted views anticipating the modern-day "misinterpretation view" of Paul on the law. According to this viewpoint, it was Judaistic perversion of the Mosaic law which accounts for Paul's negative critique of the law. Other Calvinistic interpreters recognized a merely "formal" contrast between Moses and Christ, between the Law and the Gospel. John Murray, a modern-day exponent of this Puritan doctrine, describes the law of God as a "bare" principle – as law abstracted from the covenantal context of sovereign grace and promise.[26] Part of the confusion associated with this reading of the law is to be laid at the feet of Calvin, whose teaching on the letter/Spirit contrast was, at best, confusing and, at worst, contradictory with respect to his teaching on the Law/Gospel contrast. It is the task of contemporary Reformed theology to come to grips with the weaknesses in its own theological tradition – and to do so for the sake of the Gospel of sovereign, saving grace. Exploitation of erroneous views deeply embedded in the Calvinistic tradition by the radical revisionists will only hinder the mission and witness of the Christian church to the Gospel. At worst, it results in the promulgation of another gospel, which is no gospel at all.

**ENDNOTES**

*Much of the material in this chapter was first presented in lectures to elders of the Park Woods Orthodox Presbyterian Church (Kansas, MO) in June 2000 at a retreat held in Ipswich, MA.

[1] See my *Covenant Theology in Reformed Perspective: Collected Essays and Book Reviews in Historical, Biblical, and Systematic Theology* (Eugene, OR: Wipf and Stock, 2000).

[2] Baker: Grand Rapids, 2000. This collection of essays, edited by J. B. Green and M. Turner, serves as an introduction for the launching of a new commentary series, *The Two Horizons Commentary*.

[3] *Ibid.* 2 (emphasis mine).

[4] *Ibid.* 12.

[5] *Ibid.* 97.

[6] *Ibid.* 102

[7] *Ibid.* 103

[8] See Mark W. Karlberg, "Doctrinal Development in Scripture and Tradition: A Reformed Assessment of the Church's Theological Task," *CTJ* 30 (1995) 401-418; reprinted in my *Covenant Theology in Reformed Perspective* 341-55. Much mischief has been created by the modern view – now so prevalent in Reformed circles – which says that the Hoy Spirit speaking within the faith-community leads the church into the truth of Scripture (see the argument presented by Franke, cited in the "Introduction," endnote 1). Traditional Protestant-Reformed teaching maintains that Scripture is *self-interpreting*. The interpretation of the Bible is not dependent upon the church or tradition. The Spirit bears witness to the truth of Scripture in the hearts of believers. That is to say, the truth of God is apprehended *by faith* (not reason). Enlightenment reasoning suggests that the human interpreter plays a determinative role in the formulation of Christian doctrine. To be sure, faith is not contrary to

reason. Reason, however, does not have the priority or role in the interpretive process that is advocated by the modernists. (Of course, reason illuminated by the Word and the Spirit does play a role in biblical interpretation. The Reformed understanding of the hermeneutical process, however, differs radically from that of modern-day revisionists.)

[9] Compare the current debates over the "openness of God." Proponents of this view have made full, thoroughgoing application of the Arminian doctrine regarding human freedom and divine contingency. An insightful critique of this modern-day theological heresy is found in Scott J. Hafemann's *The God of Promise and the Life of Faith: Understanding the heart of the Bible* (Wheaton: Crossway, 2001). Hafemann convincingly explains why the openness doctrine is not an evangelical option. (Disappointing, however, is his departure from traditional Protestant teaching on justification by faith alone. See Chapter 8, endnote 14.)

[10] *Between Two Horizons* 167-69.

[11] See my critique of Frame's hermeneutics, "On the Theological Correlation of Divine and Human Language: A Review Article," *JETS* 32 (1989) 99-105. Frame's rejoinder to my review essay is republished as Appendix C in his *The Doctrine of God* (Phillipsburg: Presbyterian and Reformed, 2002) 759-768. Additional interaction with my analysis of his work is found in Appendix B, *The Doctrine of God* 751-758. Frame takes this occasion to rail against one of his critics – displaying more emotion than substantive interaction. His complaints are *ad hominem,* and succeed only in evading the substantive issues in dispute. For the record, the editor of my review article (appearing in the *Mid-America Journal of Theology*) was sympathetic to my evaluation of Frame's perspectivalism and misreading of the apologetical method of Cornelius Van Til. Appendix D below was written prior to the publication of *The Doctrine of God*. Additional response is unnecessary.

[12] *Between Two Horizons* 203 (italics mine).

¹³ Specifically, it was Israel's *retention* of the land that was based on meritorious observance of the law of Moses. The original grant of land, as well as Israel's restoration to the land after Babylonian captivity, was a gift of God's unmerited grace.

¹⁴ This universal knowledge of what the law requires is the outworking of natural law written upon the human heart. See further, Mark W. Karlberg, "Reformation Politics: The Relevance of Old Testament Ethics in Calvinist Political Theory," JETS 29 (1986) 179-91; reprinted in *Covenant Theology in Reformed Perspective* 59-72.

¹⁵ This was not a "rash vow" on the part of Jephthah, who being filled by the Spirit of God was raised up to serve as one of Israel's deliverers in this unstable period in the history of the Israelite theocracy. Jephthah's vow was typological of the vow made by God the Father concerning his Son in the eternal Covenant of Redemption.

¹⁶ Contrast the teachings of the modern-day Christian Reconstructionists. See endnote 14 above and 18 below.

¹⁷ See further, Mark W. Karlberg, "Moses and Christ: The Place of Law in Seventeenth-Century Puritanism," TrinJ 10 NS (1989) 11-32; reprinted in *Covenant Theology in Reformed Perspective* 73-93.

¹⁸ See my "Covenant and Common Grace: A Review Article," WTJ 50 (1988) 323-37; reprinted in *Covenant Theology in Reformed Perspective* 297-307.

¹⁹ Contrast the views of Peter Lillback in *The Binding of God: Calvin's role in the development of covenant theology* (Texts and Studies in Reformation and Post-Reformation Thought; Grand Rapids: Baker, 2001). Compare the critical review of this book by Cornelis Venema in MJT 13 (2002) 201-209. John Frame in "Law and Gospel" (www.chalcedon.edu/articles, dated January 4, 2002) opposes the classic Protestant law/gospel distinction. Following the Shepherd-Gaffin interpretation, Frame regards this distinction as Lutheran, not Reformed. He takes vigorous exception to the position adopted by the Alliance of Confessing Evangelicals, naming

its publication *Modern Reformation* and the White Horse Inn radio broadcasts. (Sad to say, recent developments have produced division even within the Alliance.)

[20] See further my doctoral study, "The Mosaic Covenant and the Concept of Works in Reformed Hermeneutics: A Historical-Critical Analysis with Special Attention to Early Covenant Eschatology" (Th.D. dissertation, Westminster Theological Seminary, 1980) 237-242 and 250-256. Available at University Microfilms International (Ann Arbor, MI and London, England), #8024938. A recent study advancing ideas laid out in my dissertation is Michael S. Horton's *Covenant and Eschatology: The Divine Drama* (Louisville, London: Westminster John Knox, 2002). For an evaluation of Horton's formulation, see Appendix B below (previously appearing in *TrinJ* 24 [2003] 125-129). In the Spring of 2003 Horton submitted his name as a candidate for a systematics post at Westminster Seminary (to replace Trumper), and then withdraw his candidacy. Although he claims to hold to traditional covenant theology, his embrace of Gaffin's teaching – and his alignment with New School Westminster – calls that commitment into question. At the very least, there are divided interests that need to be reassessed.

[21] William Berends in "The Obedience of Jesus Christ" (*Vox Reformata: Australasian Journal for Christian Scholarship* 66 [2001] 26-51) upholds the traditional doctrine of the Covenant of Works. See also the recent study by van Willem J. van Asselt, *The Federal Theology of Johannes Cocceius (1603-1669)* (trans. by Raymond A. Blacketer; Studies in the History of Christian Thought, vol. 100; Leiden, Boston, Köln: Brill, 2001), which I have reviewed in *JETS* 45 (2002) 734-738, reprinted below in Appendix C.

[22] See Mark W. Karlberg, "The Significance of Israel in Biblical Typology," *JETS* 31 (1988) 257-69; and my "Justification in Redemptive History," *WTJ* 43 (1981) 213-46. Both essays are republished in my *Covenant Theology in Reformed Perspective* 193-207 and 157-180. The most recent textbook in Reformed theology to advance historic Reformed teaching is that written by Robert L. Reymond, *A New Systematic Theology of the Christian Faith* (Chapter 2 contains my review article of this work). Compare also Louis Igou

Hodges' discussion in *Reformed Theology Today* (Columbus, GA: Brentwood Christian Press, 1995), which I have critiqued in Chapter 1 above.

[23] Consult further, Mark W. Karlberg, "Reformed Interpretation of the Mosaic Covenant," *WTJ* 43 (1980) 1-57; reprinted in *Covenant Theology in Reformed Perspective* 17-57. A popular rendering of this teaching is found in several articles in *Semper Reformanda* 12 (2003).

[24] See Mark W. Karlberg, "The Original State of Adam: Tensions in Reformed Theology," *The Evangelical Quarterly* 59 (1987) 291-309; reprinted in *Covenant Theology in Reformed Perspective* 95-110.

[25] A few comments concerning Richard A. Muller's masterful work, *Post-Reformation Reformed Dogmatics: The Rise and Development of Reformed Orthodoxy, ca. 1520 t0 ca. 1725* (4 volumes; Grand Rapids: Baker, 2003), are in order. (Volumes one and two appeared previously, in 1987 and 1993 respectively, and have been revised for this publication. See my review of volume one in *WTJ* 50 [1988] 364-70. ) The author has not sufficiently engaged the contemporary debate. Perpetuation of the speculative, scholastic dichotomy between nature and grace in Muller's conceptualization of the original Covenant of Works renders his study inadequate for the present controversy. Specifically, his command of the Reformation, post-Reformation literature has proven to be of little help in the refutation of the views of the radical revisionists, New School Westminster in particular. One had hoped that Muller would have contributed constructively in this magisterial work for the sake of confessional Protestant-Reformed orthodoxy in our own day. But Muller's failure to reassess the scholastic formulation in the light of the teaching of Scripture only plays into the hands of the revisionists. To speak of the first covenant at creation as "gracious" is to muddy the waters and cloud the issues. Fundamentally, it is an exegetico-theological question whether God's grace is manifested in the initial order of creation or whether the manifestation of divine grace is reserved for the postlapsarian epoch of redemption. Closely related to this question are the intramural debates between the infra- and supralapsarians concerning the pri-

ority of creation to redemption (both disputants here acknowledge the distinctiveness and the eternality of the decrees of God respecting creation and redemption). Additionally, there is the question whether God's decree to create and his decree to redeem the world – comprehensive of "whatsoever comes to pass in history" – are eternal in the same sense in which God's aseity is eternal, self-existent, unchanging, simple (the doctrine of the divine *unitas simplicitatis*), and self-contained. Muller likewise gives short shrift to the matter of the interpretation of the Mosaic covenant both as an administration of the ongoing Covenant of Grace and as incorporating the works-merit principle. Muller is not wholly unaware of these issues as seen in his comments concerning the knowledge of God "under grace," in distinction from the knowledge of God in creation (*Post-Reformation Reformed Dogmatics* 3.214), and in his comments regarding the temporal administration of the covenants of God in history (3.317). Exploiting the weak point in Reformed federalism, as seen in Gaffin's work, does not advance the truth of the Gospel of grace. The speculative, scholastic construct on nature and grace only confuses and confounds the issues in theological analysis seeking to be faithful to the teaching of Scripture.

[26] Mark W. Karlberg, "Paul's Letter to the Romans in the *New International Commentary on the New Testament* and in Contemporary Reformed Thought," *EvQ* 71 (1999) 3-24; and my "Paul, the Old Testament and Judaism: A Review Article," *Foundations: A Journal of Evangelical Theology* 43 (1999) 36-44. Both articles are reprinted in *Covenant Theology in Reformed Perspective* 227-258. Consult also the comprehensive work edited by D. A. Carson, P. T. O'Brien, and M. A. Seifrid, entitled *Justification and Variegated Nomism: Vol 1, The Complexities of Second Temple Judaism* (Wissenschaftliche Untersuchungen zum Neuen Testament 2, Reihe 140; Tübingen: Mohr Siebeck; Grand Rapids: Baker Academic 2001). Volume two in this series will address the theological ramifications of the debate on Paul on the law.

[27] See especially my *Covenant Theology in Reformed Perspective* 338-339 (n. 2).

# Chapter 4

# Covenant Theology: A Post-Reformation Accretion?

The subject before us concerns the heart of the Christian message, justification by faith alone (*sola fide, sola gratia*). What is the relationship between the Law and the Gospel? To begin, we must understand that in terms of the history of Christian doctrine this manner of speaking is *theological*. The Law/Gospel antithesis is unarguably a theological construct. Saying this, however, is not to suggest that this teaching is sub-biblical. We are not to think of the classic Protestant Law/Gospel distinction as extra-biblical. The distinction is implicit in the text of Scripture. Christian theology is an explicitly exegetical enterprise; it is the explication of what Scripture teaches. Theological terminology either enhances or detracts from the systematico-exegetical task. To be sure, theological vocabulary – the product of Protestant scholasticism, old and new – is the necessary handmaid to biblical exegesis and interpretation. Some form of scholasticism is characteristic of every theological tradition. Every school of interpretation is distinguished by a particular system of doctrine and theological vocabulary – with a good deal of overlap, I might add, among the various Protestant systems. The seeds for theological shorthand are already planted in the biblical record itself – in the notions of divine immortality and incomprehensibility (1Tim 6:16 and Rom 11:33-36), the common and the holy (Lev 11:43-47 and Zech 14:21), (eternal) generation and procession (Jn 1:1-3 and Heb 1:5; Jn 14:26 and 16:7), legal (forensic) justification and imputation (Rom 5:12ff.), to name just a few. All this is to say, a biblical term is oftentimes more than a just a word.

  The Law/Gospel contrast is biblical and it is essential within the Protestant-Reformed system of doctrine. But we must first pause to ask ourselves: Are interpreters of the Bible correct in positing a "system" of doctrine within Scripture, a system reflected in the great creedal and dogmatic formulations of the Christian church? In my view, the Bible does contain a "system of doctrine," and Christian theology is correct in seeking to elucidate yet further that system of doctrine. The systematization of doctrine, the beginnings of which are already apparent in the biblical text, is essential to the church's interpretive task. What Scripture sets forth requires further elucidation, both in terms of theological definition and development of thought by subsequent Christian interpreters. Reformed covenant theology provides us with a prime example of deepening theological understanding. And it is my contention that Reformed covenant theology, in distinction from all other evangelical traditions, has done fuller justice to the Protestant Law/Gospel antithesis as regards the total witness of Scripture. Whereas this specific theological construct is an essential element within both Lutheran and Reformed teaching, credit goes to the latter for exploiting the full implications and ramifications of this biblically-based antithesis within its system of doctrine.[1]

  To what precisely does the Law/Gospel contrast refer? It has in view the manner in which God's covenant partner receives the promised inheritance. In the time of the Reformation the critical issue for Martin Luther (and all of the Protestant reformers) was how a sinner could be reconciled to a holy God. The synergistic and sacramentalist understanding of the Roman Church was judged to be in gross error. Alongside the sacerdotal system of Rome was the antiscriptural teaching concerning the role of meritorious works in the procurement of salvation. Luther's return to the Bible led him to recover the pure doctrine of justification by faith apart from the works of the law. Law stands to condemn the sinner of his/her transgression of God's commandments, including the righteous demand for full and perfect obedience. Gospel denotes the forgiveness of sins and declaration of righteousness on the basis of an alien righteousness, the righteousness of Christ, imputed to those who believe, not on the basis of inwrought righteousness. Atonement is grounded exclusively upon the obedience of the true Servant of the covenant, God's Son. For the beneficiaries of Christ's reconciling work the inheritance is received by grace through faith. The principle of inheritance is faith (that is, sovereign, saving grace). In his study of the Scriptures Luther identified an antithetical principle of inheritance, that of meritorious works, operative within the covenant God made with Israel at Sinai. Moses in his peculiar office as preacher of Law was contrasted with his preaching of Gospel. Law characterized the old covenant, and Gospel the new. John Calvin shared this same understanding of the relationship between the two testaments or covenants. In Protestant theology the historical event which necessitates the antithesis between Law and Gospel is the Fall. Subsequent to Adam's transgression of God's commandment, humanity lay in bondage to sin and death. Deliverance would come about only by means of God's singular remedy for sin, substitutionary atonement. The promise of redemption had already been announced to our first parents in the Garden (see Gen 3:15, what has been called the protevangelium, the first announcement of the gospel).

Protestant Orthodoxy, Lutheran and Reformed, is united in its adherence to the Law/Gospel contrast. Both traditions share an essentially identical understanding of the biblical doctrine of justification by grace through faith. Where the traditions diverge is in their understanding of the original state of Adam and the history and significance of the several covenants established by God in the pre- and postlapsarian epochs. Briefly stated, these two traditions differ in their formulations of biblical eschatology, what pertains to the goal of God's original creation. In the interest of further systematizing the biblical data with regard to the history of revelation, Reformed interpreters came to recognize that the original arrangement between God and Adam was federal, that is, covenantal. Several features stand out in this initial state of affairs. Not only was the first covenant at creation informed by the works-inheritance principle – as opposed to the faith-inheritance principle associated with God's provision of redemption – but this order was qualified by the specific demand of the covenant, the probationary command not to eat of the tree of the knowledge of good and evil. It had in view a particular, limited period of time. The original state of creation was provisional, looking forward to its eschatological goal, consummation in Glory. So long as the principle of inheritance by works was operative, Adam, as federal head of the human race, was on probation. (Wherever in Scripture we find this works-principle in effect, we are addressing a situation involving probationary testing – thus not only in the case of Adam at creation, but also with respect to Israel under the law of Moses and Jesus in his earthly mission, the purpose of which was to fulfill all righteousness.) Had Adam successfully completed his time of probation, had he rendered to God full and perfect obedience, his "one act of righteousness" would have been imputed to the account of the entire human race. As it turned out, Adam's transgression resulted in the guilt of all humankind. A further consequence of Adam's rebellion was the depravity of human nature and the reign of sin as a dominating power. Each individual of the human race was not only accounted guilty for Adam's act of treason, but was now also prone to do evil, not good, continually. The human will, as Luther learned from Scripture, was bound to sin and disobedience. All humanity lay under God's wrath and displeasure.

In mercy God was moved to establish a second covenant wherein life and righteousness would prevail. That covenant, according to the Reformed tradition, was the Covenant of Grace, spanning the time from Adam's fall in the Garden to the consummation of history at the return of Christ, the inauguration of the new heavens and new earth. Covenant theologians uniformly stressed the continuity of the covenants in the entire epoch of redemption. At the same time, these theologians recognized the unique operation of the works-inheritance principle within the Mosaic economy. It would be the peculiar task of Reformed covenant theology from the time of the Reformation onwards to elucidate the precise manner in which these two antithetical principles of inheritance – one of works, the other of grace – were fully compatible within the Mosaic administration, what was itself a manifestation of the single, overarching Covenant of Grace. The core significance, the "proper purpose," of redemptive covenant throughout the course of history is the salvation of God's elect. But under the old economy the elenchtic, tutelary function of the Mosaic law was to work death in Israel. The final judgment was symbolically represented in Israel's captivity in Babylon. On the basis of her own obedience to the law of Moses Israel was unable to secure God's favor and blessing in the promised land. The principle governing Israel's retention of the land was that of works, not faith.²

Turning to another aspect of the Law/Gospel doctrine, a somewhat subtle difference appears between Lutheranism and Calvinism in their respective understandings of the role of good works in the life of the Christian, in the life of the one justified by grace through faith. That difference pertains to what has been dubbed the "third use of the law." There is no question that Calvin emphasized this use of the law. Obedience to the law of God, though not the meritorious ground of salvation, nevertheless was necessary as *evidence* of spiritual regeneration and renewal. In substance, Luther and those in his theological train were in full agreement concerning the necessity of good works as demonstrative of true faith. However, Lutheranism accented the law's "second use," what consists in the law's pedagogical function in the condemnation of all humankind since the Fall. On all essential points Lutherans and Calvinists were in agreement. The differences are largely – though not exclusively – semantic. They are doctrinally systemic; that is to say, these differences have exercised a formative role in the exposition of the respective systems of doctrine.

Study of the Reformation creeds reveals genuine development in doctrinal understanding, as well as consensus within historic Protestant orthodoxy. My paper entitled "The Impact of Norman Shepherd's Teaching within Westminster Theological Seminary," published here as Chapter 7, addresses one important modern-day dispute concerning the teaching of Scripture and the creeds of the Protestant Reformation. It addresses the fierce battle between orthodoxy and neoorthodoxy, a battle that has penetrated deeply within the ranks of contemporary evangelicalism. The so-called "new perspective on Paul and the Mosaic law" is but one facet of this controversy. The allegation has frequently been made that Dutch Calvinism differs significantly from English Calvinism, a difference reflected in the *Three Forms of Unity* and the *Westminster Confession of Faith* and *Catechisms*. The argument advanced in support of this reading of international Calvinism, in my judgment, lacks any support in the literature of the Reformation. What this argument does show is a lack of appreciation for and understanding of genuine development in doctrinal formulation, and more significantly, a misinterpretation of the fundamental doctrines of the Protestant-Reformed faith, specifically, justification by faith alone and decretive election (also known as "double-predestination"). More germane to the theological tradition presently under review, the Reformed doctrine of the Covenant of Works as espoused in the Westminster standards is in the mind of some critics foreign to the system of doctrine taught in the creeds of the Dutch Reformed churches. As I see it, it is not enough to argue from the fact that the covenant-of-works terminology is not employed in the Dutch confessions. Such an argument is overly simplistic.

The root of modern-day antipathy for the Reformed doctrine of the Covenant of Works is distaste – even revulsion – for the biblical teaching that God relates to humankind on the basis of law (merit). Complicating the picture drawn from the history of Reformed dogmatics is the uncritical adoption of the Thomistic nature/grace (nature/covenant) dichotomy by the early orthodox scholastics in their formulations of the doctrine of the Covenant of Works. Simply put, this view teaches that at the outset of creation Adam's "natural" relationship to God was one of works. So long as Adam rendered perfect obedience to God he was worthy of divine blessing and approbation. The covenant arrangement, understood as superimposed upon the (initial) order of nature, opened up the prospect of confirmation in righteousness (wherein transgression of God's law was no longer a possibility). In this scholastic conceptualization the reward of the covenant was one of grace, not meritorious works. Contemporary Reformed theologians now have the arduous task of untangling disparate theological elements found within their own tradition. Despite the difficulty in this effort, I maintain that Reformed covenant theology continues to offer evangelicals the best interpretation of redemptive history and revelation. It is the Reformed doctrine of the covenants which has done fuller justice to the classic Protestant contrast between Law and Gospel. The outcome of this reading of the Bible is a more satisfying restatement of the system of doctrine contained in the Scriptures. A crucial feature of Reformed hermeneutics is the role given to biblical typology in the exposition of the relationship between the Testaments.

Time does not permit more than a passing glance at recent developments within contemporary theology, namely, "progressive dispensationalism" and the "new perspective on Paul and the law." In my judgment, the first of these is but a variation within evangelicalism; the second entails a repudiation of the message of justification by faith alone hailed by the sixteenth- and seventeenth-century Protestant reformers. The latter teaching is essentially a return to medieval nominalism, specifically, the teaching that God covenants with that individual who seeks God's favor on the basis of his/her best moral efforts. Critics of the Protestant doctrine suggest that the root or source of Luther's trouble and anxiety is what has been dubbed "the introspective conscience of the West." If only Luther had lived in the enlightened age of E. P. Sanders, James Dunn, and N. T. Wright![3] For the most part, dispensationalism today no longer teaches that God tested Israel through the giving of the law at Sinai as a means of salvation. On this point most dispensationalists have now joined Calvinists in denying that the Mosaic covenant was ever anything other than a manifestation of the single

Covenant of Grace. Differences remain, however, over the meaning and significance of ancient Israel's election and over the nature and content of saving faith under the two economies of redemption. Regrettably, too many of the progressive dispensationalists have fallen prey to the error of Daniel Fuller and others in denouncing the covenant-of-works idea. Most modern interpreters come to Leviticus 18:5 – *the* critical Old Testament text in the current debate – with a radically different presupposition at work, one which results in the dissolution of the traditional Law/Gospel contrast. According to this interpretation, the "doing of the law" is equated with the "obedience of faith" (to use Paul's expression in his letter to the Romans). It is at this point that we see the convergence of modern-day "evangelicalism" – represented by many of the progressive dispensationalists – with the "new perspective on Paul and the law." What all these interpreters share in common is their anti-juridical bias. We are told that God is a God of grace who never relates to humankind in terms of legal satisfaction. God is a loving, indulgent Father who does not count disobedience against transgressors. (The love of God, on this view, is unconditional.) I ask: Does the redemptive work of God in Christ restore the sinner to the position of Adam before the Fall, so that the keeper of the covenant now works out his/her salvation, that is, justification, through the exercise of faith and obedience? Is the notion of Adam's probation in the Garden a speculative element within Calvinism? Does theocratic Israel's experience of exile – as the representative experience of Everyman – suggest that salvation is losable?

The current issue of the *Journal of the Evangelical Theological Society* contains an essay by Craig Blaising, entitled "The Future of Israel as a Theological Question." There are a number of strong exceptions I take to Blaising's take on biblical and historical theology. Here I only address the major plank of his argument, the contention that supersessionism, in whatever form, is a distortion of Scripture. Blaising's attack is aimed more directly at the teachings of amillennialism, what is Reformed covenant theology in its most consistent expression. "Supersessionists," Blaising asserts, "developed ways of reading the Bible that not only eliminated Israel from the main story, but turned it into a symbol of the Gentile Church and the spiritual realities that characterized the Church's supposed future."[4] Throughout this essay Blaising makes sweeping statements without substantiation or documentation. More seriously, Blaising's own interpretation – what is intended as the answer to supersessionism – ends up sacralizing the Jewish people, seeing them as a holy, sanctified people singularly favored by God, the chosen nation for time and, in the thinking of most dispensationalists, eternity. "Israel and the Jewish people," writes Blaising, "are taken up into God's ways of blessing human life on this side of the parousia – a point which might be seen in Thomas Cahill's recent work *The Gifts of the Jews*."[5] Ethnic Israel is thereby granted a *mediatorial* role, a role that belongs uniquely to Christ. Lastly, by way of critique, Blaising's distinction between his brand of "new creation eschatology" and the "spiritual-vision eschatology" attributed to amillennialism is not helpful at all. The real issue in the theological dispute is one's understanding of the nature and significance of ancient Israel's theocratic election. To be sure, how one answers this question brings into view the discipline of biblical hermeneutics in its comprehensive scope and application. Pivotal in this discussion is one's grasp of biblical typology, including the matter of the relationship between the old and new covenants. Evangelicalism today (as in the past) contains several disparate systems of doctrine. The alleged consensus within contemporary scholarship, of which Blaising speaks, is an illusion. The case against amillennialism has not been made – certainly not by Blaising.[6]

One closing observation: Christian theology does not have one new word to add to the deposit of truth contained in the canons of Scripture, Old and New Testaments. Rather, the history of Christian interpretation is the history of the church's *apprehension* of God's Word. That apprehension is set forth in polemical formulation as the church's restatement and defense of what Scripture teaches concerning the whole counsel of God, what is necessary for faith and life in the Covenant of Grace. In the biblical account of the history of redemptive revelation and in the history of Christian interpretation what we find is progressive development in doctrinal formulation. In the former it is from seed to full flowering; in the latter it is from elemental to complex. The church's theologizing is characteristically polemical in formulation. The history of Christian interpretation witnesses to periods of intense conflict and debate. There is progression as well as retrogression as regards the accurate restatement of what Scripture teaches. It should be emphasized, of course, that doctrinal exposition in every age of the Christian church reflects the historical setting in which biblical interpreters find themselves. This can be seen both in terms of theological methodology and philosophico-dogmatic orientation (that is, presuppositionalism and what falls under the rubric of theological prolegomena). In acknowledging this, however, we are not suggesting that truth is relative. To the extent that church doctrine, that is, dogma, faithfully reflects the teaching of Scripture, to that extent it is binding upon the people of God. Here we must give full credence to the illuminating work of the Holy Spirit, the supreme interpreter of God's Word. Creedal doctrine, though subordinate to Scripture, is nevertheless authoritative as ecclesiastical statements of faith. The creeds and confessions of the church are always subject to revision, correction, modification, clarification and expansion in the ongoing articulation of Christian theology. Reiterating a point I have made elsewhere, to the extent that the creeds accurately convey the teaching of Scripture, to that extent they are to be believed. The great creeds of the Protestant Reformation continue to shed light on the church's interpretation of Scripture.[7]

The characterization of covenant theology as the distinctive teaching of the Reformed faith at the opening of my presentation is not intended to incite partisanship, but rather to emphasize that Calvinistic federalism indeed has something unique to bring to the table. To paraphrase the words of one of Paul's inquisitors recorded in the Book of Acts: Are you now seeking to make covenant theologians out of all of us here today? I pray that you will receive the clear testimony of Christ speaking through the Scriptures, what the Protestant reformers identified as the Scripture principle (*sola scriptura*). The biblical doctrine of justification by faith alone, what is the heart of the Christian gospel, finds its most consistent and comprehensive exposition in covenant or federal theology. Here the classic Protestant Law/Gospel antithesis and the reformational hermeneutic of the analogy of faith – the principle that Scripture is self-interpreting – find their proper home. Is Reformed covenant theology a post-Reformation accretion? Hardly so. It is simply the outworking of Protestant-Reformed principles of interpretation. At the very least, may we embrace the fundamental truths of the Protestant Reformation, and in so doing may the Spirit of God enable us once again to come together on the orthodox, biblical doctrine of justification by grace through faith, the article of faith upon which the church stands or falls.

## ENDNOTES

[1] Jack Rogers, no friend of Reformed orthodoxy, acknowledges: "One doctrine which may serve to focus on the distinctively Reformed contribution to ecumenical Christianity is *covenant*. The concept of covenant sums up much of what being Reformed is all about" (cited in my *Covenant Theology in Reformed Perspective* [Eugene, OR: Wipf and Stock, 2000] 95). This assessment of Reformed teaching is widely sounded in the theological literature.

[2] Reformed theology has given expression to three distinct interpretations of the Mosaic Covenant: (1) the formative principle "do this and life," the principle of works-inheritance, when rightly interpreted, pertains exclusively to temporal life in the land of Canaan; (2) this works-principle of inheritance is purely *hypothetical* throughout the postlapsarian epoch, so that in this view the Mosaic Covenant only has the (external) "form" of a covenant of works; and (3) "do this and live" describes the way of unmerited grace and favor, and is equivalent to what the apostle Paul identifies as the "obedience of faith" (the principle of faith-inheri-tance). The teachings of the Westminster standards accommodate the first two points of view; the latter reading of the law came to the fore in a later period in the history of doctrine. Calvin held to the second position, which led him then to speak of law as a "bare principle" (law in the "narrow sense"). All factors considered, however, Calvin's formulations did anticipate the first of these. See my "Reformed Interpretation of the Mosaic Covenant," reprinted in *Covenant Theology in Reformed Perspective* 17-57.

[3] See Donald Hagner, "Paul and Judaism: Testing the New Perspective," in Peter Stuhlmacher, *Revisiting Paul's Doctrine of Justification: A Challenge to the New Perspective* (Downers Grove,IL: InterVarsity, 2001) 75-105. This essay, though brief, is a masterful overview and critique. One major drawback, however, is that the author does not satisfactorily explain what he means by old covenant nomism, what is descriptive of the legal economy under Moses. Not unrelated to this matter is the question how Hagner's view compares to that of Stuhlmacher on the doctrine of justification by faith (apart from the works of the law). The latter assumes

justification to be a process. This is not the teaching of the Protestant reformers, which Stuhlmacher seeks to defend in his criticism of the new perspective on Paul and the law. Critical to this debate is one's assessment of Judaism. For discussion of the varieties of teachings within ancient Judaism, see *Justification and Variegated Nomism. Vol 1, The Complexities of Second Temple Judaism,* ed. D. A. Carson, P. T. O'Brein, and M. A. Seifrid (Wissenschaftliche Untersuchungen zum Neuen Testament 2. Reihe 140; Tübingen: Mohr Siebeck [Grand Rapids: Baker Academic] 2001. Of particular interest will be the forthcoming installment of this two-volume study.

[4] *JETS* 44 (2001) 436.

[5] *Ibid.* 444.

[6] *Ibid.* 450. On this point, see my critique of the views of Willem VanGemeren in *Covenant Theology in Reformed Perspective,* esp. 278-279.

[7] See my essay, "Doctrinal Development in Scripture and Tradition: A Reformed Assessment of the Church's Theological Task," reprinted in *Covenant Theology in Reformed Perspective* 341-35.

# Chapter 5

# John Piper on the Christian Life:
# An Examination of His Controversial View of "Faith Alone" in Future Grace*

The popularity of the writings of John Piper in both evangelical and Reformed communities attests to the timeliness and urgency of the author's call for a renewed awareness of God's sovereign grace, the mainstay of "practical," biblical Christianity. There is no question that Piper's books do embody much that is good as regards a devotional and experiential commentary on the Christian life in our day. This twentieth-century author also conveys something of the spirit and ethos of the seventeenth-century Puritans; Piper himself demonstrating the uncommon blend of pastor and scholar. His theological pursuits are, therefore, both practical and academic: the scholarly questions are raised for their practical implications; and the practical concerns are subjected to scholarly investigation. There is a healthy mix of the two. (This serves to prove that the academic and the pastoral disciplines are not incompatible, as many Christians are prone to argue.)

The weightier question, however, is whether the author stands in the same theological tradition as English (and international) Calvinism. Clearly, Piper articulates many sound points of orthodox Reformed theology in new and refreshing ways. But does his doctrine of the Christian life rest securely upon the foundation of Jesus Christ as Saviour of, and Substitute for, sinners? Since his early years of preparation for the gospel ministry, Piper has been heavily influenced by the teachings of his revered professor and mentor, Daniel Fuller. Together, Fuller and Piper have developed a particular understanding of the Creator/creature relationship – that is, the *covenantal* bond between the Father and his sons and daughters – which serves as the foundation of their theological analysis of the Christian life. Piper remarks:

> Daniel Fuller's vision of the Christian life as an "obedience of faith" is the garden in which the plants of my ponderings have grown. Almost three decades of dialogue on the issues in this book have left a deep imprint. If I tried to show it with footnotes, they would be on almost every page. His major work, *The Unity of the Bible* (Zondervan Publishing House, 1992), is explanatory background to most of what I write. [7]

Like many other contemporary restatements of Protestant theology, the Fuller-Piper theology represents a major *revision* of traditional Protestant teaching. It is the purpose of this review to explore the nature and significance of this revision for biblical Christianity.

## 1. Theme and Variations

Piper states as the major theme of his theology: "God is most glorified in us when we are most satisfied in him" (386). Here and in his earlier book, *Desiring God* (Leicester: InterVarsity, 1986), Piper labels his theology of the spiritual life as "Christian hedonism." It is intended to be a reaffirmation (and adaptation) of the first question and answer of the Westminster Shorter Catechism. It is also intended as a restatement of the theology of Jonathan Edwards, the second theological figure to whom Piper is most indebted. In his closing chapter, Piper attempts

> to show that living by faith in future grace and Christian hedonism stand in faithful continuity with the thinking of Jonathan Edwards. I do not claim that Edwards would have chosen my way of bringing biblical truth to bear on the modern church. Nor do I assume it is the only or even the best way. But I do want to claim that it is biblical and that it is in the Reformed tradition of Jonathan Edwards, and that, if properly understood and applied, it leads to a God-centred life of joyful and sacrificial love. [387-88]

Piper's claim of adherence to the teaching of Puritanism (English and American), however, must be contested.

The new element in his understanding of the Christian life is what the author describes in this treatise as *the future orientation of justifying faith*. Genuine love and obedience find their motivation in God's promise of future grace, not in gratitude for God's past mercies. In this discussion Piper sets up a false dichotomy between gratitude for past blessings and confidence in future grace. The sharp distinction between these two plays a formative role in Piper's thinking. *It is the reason for writing this book.*

Piper concedes that "gratitude is a beautiful and utterly indispensable Christian affection" (11). And he recognises that "Past grace is the foundation of life-transforming faith in future grace" (18). "But," argues Piper, "you will search the Bible in vain for *explicit* connections between gratitude and obedience. . . . Gratitude was never designed as the primary motivation for radical Christian obedience" (11). Contrary to the biblical witness, the author drives a wedge between "*living by faith in future grace*" and "living by gratitude for past grace" (18). He asks: Does obedience out of gratitude for God's past goodness become payment of debt for God's former grace? The first chapter of the book is devoted to the question, "The Debtor's Ethics: Should We Try to Pay God Back?" According to Piper's understanding of the Scriptures, gratitude is itself an expression of *free grace*. "We easily forget that *gratitude* exists because sometimes things come to us *gratis* – without price or payment" (31). Simply put, "Gratitude corresponds to grace (*gratis*)." What we find in Piper's writing is a theology of grace, from beginning to end. Is this understanding not the essence of Reformed teaching on the Christian life? On the surface, Piper's theology sounds good – until we uncover the theological presuppositions underlying his "ponderings."

### 2. Critique: Is Piper's theology a theology of grace?

A Christian theology of grace requires a theology of divine justice and holiness. In terms of the traditional categories of dogmatics, interpretation of the doctrine of man is dependent upon the (prior) doctrine of God. Man knows himself, as John Calvin taught, only in relation to the triune God (the two doctrines are mutually interpretative). Theology begins and ends *with God*. From the standpoint of the Creator/creature distinction, is it proper to speak of the creature as being indebted to the Creator? Piper answers:

> I don't deny that we are debtors to God. . . [W]hen the Bible focuses on our being in debt to God it has reference to our sins that need to be forgiven, not our obedience that needs to be paid.
>
> It would seem more appropriate to say that we are debtors to God's justice, not to his grace. That is, if we deal with him in payments of debt, he will deal with us in terms of justice: value for value (see Romans 4:4). We will not get very far in this transaction. That is why we plead for forgiveness of our debts instead of proposing a schedule of payments. To

be more biblical, let us not say that grace *creates* debts: let us say that grace *pays* debts. [46]

What more does Piper say about the justice of God? Nothing more in *Future Grace*, or in his other writings bearing on this subject. But what more needs to be said in this regard? Most importantly, all God's works in creation and redemption are just and righteous. There is no tension or dialectic between love and justice in God himself, nor in his external works. No less in redemption than in creation. For a proper interpretation of the Christian life, it is essential to understand how the biblical doctrines of sin, atonement, and justification are inextricably tied to the doctrine of God's justice.

In "Introduction Two: For Theologians," Piper aligns his teaching with the confessional theology of the Protestant Reformation. Central to the subject of this book are the doctrines of justification and sanctification. "In its popular form, the classic Reformed, Protestant expression of faith's relation to sanctification goes like this: 'It is faith alone which justifies, but the faith which justifies is not alone.' That is, justifying faith is always accompanied by good works" (21-22). Echoing the confessional formulations, Piper regards good works to be "the *evidence* of authentic faith" (24, emphasis mine). Works are the outworking of true, saving faith. The Reformed creeds typically speak of the merit of Christ's substitutionary obedience imputed to believers through the sole instrumentality of faith. Regrettably, it is here that the Fuller-Piper revision parts company with historic Protestant orthodoxy. It does so by rejecting the concept of merit in connection with the legal requirement placed upon Adam in his time of probation under the original Covenant of Works in Eden, and upon Christ, the Second Adam, who in submission to the will of his Father, was obligated as Adam's substitute to render full and perfect obedience to God's law.

Piper shows some understanding of the Reformed doctrine of the consequent absolute necessity of the atonement. He states:

> God did not spare his own Son, because it was the only way he could spare us. The guilt of our transgressions, the punishment of our iniquities, the curse of our sin would have brought us inescapably to the destruction of hell. But God did not spare his own Son; he gave him up to be wounded for our transgression, and bruised for our iniquities and crucified for our sin. [113]

But his formulation falls far short of Reformed (biblical) teaching. This doctrinal matter deserves our closest attention. In an extended endnote, Piper indicates his misgivings concerning the Reformed doctrine of the Covenant of Works. He maintains that this doctrine posits a false antithesis between law and grace. (The classic Protestant contrast between the "Law" and the "Gospel" is thereby jettisoned.) The concept of "works" in the traditional doctrine, writes Piper, "implies a relationship with God that is more like an employee receiving earned wages than like a Son trusting a Father's generosity" (413, n. 4). According to Piper's interpretation of the biblical covenants, grace is likewise "the basis of (God's) relationship with Adam and Eve before the fall." The author explains further: "I see Christ, the Second Adam, fulfilling this covenant of grace (not works) perfectly by trusting his Father's provision at every moment and obeying all his commandments by faith."

In his exegesis of Philippians 2:9, Piper mistakenly contends that God's bestowal of "the name which is above every name" upon Christ was an act of grace, not the granting of reward on the ground of meritorious achievement. He concludes:

> This does not nullify the substitutionary work of Christ nor does it make his obedience any less the ground of our justification and the vindication of the Father's righteousness. Rather it says that the obedience that Adam failed to perform by faith, Christ has perfectly performed by faith. In this way Christ is indeed a perfect example to us how we should live and love by faith in future grace, even if grace for him was Fatherly beneficence without having to overcome sinful deficiency – except in the sense of the Father's overcoming Christ's taking our sin upon him. [413-414, n. 4]

How are we to construe Piper's affirmation that Christ's obedience is "the (exclusive) ground of our justification and the vindication of the Father's righteousness," when, in his view, Christ is not obliged to satisfy the justice of God as the *legal* means of inheriting (that is, earning) the reward promised by the Father? The Fuller-Piper theology marks a clear departure from historic Protestant teaching. The crucial question posed by the new theology is this: How necessary or important is the Reformed and Protestant doctrine of meritorious reward for orthodox, biblical theology?

According to Piper, the perfect righteousness of Christ is *imputed* to believers by grace through faith. It alone is the ground of life and salvation. Yet, if Christ's obedience is not the *meritorious* ground of divine blessing, as Protestant orthodoxy maintains – if Christ does not satisfy the legal demand of God's first covenant with Adam – how can one speak meaningfully of Christ's obedience (both active and passive) as the basis or ground of salvation? (The covenantal concepts of "ground" of justification and "meritorious reward" are inseparable.) The parallel drawn by the apostle Paul in Romans 5 makes clear that Christ's substitutionary obedience not only achieves the forgiveness of sins, but also the right to life eternal. Probation, either for the First Adam or the Second, is part and parcel of the Covenant of Works. According to God's eschatological design for humankind, confirmation in righteousness is granted after fulfillment of the conditions of the Covenant of Works. The expression used by Paul in his letter to the Romans, the "obedience of faith," is descriptive of the obedience of all those who have been justified in Christ. It does not describe the nature of Adam's or Christ's obedience under the Covenant of Works, contrary to Piper's argument.

As we noted earlier, there is no Law/Gospel contrast in the Fuller-Piper theology. This omission has immediate consequences for one's interpretation of the relationship between justification and sanctification, faith and works, old and new covenants. We shall consider each in turn.

### 3. Piper's Challenge to the Protestant Reformation: No law/gospel antithesis

The crucial text in Piper's understanding of justification is Galatians 5:6, which speaks of "faith working through love" (25). The author complains that so little attention in the history of Christian theology (including the Reformed tradition) has been given to "the spiritual dynamics of how faith sanctifies" (25). He comments:

> I could be wrong about this, since I am not an expert in the history of doctrine. But my sense is that both historically and currently, the claim that justifying faith *"is it [sic] not alone in the person justified, but is ever accompanied with all other saving graces"* is usually left dangling without any extended reflection on *why* this is the case, and how it works out in the spiritual dynamics of real Christian living. Such an extended reflection is what this book is meant to be. [25]

Piper contends that the Protestant Reformation did not arrive at a fully biblical doctrine of justification by faith. (Of course, it is the ongoing task of Christian theologians not only to build upon the insights of the past, but also to reformulate or revise churchly doctrine when demanded by the teaching of Scripture. But the question here, however, is whether or not Piper is correct in thinking that the Protestant reformers missed something important in their understanding of the doctrine of justification by faith alone.) Piper begins by stating that he has no desire

> to confound justification and sanctification. They are distinct. . . Justification is an act of God's reckoning; sanctification is an act of God's transforming. Thus the function of faith in regard to each is different. In regard to justification, faith is not the channel through which a power or a transformation flows to the soul of the believer, but rather faith is the occasion of God's forgiving and acquitting and reckoning as righteous. These justifying acts of God do not in themselves touch the soul of man. They are *extra nos* – outside ourselves. [26]

The author views faith as "the instrumental cause" of good works (22) . That is to say, faith is the source of good works; good works inevitably flow out of true, justifying faith.

> Thus it is proper to speak of the moral effectiveness of justifying faith not merely because it brings us into a right standing with God at the first moment of its exercise, but also because it is a persevering sort of faith, whose effectiveness resides also in its daily embrace of all that God is for us in Jesus. Justifying faith necessarily sanctifies. This book is an extended reflection on the biblical underpinnings and practical spiritual dynamics of the sanctifying power of justifying faith. [27]

With respect to the so-called "Lordship controversy" in present-day evangelicalism, Piper's book is a powerful argument against those who would *separate* God's justifying and sanctifying acts from one another. Justification and sanctification are distinct, yet inseparable. What is the precise relation between these two? Were the Protestant reformers correct in seeing the former as the definitive, finished act of God at the beginning of the Christian life, and the latter as the progressive, ongoing work of the Spirit of holiness? (The distinction here is between *imputed* righteousness and *inwrought* righteousness.) In an end-note, Piper asserts that

> . . . justification is not an act that comes in varying degrees, but one that is a once-for-all and total reckoning of righteousness to us for Christ's sake. It is not mediated to us in varying measures as sanctification is. However, when it comes to sanctification, while faith is always the essential element in appropriating the power of transforming grace, there are other acts of the soul that the Word of God prescribes as a means of experiencing the ongoing empowerment of sanctifying grace, though I would say that all of these "means of grace" are exercised "from faith" (*ek pisteos*) and not "from works" (*ex ergon*), as Romans 9:32 says. Thus faith is the decisive human agency that connects with the sanctifying grace of God. [402, n. 1]

So far, so good. In fact, most of what Piper says here is excellent and can hardly be improved upon. Problems surface, however, in his understanding of the relation between faith and (good) works, including the subject of judgment according to works.

In his discussions of the nature of faith, Piper does not succeed in keeping the evidential or demonstrative aspect of justification ("faith working through love") distinct from the *constitutive* aspect (faith apprehending Christ apart from the works of the law). This point must not be missed, for the difference between Piper and the Protestant reformers is not insignificant. Piper begins cautiously:

> I want to say a bit more than [Charles] Hodge does. I don't want to say merely that faith in promises produces "confidence, joy and hope," but that an *essential element* in the faith itself is confidence and joy and hope. It is not false to say that faith *produces* these things. But that does not contradict the other truth: that confidence and joy and hope are part of the warp and woof of faith. [205]

The classic Protestant formulation, as noted earlier by Piper, states that believers are justified by grace through the sole instrumentality of faith (*sola fide*). Faith alone – in distinction from all other saving graces – receives the righteousness of Christ imputed to all those who believe. Such faith, however, never stands alone. Justifying faith necessarily produces good works. What is the precise nature of justifying faith? Specifically, is faith (as the instrumental cause of justification) distinct from good works, as Piper acknowledged earlier in the book? Or is faith identical with the good works which flow from it, as Piper contradictorily argues in his subsequent discussion? Are faith and good works in some way synonymous? Piper rightly observes: "If we go wrong on the nature of faith, everything in the Christian life will go wrong" (209).

In contemporary theological debate, biblical scholars remain divided over their interpretation of Paul and James on justification. Recent challenges to the traditional understanding of the relationship between Paul's teaching and that of Judaism have added further fuel to the fire. The chief issue is this: When Paul affirms that justification is by faith apart from the works of the law, is he excluding the good works of regenerate believers, those acts of love and obedience which faith inevitably produces? Or is Paul excluding only those works which are performed in order to merit God's saving favour? In this debate the critical text is Leviticus 18:5. Does the apostle Paul see in this verse the principle of works in contrast to the principle of faith (as the Protestant reformers uniformly taught)? Or is the principle enunciated in Leviticus 18:5 identical with the principle of faith underlying the Covenant of Grace? Does Paul lift Leviticus 18:5 out of its proper, covenantal context for rhetorical effect in his argument against the Judaisers, those who have perverted God's law into a religion of legalism (that is, salvation by works)? Or does the principle of works legitimately operate within the restricted temporal sphere of the Israelite theocratic kingdom? (These questions arise again in connection with the issue of the relationship between the old and new covenants discussed below.)

Returning to the immediate question: Does Paul exclude good works from God's definitive, once-for-all act in justifying sinners? For Piper, the answer is tied to the question whether salvation is conditional or unconditional. Piper states:

> We must keep in mind that love relates to faith as evidence to origin. Love is the necessary evidence of faith. Faith apprehends and embraces the spiritual beauty and worth of all that God is for us in the promises of future grace. This spiritual awakening to the glory of God in the promises is the means by which God unites us to Christ and to the Spirit's flow of future grace. But this kind of faith inevitably "works through love" (Gal 5:6), so that love confirms the authenticity of faith. . . Thus love for others is a condition of future grace in the sense that it confirms that the primary condition, faith, is genuine. We could call love for others a secondary condition that confirms the authenticity of the primary condition of faith. [257]

Piper faults Calvin for not probing sufficiently into the nature of justifying faith in his commentary on Galatians 5:6.

Such neglect "seems to continue into our own day" (277). Again, we ask: What is missing in the Protestant orthodox formulation? In the opinion of Piper, the Reformers failed to see that the *efficacy* of true, justifying faith *is conditioned upon good works* (that is, faith persevering in good works to the end of the Christian life). The author states emphatically: "The promise of future grace is conditional. But it is not earned" (237). "Faith alone is necessary for justification, but the purity that confirms faith's reality is *also* necessary for *final* salvation" (333). Justification, according to Piper, includes both the initial act *and* its accompanying fruit, the evidential working of faith. This brings us to the matter of judgment according to works (or "*final* salvation").

Piper sees this future judgment as twofold: (1) "the public declaration of our differing rewards in the kingdom of God, according to our deeds;" and (2) "the public declaration of our salvation – our *entering* the kingdom – according to our deeds" (364). Since there is no place for a doctrine of merit in the Fuller-Piper theology, gradations of reward in heaven are not earned by believers on the basis of (meritorious) works, any more than salvation itself. Such reward, nevertheless, *is* "according to works." The traditional Protestant interpretation of judgment according to works is problematic. How can we say that degrees of reward in heaven are based on good works, yet unearned? Resolution of this theological dilemma necessitates reformulation of the Reformed doctrine of rewards. For Piper, salvation is based on faith *and* works because the works excluded from justification are the works of merit, not the evidential works of true, justifying faith. Piper comments:

> Salvation is *owned* by faith. Salvation is *shown* by deeds. So when Paul says (in 2 Cor 5:10) that each "[will] be recompensed. . . according to what he has done," he not only means that our *rewards* will accord with our

deeds, but also our *salvation* will accord with our deeds. [365]

What is lacking in Piper's presentation is a consistent and unambiguous affirmation that justification is God's declaratory act rendering the *final* verdict of justification (that is, salvation) in the believer's present experience of regeneration and spiritual union with Christ. Those united to Christ are *already* saved (that is, justified), although *not yet* glorified (transformed into the consummate image of Christ). Glorification coincides with judgment according to works. Corporately speaking, the New Man (the body of Christ) is declared/judged righteous according to works, but not on the ground of works. This teaching is what Piper's theology cannot accommodate, because Piper has no doctrine of the Covenant of Works and his system of doctrine makes no allowance for the classic Protestant law/gospel antithesis. The Fuller-Piper reformulation of Christian theology transforms the older dogmatic distinctions into something radically different. The *sola fide* formula is understood in vastly different ways. On the surface, the two schools of theology give the appearance of saying the same thing. But that is so only on the surface.

According to Piper's theology of grace, what overshadows all God's covenants with humankind is (future) grace – the grace of God infused into the human heart, the channel for the reception of all future blessings derived from the goodness and love of God. For man, life in covenant with God is the appropriation of grace upon grace. Piper explains:

> Before sin entered the world, Adam and Eve experienced God's goodness not as a response to their demerit (since they didn't have any) but still without deserving God's goodness. You can't deserve to be created. You can't deserve, as a non-being, to be put into a lavish garden where a loving Father meets all your needs.

> So even before they sinned, Adam and Eve lived on grace. And God's will for them was that they live by faith in future grace – God's daily, fatherly care and provision. *This is important because it is customary among some theologians to give the erroneous impression that God wanted Adam and Eve to relate to him in terms of meritorious works rather than childlike faith.* [76, italics mine]

By misstating the view of "some theologians," Piper caricatures the position he opposes. Two factors are to be noted by way of response: (1) the position he opposes is that which was held *unanimously* among the Reformed orthodox; (2) the Fuller-Piper theology denies that Adam was placed on *probation* according to the stipulations of the covenant established by God with Adam at creation. The Scriptures teach that Adam was given a particular task to perform, namely, to guard the Edenic sanctuary, the site of God's theocratic presence, against the encroachments of Satan. On the basis of his meritorious accomplishment of that mission, Adam would have moved from an original state of mutability to one of immutability, from the state of unconfirmed righteousness to the state of confirmed righteousness. That would have been Adam's reward had he persisted in well doing during the course of his probation. Christ has now secured that reward for God's elect. Whereas the first Adam failed to achieve the promised blessing for himself (and the entire human race in whose place Adam stood as federal representative), the Second Adam succeeded. Christ merited the reward covenanted by the Father from all eternity. This was the lesson to be drawn from the history of the ancient Israelite theocracy. According to the teaching of the apostle Paul in his letters to the Galatians and the Romans, the Mosaic law was added to the Abrahamic promise, in order that Israel – together with all human flesh – might be consigned under sin, subject to the wrath of God. (Under the Mosaic economy, that state of death and condemnation was symbolically portrayed in Israelite history during the time of Babylonian captivity and exile.)

In Piper's theology, testamental discontinuity is obscured at the expense of continuity. There is, says Piper, only one covenant in the Bible, the Covenant of Grace. There is no place for "works" in the original covenant at creation, nor under the Mosaic economy. Rather, insists Piper, the obedience demanded by the Old Testament is "the obedience of faith" (143). No probation, no works, no "Law" (in antithesis to "Gospel"). What, then, is the difference between old and new covenants, according to Piper?

The difference, says Piper, lies in the fuller manifestation of the Spirit's working in the new covenant era. It pertains to the measure of the Spirit's work before and after Pentecost. "The basic difference (between the old and new) is that in the old covenant the gracious enabling power to obey was not poured out as fully as it is since Jesus" (158). Dispensationalism teaches that Pentecost marks the beginning of the regenerating work of the Spirit in the hearts of believers (such was lacking under the old economy of redemption). Piper, happily, does not resort to that popular explanation. Rather, he states:

> My conclusion is that already in the Old Testament God meant for the law to be fulfilled by faith in future grace. This was possible for the true saints even before the outpouring of the new covenant promise, because God gave foretastes of his enabling power before the coming of Christ and the outpouring of the fuller measure of the Holy Spirit. [154]

To be sure, what Calvin identified as the normative (or "third use") of the law is relevant to the spiritual life of the saints before as well as after Pentecost. However, alongside the "normative" application of the Mosaic law is the *typological* application/interpretation. On the one hand, the heavenly inheritance – life everlasting – is the gift of God's sovereign, electing grace. According to the grace of justification under old and new dispensations, true faith is productive of godly living. Good works are tokens of gratitude to God, what Paul calls the "spiritual worship" of the saints (Rom 12:1). On the other hand, temporal life and prosperity in the land of Canaan was contingent upon Israel's obedience to the Sinaitic covenant. With respect to the earthly inheritance, the governing principle was one of works, not faith (Lev 18:5). The ancient theocracy endured from the time of Sinai to the Cross. This was the period of Israel's national probation. That probation was terminated with Christ's fulfillment of the law and the satisfaction of divine justice.

Of course, the Pentecostal outpouring of the Spirit "was reserved for the New Testament time" (148). But that anointing of the Spirit must be understood in terms of the redemptive-historical transition from shadow (the old covenant) to fulfillment (the new covenant). The fuller measure of the Spirit's working is *eschatological* in nature, not quantitative. The Spirit-temple, not the Solomonic temple, is God's true dwelling place in the midst of his people. And the establishment of the new covenant means more than the abrogation of certain cultic and ethnic distinctives within theocratic Israel. Piper argues:

> The reason that parts of the Old Testament law are no longer binding on God's people is that there has been a great fulfillment in Christ; and the way God is pursuing his redemptive plan is very different now than it was in the Old Testament, when most of his focus was on the ethnic people of Israel. [159]

What Piper needs to recognize is that the Mosaic covenant – as the legal instrument regulative of Israel's life in

Canaan – had been terminated, not just in part, but in whole, with the coming of Christ. What chiefly resulted was the cessation of probation for the people of God and the abrogation of the works-inheritance principle operative within – what Geerhardus Vos has called – the symbolico-typical sphere of the Israelite theocracy. Piper is wrong when he says: "All the covenants of God are conditional covenants of grace – both the old covenant and the new covenant" (248). According to Romans 9:31-32, Israel failed to attain that righteousness which the law required. The Law of Moses set forth the principle of works-inheritance, not faith-inheritance. The Gentiles, however, attained the righteousness of God through faith in Israel's Messiah.

## 4. Conclusion

Looking back to Jesus' ordeal at Calvary and the subsequent triumph of his resurrection from the dead, we can rejoice and find comfort in the certainty of our salvation in Jesus Christ. "Past grace" is not only a stimulus for perseverance in grace and assured victory for the people of God; it is the *source* of our great salvation. Christ has secured for the elect our eternal rest on grounds of his meritorious work of redemption. Unlike the good angels who were confirmed in righteousness on the basis of their own strength and integrity, the redeemed of the Lord are clothed in the righteousness of Christ and will be resurrected to glory greater than that of the angels. The redeemed have been washed in the blood of the Lamb. What evangelical and Reformed Christians need today is not a revision of Protestant teaching on justification by faith, but a rediscovery of those truths which our Protestant and Reformed forefathers recovered in their day.

Piper says many things good and important in themselves about the Christian life. But when we bring all the strands together for a *coherent* doctrinal statement on justification, Piper's interpretation is found wanting. Not only does Piper lose the proper balance between gratitude for past grace and confidence in future grace as motivations for spiritual growth, but he also denies the meritorious accomplishment of Christ's work on behalf of the redeemed. Apart from that sure foundation for Christian living, all else is shifting ground. Piper's subtle, and not so subtle, challenge to evangelical theology is at the same time a renunciation of Protestant orthodox teaching. Piper attempts to find a place for the good works of the godly in God's declaration of (final) salvation on the Day of Judgment. *Future Grace*, though written for a popular audience, is actually difficult going. To read this work lightly, or to recommend it to others, might well prove to be perilous. May God preserve in our day the biblical doctrine of justification by faith alone. In the words of the hymn-writer Edward Mote (1834) may every believer declare:

> *My hope is built on nothing less*
> *than Jesus' blood and righteousness. . . .*
> *His oath, his covenant, his blood*
> *support me in the whelming flood. . . .*
> *On Christ, the solid rock, I stand;*
> *all other ground is sinking sand,*
> *all other ground is sinking sand.*

---

\* This essay was first published by the Christian Research Network (Great Bromley, 1999).

# Chapter 6

# The Changing of the Guard: Westminster Theological Seminary in Philadelphia*

At Buckingham Palace, England, the grand tradition of the changing of the guard captivates tourists the world around. Periods of social change, however, lead more often than not to the undoing of tradition, where it counts the most. The teaching at Westminster Abbey – viewed as representative of Her Majesty's religion (the Church of England) – has moved significantly from its historical-theological moorings, away from Calvinistic Puritanism to religious pluralism. The story of Westminster Seminary in Philadelphia is also a story of change, not as radical as that of the Abbey, but radical nonetheless. The change here, though not as obvious, is equally destructive of the Christian Gospel. Comparatively speaking, the size and influence of Westminster Seminary are minuscule; judged from other considerations, however, Westminster has been highly influential, far more than its size would seemingly warrant. The Orthodox Presbyterian Church, to which Westminster Seminary has had close ties from the beginning, has been described by historian Mark Noll as the pea under the mattress.[1] All this is to say that size does not tell the whole story; nor should one small book, the focus of this critical analysis of a theological institution, be deemed insignificant with respect to the history of ideas (theological or otherwise).

In *The Call of Grace*,[2] subtitled *How the Covenant Illuminates Salvation and Evangelism,* author Norman Shepherd offers a popular treatment of his theological ruminations that date back to the early 1970s, if not earlier. The book is highly readable; but whether or not the distinctive argument against traditional Reformed covenant theology set forth in these pages is readily grasped by the reader is another question altogether. *Let there be no doubt about it – this study is highly controversial, not only in the Seminary community in which Shepherd ministered for many years, but in the wider arena of contemporary evangelical and Reformed theology.* The views expressed in this book resulted in the dismissal of Shepherd from the faculty of Westminster Seminary in 1982. Now that he has retired from pastoral ministry in the Christian Reformed Church, he has found this to be the opportunity to lay out once more his thinking concerning the covenants of God, election, and evangelism. Here is theological writing with a very practical bent to it. Of course, not only are there practical implications in all theological discourse, but it is helpful when the church theologian gives focused attention to the practical (that is, pastoral) side of his theology. Shepherd continues to believe that he has something that must be said to the Reformed churches, and that by way of exhortation and confrontation (however much this second feature of Shepherd's presentation lies under the surface).

Part 1, as Shepherd describes it, "deals with the problem of faith and works, or grace and merit," the subject previously developed in the Robinson Lectures at Erskine Theological Seminary in April 1999, now "with only minor revisions." Part 2 (re)presents material first given at an ecclesiastical gathering sponsored by the Reformed Presbyterian Church of North America in May 1975 and subsequently published in *The New Testament Student and Theology* (1976). The reason furnished by the author for this reissue of old material is "because of continuing interest in the perspective developed in this article." Here the argument receives "a revised form" (viii). This reviewer, fully acquainted with the author's views since the mid-1970s, looks in vain for any modification or reworking of his thinking since that formative period. That being the case, this book is merely a regurgitation of long-held views, views that remain controversial. One would have hoped to find in these pages, at the very least, added clarification and defense of the author's position. But no advance in the author's argument is to be found here. My evaluation of Shepherd's covenant theology can be summed up, in part, in the words of one important document, to which we will return later: in the teachings and writings of Shepherd explicating the Reformed faith there are "deep inherent problems in the structure and the particular formulations of [his] views."[3]

## 1. Norman Shepherd's Proposal for the Reconciliation of Roman Catholics and Protestants Concerning the "Way of Savation"

Placing the topic of this book in the broader context of contemporary evangelical-Reformed debate, one has only to note Shepherd's assault on Reformation doctrine in his assessment of the *Alliance of Confessing Evangelicals*, an organization noted for its stand against modern-day challenges to the historic Protestant-Reformed doctrine of justification by faith (*sola fide*). Shepherd is persuaded that the members of this *Alliance* are misguided and misinformed concerning the biblical and "true" Reformed teaching (as he understands it). It is his objective in *The*

*Call of Grace* to set the Reformed churches straight, once and for all, on this score. Echoing commonplace sentiment today, Shepherd alleges that for too long a time Reformed thinking has been distorted by utilization of the scholastic, rationalistic notion of law (that is, covenant) as contract. What he finds particularly repugnant is the notion of "merit" in connection with the procurement of eternal life, what was first offered to Adam, the federal head of the entire human race, in the Garden of Eden. Never, contends Shepherd, was the First or Second Adam placed in a position of having to merit the covenantal reward on grounds of legal obedience. What Shepherd identifies as the "Lutheran" notion of *law versus gospel* (or *law versus grace*) is, in his thinking, wholly unscriptural; it is what lies at the root of serious, widespread theological error in much of evangelical thinking, past and present. According to Shepherd's argument, the problem afflicting the thinking of those associated with the *Alliance* (among other such groups within the evangelical-Reformed camp) is itself the legacy of the Protestant Reformation. This particular theological dilemma, suggests Shepherd, resurfaces time and again in the history of Christian theology, for example, in the Marrow controversy in eighteenth-century Scotland and in the modern-day "Lordship" controversy.

> It is the controversy between antinomianism and legalism. It is the controversy between Rome and the Reformation [here Shepherd means the "pure" Calvinistic branch, as he understands it]. It is the historic difference between the Lutherans and the Reformed with respect to the use of the law. [8]

Shepherd opens his popular disputation with the question, "What distinguishes the Reformed faith from all the other confessional options found among sincere Christians" (p. vii)? Behind the author's thinking is the supposition that what lies at the heart of genuinely Reformed theology is the doctrine of God's "sovereign grace and promise," to use the language of John Murray, Shepherd's predecessor in the Systematics Department at Westminster Seminary where Shepherd taught from 1963 to 1982. It is this that informs – in a decisive way, Shepherd argues – the Reformed understanding of all the divine-human covenants in the Bible, as well as the covenant between the Father and the Son in eternity. More significantly, the paternal Father-Son relationship is the model or paradigm for all the covenantal transactions in the history of revelation, from the Fall to the Consummation. And what characterizes this relationship or bond between the parties of the covenant is the *grace* of God as Father, the One who is the Creator and Redeemer of the world. The gift of God's grace and favor to creatures of the dust – whether before or after the Fall – is ever and always sovereign and unmerited. Another way of making the point is to say that the notion of meritorious reward is wholly incompatible with the attribute of divine goodness (which Shepherd calls "grace"). The erroneous idea of merit, Shepherd contends, originates with the fallen sinner's attempt to contract God's love and blessing. The doctrine of an original "Covenant of Works" (wherein works are meritorious of divine favor and reward) is thereby rejected. So then, in this line of reasoning where do we turn for a resolution of the alleged theological dilemma created by Reformed scholasticism? The answer is found "in the light of the biblical doctrine of covenant" (9). This doctrine of the covenant, as interpreted by Shepherd, is the distinctive contribution of pure, unadulterated Calvinism. We have no quarrel with the significance Shepherd attaches to covenant theology in the Reformed tradition, but rather with his exposition of it.

After the introductory chapter, "Facing a New Challenge," Part 1, titled "Covenant Light on the Way of Salvation," advances a very brief overview of the leading covenants in the Bible, namely, the Abrahamic, the Mosaic, and the new covenants. Shepherd explains: "We can describe a covenant as a divinely established relationship of union and communion between God and his people in the bonds of mutual love and faithfulness" (12). Implicit in the covenant relationship between God and humanity is creaturely compliance with God's law and commandments. The element of conditionality, according to Shepherd, is the underlying feature in covenants, human or divine. More particularly, the conditions of rightful membership in God's covenant (before and after the Fall) are faith and good works, which are viewed by Shepherd as *the means of justification, that is, life with God*.

One of the major disputants in the controversy surrounding Shepherd's teaching – the controversy which first occupied the time and energy of faculty members at Westminster Seminary from 1975 to 1982 – is Professor Meredith G. Kline. Reflecting the teaching of historic Reformed covenant theology, Kline opposes Shepherd's definition of covenant conditionality, comprehensive of the pre-redemptive and redemptive covenants (as well as the pre-temporal covenant between the Father and the Son established in eternity). According to classic Reformed theology, the conditions of the covenant vary with the historical circumstance. The *Westminster Confession of Faith*, which embodies the consensus of teaching within orthodox Reformed Christianity at the close of the Reformation age, distinguishes between *two antithetical covenants*, the initial "Covenant of Works" with Adam at creation and the subsequent "Covenant of Grace" after the Fall (the proper purpose of this latter covenant is the redemption of God's elect). In Shepherd's exposition the notion of "grace" as descriptive of "the way of salvation" proffered to the fallen sons and daughters of Adam is not sufficiently distinguished from "grace" as descriptive of the the way of life established in the covenant of creation, more expressly in terms of Adam's representative headship and probationary test. Neither Adam's federal headship nor the probation is given its proper due in Shepherd's elucidation of this first covenant. (We have already indicated Shepherd's distaste for the notion of works-inheritance, a formative element in confessional Reformed theology. Furthermore, application of the theological term "grace" to the prelapsarian covenant with Adam is erroneous and misleading. Grace pertains specifically to God's provisions of *redemption*.)

According to Shepherd, Abraham (like Adam) was required to fulfill the obligations of the covenant (16). Our author reasons: "If the promises of the Abrahamic covenant had been unconditional, the Israelites would have been able to march right into the Promised Land regardless of their behavior" (18). Abraham's own righteousness or obedience to God's law and commandments is anticipatory to that of Jesus Christ, what Shepherd regards as "the ultimate proof of the conditional character of the Abrahamic covenant" (18, original italicized). The Abrahamic covenant, like the first covenant with Adam, has two parts – promise and obligation. (There is no covenantal discontinuity, in Shepherd's thinking, between the covenant with Adam at creation and the covenant with Adam after the Fall, the latter finding its realization in the promise made to Abraham.) The fulfillment of the covenant obligations on the part of Abraham, Shepherd reiterates, is not meritorious. And what is true for the First Adam is also true for the Second. The Son's fulfillment of the covenant obligations laid upon him by the Father in the Counsel of Redemption – realized in the historical life, death, and resurrection of Jesus – must not be construed in any sense as meritorious. Shepherd further explicates:

"Whereas promise is in the foreground in the Abrahamic covenant, obligation comes to the fore in the Mosaic covenant" (24). The obligations of this covenant of law, we are told, do not differ principally from those of the Abrahamic. Shepherd contends that there are no contrasting principles of inheritance (one of faith and one of works) as taught in scholastic Protestant orthodoxy, Lutheran and Reformed.

> Because of the promise of blessings for obedience and the threat of punishment for disobedience, the Mosaic covenant has often been described as a *covenant of works*. It is understood to be a republication of the covenant of works that God made with Adam in the Garden of Eden, and in him with the whole human race. Representative of this view is the great Princeton theologian of a former generation, Charles Hodge. [25]

Shepherd correctly points out: "The basic principle embodied in this conception of the covenant of works can be called the 'works/merit' principle." Under the constraint of time and space Shepherd abruptly ends discussion of this matter with the following remarks – remarks that indicate Shepherd's radical departure from the theological tradition he seeks to represent:

> Different theologians describe the covenant of works with a variety of nuances that we cannot get into here. What interests us is the idea that perfect obedience merits the reward of eternal life as a matter of simple justice. Is this how we are to understand the covenant that God made with Moses and all Israel? [26]

The answer to that question – one of the central concerns in Shepherd's book – is an emphatic *No*. Neither the Mosaic nor the Edenic covenant can be classified as a Covenant of Works. Shepherd maintains that the alleged antithesis in Scripture between works and grace, between law and gospel, is nonexistent – Shepherd views the classic Protestant *law versus gospel* construct as wholly unbiblical, wholly speculative. Shepherd construes the critical Old Testament text Leviticus 18:5 and its New Testament citation/interpretation to teach that *covenantal obedience – obedience to the law of Moses (or the law of God more generally) – is synonymous with "a living and active faith,"* the response of every sincere believer to the beneficence and love of God, whether in the pre-redemptive or the redemptive epochs. It is the very same living, obedient, and active faith that in every age justifies the ways of the sons and daughters of the covenant in the eyes of their heavenly Father. Justification according to this interpretation is not once-for-all, but rather *ongoing*. Part of Shepherd's misreading of the Biblical doctrine is his failure to reckon with the probationary test affixed to the original covenant with Adam, as well as the covenant with Christ, federal head of the elect seed. At the close of the probation period, Adam would have been *confirmed in righteousness* had he remained obedient to God's law. And where the First Adam failed, the Second succeeded. Christ's righteousness imputed to the believer in the divine act of justification is the ground of life and salvation. The justification of the sinner is the definitive, once-for-all act of God, the permanent possession of those saved by faith. Shepherd counters this interpretation by saying that obedience to divine law is never meritorious of the Father's love and favor. At the same time Shepherd contends that the reward is a matter of promise and obligation – gratuitous promise on the part of God who showers favor and mercy on creatures of the dust and obligation on the part of the sons and daughters of God, those who are called to be the keepers of God's covenant. Such is the substance of Shepherd's argument in *The Call of Grace*: the way of salvation, that is, justification, is the way of faith *and* (non-meritorious) works.

In Shepherd's formulation of the new covenant there is an almost exclusive emphasis upon the *continuity of the covenants*. Shepherd writes: "We discover in the New Testament that the new covenant, like the Abrahamic and Mosaic covenants, also has two parts, promise and obligation" (44). We need not detain ourselves here as to what our author sees as the "newness" of the covenant in Jesus' blood, nor what makes it a "better" covenant than the old (see below). What is critical in Shepherd's discussion is the attention he gives to the underlying continuity of the covenants throughout Scripture, which continuity is explained in terms of the way of salvation, the way of faith and good works. What is the nature of justifying faith? Shepherd reasons: "Faith and repentance are indissolubly intertwined with one another" (47). "A living, active, and abiding faith is the way in which the believer enters into eternal life" (50). As regards the interrelationship between promise and obligation, faith and works, in the covenant of God, Shepherd offers this explanation, citing 1 Corinthians 10:1-13 and related passages:

> Note that Paul can take an example from life under the Mosaic covenant and apply it to those who live under the new covenant. This shows that the principles operative under both covenants are the same. There is promise and there is obligation. The land promised to the wilderness generation was the Promised Land. It was an unearned and unmerited gift of grace. Yet the first generation did not inherit the land because of their unbelief and disobedience. This is the point made in Hebrews 3:18-19. Similarly for us, eternal life is an undeserved gift of grace; we enter into it by way of a living, active, and obedient faith.
>
> The relationship between promise and obligation is also illustrated in Hebrews 10:35-36: "So do not throw

away your confidence; it will be richly rewarded. You need to persevere so that when you have done the will of God, you will receive what he has promised." The requirement is perseverance in faith, which includes doing the will of God. The benefit is receiving what God has promised. But what is promised cannot be earned or merited. [51-52]

Shepherd's exegesis of these biblical texts is overly simplistic. According to Shepherd, faith, repentance, and good works are all part of one package: They are "indissolubly intertwined with one another." Faith is "living, active, and abiding." Faith "perseveres." *Here is the crux of the theological dispute concerning the doctrine of justification by faith (sola fide): Is Shepherd affirming the view taught in traditional Protestant-Reformed theology that the faith which alone justifies is a faith which is living, active, and abiding? In other words, is faith the alone instrument of justification? Or is Shepherd saying that faith and works together are the "instrumental" means of life and salvation?* Shepherd is a master of theological subtlety. What is clearly lacking in Shepherd's discussion is mention of the term "instrument" with respect to justification. It is the case that Shepherd regards this and other traditional terminology as unnecessary theological baggage – more precisely, theological terminology that, in his view, is scholastic, speculative, unbiblical in origin. What is particularly striking in this book, a book that gives central place to Shepherd's understanding of the doctrine of justification by faith (and the related doctrines of election and the covenants of God), is the avoidance of such terminology as "justification," "imputation, "ground of salvation," and "instrument" (as previously noted). According to Protestant-Reformed theology, the righteousness of God imputed to the believer is received through the sole instrumentality of faith; and this righteousness of Christ imputed is the sole grounds of salvation. Clearly, terms such as these have no formative role in Shepherd's theology, one that – on close examination – is at odds with Protestant orthodoxy. For Shepherd, the slogan "faith alone" is understood to exclude *meritorious* works, not the works of faith (those good works which manifest, in Shepherd's words, the "grace of justification").

We still have not heard all that Shepherd has to say regarding the Mosaic covenant. Contrary to all that we have read thus far, Shepherd now informs us that in spite of the continuity between the two covenants, the old and the new, "[t]here was something wrong with the Mosaic covenant. It was defective because it could not succeed in doing what it was designed to do" (54). What is different about the "design" of the new covenant that makes it effective and successful in achieving its purpose? Shepherd answers: the Holy Spirit now, unlike former times, is actively applying the law to the hearts of believers so that they *can* obey the law and commandments of God.

> The defect in the law was correspondingly twofold. First, the blood of bulls and goats could not really handle the problem of sin. . . . Second, the commandments could not impart life. . . . For both of these reasons, Israel never succeeded in being the holy people of God that the Lord called them to be under the Mosaic covenant. That covenant was faulty. It was defective. That is why it was set aside when Jesus established the new covenant. [54-55]

> Paul declares repeatedly that observing the law cannot save a person. The reason for this is not that no one can keep the law perfectly as a covenant of works. Rather, observing the law cannot save a person because the Mosaic system is no longer operative. Salvation comes through faith in Jesus Christ. [56]

I leave it to the reader to compare this dispensational, non-Reformed explanation to the author's previous argumentation in *The Call of Grace*. After refuting the teaching of classic covenant theology which sees two antithetical principles at work within the Mosaic covenant (one on the typical level, the other on the antitypical), Shepherd ends up acknowledging that the Mosaic law cannot make alive. On first impressions, Shepherd seemingly accommodates the Pauline contrast between "letter" and "Spirit," that is, the contrast between the Law (which works death and condemnation) and the Gospel (which brings life and justification). But this redemptive-historical contrast remains an anomaly in Shepherd's theology of law, a theology that is poorly and inconsistently formulated.

Moving beyond the subtleties implicit in Shepherd's interpretation of justification by faith, we turn once again to his doctrine of the covenants, specifically to his repudiation of the Reformed doctrine of the "Covenant of Works." From the start, Shepherd informs his readers that he will not agree to a theology of law which incorporates the idea of *works-inheritance*. The Apostle Paul's negative critique of the law (pre- or post-Fall) hinges on *ad hominem* argumentation, claims Shepherd. That is to say, Paul assumes – for the sake of argument only – the validity of the principle of *inheritance-by-works* (meritorious reward) as taught by the Judaizers. "When the law is conceived of as a works/merit scheme, Paul is opposed to the law" (38). But Shepherd contends:

> God does not tempt his children to try to earn their salvation [or, in the case of Adam before the Fall, life and communion with God] by the merit of their works. Nor does he tease them by offering a way of salvation that he knows will not work. More pointedly, the very idea of merit is foreign to the way in which God our Father relates to his children. [39]

In the case of the Israelites, Shepherd explains further: "The obedience required of Israel is not the obedience of merit, but the obedience of faith. It is the fullness of faith. Obedience is simply faithfulness to the Lord; it is the righteousness of faith" (39). With respect to the typological reward of life and prosperity in Canaan, the land of promise, Shepherd is simply wrong. Reformed theology has correctly recognized two separate covenants made with the federal heads, Adam and Christ (the "Covenant of Works" and the "Covenant of Redemption" respectively): The inheritance-principle in both of these covenants is that of works/merit. The Mosaic covenant in its peculiar and distinctive way reintroduces the works-principle on the *typological level* of kingdom inheritance. (The issue here is not the mistaken notion of God tempting fallen creatures to earn something beyond their grasp or ability, specifically the procurement of that righteousness which alone justifies. In agreement with Shepherd, we too oppose the notion of *hypothetical salvation by works* as an administrative principle operative within the Mosaic economy.) At the root of Shepherd's error is faulty exegesis of Scripture, including theological synthesis – what belongs to the domain of biblical theology and systematics.

Spurred on by the writings of E. P. Sanders in the 1970s, and others following in his wake, the so-called "new perspective on Paul and the law" – what actually is a modification and reworking of Sanders' thesis – has become the dominant view in present-day biblical and theological studies. This revolution in contemporary theology makes possible the realignment between Roman Catholicism and Protestantism currently underway. Should agreement be reached between these two communions, the outcome would indicate that neither ecclesiastical tradition holds firm to its own historical-theological moorings. With respect to the long-standing dispute over the doctrine of justification by faith, what specifically is needed to bring about reconciliation? How promising does the union between Roman Catholics and Protestants appear to Shepherd? He modestly writes: "May I suggest that there is at least a glimmer of hope *if both sides are willing to embrace a covenantal understanding of the way of salvation*" (59, emphasis mine). And in Shepherd's judgment, this is the *only* real prospect for reconciliation between the two communions.[4] In this connection two observations are quite telling: (1) Shepherd in his opening attack on the *Alliance of Confessing Evangelicals* in this book faults both sides in the Reformation debate, Roman Catholic and Protestant, for misinterpreting the Scriptures concerning the way of salvation; and (2) students of Shepherd in recent years have been led to join/rejoin the Church of Rome precisely for the theological reasons Shepherd offers in *The Call of Grace*. On the one side of the dispute, observes Shepherd, the Church of Rome is to be faulted not only for making room for human merit in salvation, "[b]ut on a deeper level, what must be challenged in the Roman Catholic doctrine is the very idea of merit itself. God does not, and never did, relate to his people on the basis of a works/merit principle" (60). On the other side, a similar, grievous error has been committed by the orthodox Protestant-Reformed scholastics. Shepherd informs his readers: Were Rome to rethink (paradigmatically) its theology of law "this change in paradigm would provide a proper basis for Rome's legitimate insistence that full credence be given to James 2:24, Galatians 5:6, and similar passages" (61). Protestantism, on the other side of the aisle, would need to recognize and relinquish those errors which had crept into its confessional and dogmatic formulations. Here again, Shepherd assumes that his interpretation of *justification by faith and (non-meritorious) works* is the teaching of genuine, pure Calvinism (Calvinism of the non-scholastic variety). This assumption on the part of Shepherd is simply false. *The Call of Grace* makes no real attempt to prove the author's case on the basis of Scripture or the history of doctrine. For the most part, the argumentation is specious and shallow.

Without the painstaking exegesis of Scripture and the accurate reading and critique of historical theology, Shepherd simply asserts as the substance of his argument: "if we do not reject the idea of merit, we are not really able to challenge the Romanist doctrine of salvation *at its very root*" (61-62, italics mine).[5] The old Roman-Protestant scholastic theology, Shepherd argues, cannot accommodate the teaching of Scripture on covenant conditionality – including repentance and obedience, the warning against falling away, and the need for perseverance. Galatians 5:6, James 2:24, and like passages "are almost uniformly treated as problem texts because they do not fit into *a non-covenantal paradigm of salvation by grace*. Various exegetical and dogmatic devices of dubious validity are used to defuse and tame these texts so that they do fit" (62, italics mine).

Those in the Reformed camp who do not see the issues Shepherd's way are deemed antinomian. Shepherd claims that contemporary evangelical Protestants are eager

> to ward off the clear danger of legalism, but in doing so, [they] gravitate toward antinomianism. . . . This is the dilemma that has plagued evangelicalism even to our day, as evidenced by the lordship salvation controversy and the more recent discussion surrounding *The Gift of Salvation* and the *Appeal to Fellow Evangelicals*. [62]

What is totally lacking in the writings emanating from members of the *Alliance of Confessing Evangelicals*, in Shepherd's estimation, is any (legitimate) appeal to the covenant.[6] Parenthetically, it was not until Shepherd's teaching on the covenants moved to the forefront of discussion at Westminster Seminary – notably his repudiation of the Reformed doctrine of the "Covenant of Works" – that many more became convinced of the error of his doctrinal formulations. But there are other equally problematic issues surrounding Shepherd's theology. And to those we now turn.

### 2. Evangelism and the Sovereignty of God: Shepherd's new perspective

Shepherd begins Part 2 by challenging the view of Karl Barth on election. In the previous section, Shepherd was less combative in his attack on modernist teaching. (Barth is a pivotal figure in the neoorthodox school, influential especially for its reformulation of the doctrine of justification and the covenants. As a follower of apologist and theologian Cornelius Van Til, I consider Barthianism to be a variation of modernist theology. On this score, compare the penetrating case made against modernism by J. Gresham Machen in *Christianity and Liberalism*.) What accounts for this, in part, is the fact that Shepherd implicitly embraces Barth's *mono-covenantalism*. According to Barth's schematization of history, there is only one covenant, namely, God's single, unchanging *covenant of grace* beginning at creation. Coordinate with this understanding of covenant, the classic Protestant law/gospel antithesis is rejected outright. In its place the neoorthodox and modern-day revisionists speak of *law in grace* or *grace in law*. As we shall now see, this interpretation has a direct bearing on the doctrine of election. With respect to the role of human decision in salvation Barthianism is, at the same time, a hybrid of Arminianism.[7]

    The Synod of Dordt (which produced the *Canons of Dordt*) met in the seventeenth century to draw up five major points of doctrine to refute the teachings of the Remonstrants, who were proponents of an Arminian understanding of free will, the decrees of God, the fall of Adam from an original state of integrity, and the accomplishment/application of Christ's atoning work on behalf of sinners saved by grace. Lacking in this confessional writing (and, as noted earlier, in the writings of the *Alliance of Confessing Evangelicals*), argues Shepherd, is the doctrine of the covenant, that which is essential to the church's understanding of election and the way of salvation. Shepherd compares and contrasts his view on these matters by distinguishing between "election-evangelism" or "regeneration-evangelism" and his own brand of "covenant-evangelism." Those who practice the latter methodology are almost guaranteed to see results. "The New Testament represents the present age as one of unprecedented and superabundant blessing. Reformed churches ought to be experiencing that blessing in both the numerical and the spiritual growth of their congregations" (71). (One seriously wonders if this was the case in the churches Shepherd pastored.) In short, evangelistic methodology, Shepherd instructs his readers, must be oriented to the doctrine of the covenant, rather than the doctrines of election and regeneration. Shepherd claims that the particularism intrinsic to Calvinistic theology has too often inhibited evangelistic zeal and outreach. Shepherd says of the Calvinists: "Some would go so far as to say that there is no good news in any sense for the reprobate" (80). (Shepherd's use of the term "reprobate" here is infelicitous; prior to the consummation God alone is able to discern those who are elect and those who are reprobate.) Shepherd's assessment of Calvinism ends up being nothing more than a caricature, one all too familiar at that. Shepherd erroneously states:

> Because the Calvinist has an accomplished redemption that is particular in scope though always effective for the elect, he cannot apply it to particular persons. The ap-

plication has to be more general and abstract because he cannot distinguish between the elect and the reprobate in real life. [81]

In *The Call of Grace* Shepherd transforms the Reformed doctrine of the indiscriminate offer of the Gospel into the belief that Christ died for all indiscriminately. Clearly, Shepherd's view is in conflict with Calvinistic teaching concerning the particularism of Christ's atonement. What Shepherd fails to understand is that although the Gospel is preached to all sinners indiscriminately, as the Great Commission requires, we cannot say indiscriminately that Christ died for "you." To declare "Christ died for (an equivocal) you" is not the Gospel. That assertion is true only for the elect of God. Election to salvation is the *proper purpose* of redemptive covenant. But until the return of Jesus Christ at the end of the age there are both elect and non-elect within the covenant household. The present ministry and discipline of the Word within the community of faith provides only an approximate reading of the true church, fully known by God. The revelation of the true, final, eschatological assembly of the saints awaits the Consummation, when the Bridegroom meets his Bride, and the sons of God shall be revealed.

Shepherd's exegesis of Ephesians 1:1-14 is marred by underlying confusion concerning the biblical doctrine of election. Contrary to Shepherd's teaching, election to salvation is *definitive* by virtue of the death and resurrection of Christ (that is, the accomplishment of redemption). Paul's address to the Ephesian church as the "elect of God" must be understood, accordingly, in terms of what we have identified as the *proper purpose* of redemptive covenant. *Over the course of redemptive history covenant is broader than election.* (Esau, it will be remembered, was a covenant child, but not numbered among the elect.) Shepherd presumes an election to salvation with respect to all those who are members of the covenant community: "In Ephesians 1, Paul writes from the perspective of observable covenant reality and concludes from the visible faith and sanctity of the Ephesians that they are the elect of God" (87-88). On the one hand, Shepherd acknowledges that such "election" is *losable*: "It is true that some in the congregation may fall away and leave the church. Paul issues a warning in view of that possibility. Were some to fall away, he would no longer speak of them as the elect of God" (88). Contrary to Shepherd's interpretation, Calvinism teaches that election is *unlosable*. Parenthetically, Shepherd equates the election of individuals within the community of the new covenant with Israel's national election under the Mosaic economy: Both are *losable*.

When does one have the "right" to be called a child of God (see Jn 1:12)? Is it at the time one professes faith in Jesus Christ as Lord and Savior? Or is it at the occasion of baptism (rightly administered), when one receives the name "Christian" – the new name given only to the saints of God (see Jn 3:3-8 and Rev 3:12)? The answer is the latter. (A covenantal understanding of conversion brings together personal profession of faith and institutional baptism. Membership in the church of Christ is outwardly marked by baptism, the covenantal sign and seal of that inward grace which is sovereignly bestowed by the Spirit of God upon the elect, and the elect alone. Not all who are outwardly baptized are regenerated from above. But the *proper purpose* of baptism is the salvation of the elect.) From this biblical point of view, however, Shepherd mistakenly reasons:

> [I]nstead of looking at covenant from the perspective of regeneration, we ought to look at regeneration from the perspective of covenant. When that happens, baptism the sign and seal of the covenant, marks the point of

> conversion. Baptism is the moment when we see the transition from death to life and a person is saved. . . .
>
> This covenant sign and seal marks his conversion and his entrance into the church as the body of Christ. From the perspective of the covenant, he is united to Christ when he is baptized. [94]

It is at this point that Shepherd confuses election – God's secret work – with the church's administration of baptism, the *sacramental* sign and seal of union with Christ. (We cannot enter here into the theology of the sacraments in any full way. That is a subject requiring extended discussion. The biblical-Reformed interpretation has no kinship with sacramentalism. There is no *ex operato* benefit in its administration – no automatic bestowal of grace to the recipient. Only by means of the regenerating work of the Spirit of God among the elect is the proper purpose of baptism realized at some point in time, before or after the actual administration of the sacrament. See endnote 11 below.) Shepherd would no doubt respond to my criticism by saying that the "election" of which he speaks is different from *decretive* election. But here lies the problem: Shepherd defines terms contrary to their proper biblical and theological usage – he employs his own special vocabulary. The attentive reader must understand that Shepherd's objections to traditional Calvinistic formulation are not semantic, but theologically substantive. Shepherd faults the orthodox Calvinists not only for their employment of scholastic distinctions and terminology which he regards as speculative, but also for their misconception and misformulation of biblical teaching.

According to Shepherd, some of the by-products of Calvinistic theology oriented to the doctrines of election and regeneration – most evident its teaching on covenant and evangelism – include preparationism, that is, reliance on the preaching of Law (God's word of wrath and condemnation) prior to the preaching of the Gospel (the call to faith and repentance) and the problems created by Calvinism in its emphasis upon personal introspection – either on the part of sincere inquirers seeking entrance to the kingdom of God or on the part of longtime members of the covenant household uncertain of their election. Such introspection frequently results not in salvation by works, but in "assurance by works," an equally fatal error (99). Accordingly, Shepherd reasons, the Calvinist is led to believe that one can be certain of his election by producing the fruits of regeneration, namely, good works.

> When the call to faith is isolated from the call to obedience, as it frequently is, the effect is to make good works a supplement to salvation or simply the evidence of salvation. Some would even make them an optional supplement. According to the Great Commission, however, *they belong to the essence of salvation*, which is freedom from sin and not simply freedom from eternal condemnation as the consequence of sin. Because good works are done in obedience to all that Christ has commanded, they are suffused with and qualified by faith, without which no one can please God (Heb 11:6). [104, emphasis mine]

Shepherd's understanding of the way of salvation, his readers are reassuringly told, is the only real solution to the theological dilemmas created by Calvinists. Only his understanding offers the sure confidence sinners need to rest in Christ for life and salvation. We have now come full circle. In *The Call of Grace* the author's primary thesis can be summarized as follows: The way of salvation, that is, justification, is the way of faith and good works. The faith that saves – the faith that justifies – is active, living, and abiding. It perseveres to the end. The way or "instrument" of justification (though Shepherd does not employ the term "instrument") is faith *and* works.

## 4. Advice and Consent:
## Hearing from and responding to Shepherd's critics

Discussion of and debate over Shepherd's theology have taken place in various contexts over many long years, down to the present. In what follows we will draw from the body of published and unpublished writings addressing these controverted issues. Unaware of the heated dispute taking place at that time on the campus of Westminster Seminary, Sinclair Ferguson in the pages of the Scottish magazine *The Banner of Truth*, popular among Calvinists (of the Puritan type), criticized Shepherd's essay appearing in *The New Testament Student and Theology* edited by John H. Skilton. Ferguson, who was later to become Shepherd's replacement at Westminster, took Shepherd to task for his views on covenant evangelism.[8] Ferguson wrote:

> Shepherd appears to adopt the view of the prevailing academic critique of the covenant theology of the seventeenth century (forcefully presented decades ago by Perry Miller), which suggests that the doctrine of covenant somehow makes God's secret counsels less harsh. We ought therefore to look at covenant, and not at election. This analysis, both historically and biblically we reject. . . . From a more practical point of view – was it because Whitefield and Edwards, Spurgeon and M'Cheyne managed to escape the old Reformed straitjacket and discover election in its covenant perspective that they were such great evangelists? It seems highly doubtful. And therefore we are justified in wondering whether this is really the true solution at all.
> 
> Shepherd has had the courage to state to the Reformed reader that a question mark hangs over the commonly accepted notion that the preacher cannot

> say: "Christ died for you." In fact Shepherd goes so far as to say that, from this covenantal perspective [of his], the Reformed preacher is *under obligation* to say "Christ died to save you." But that cannot possibly be a proper assessment, for no evangelist in the New Testament shows himself to have been under an inescapable burden to say that.[9]

Another major point to which Ferguson took exception is Shepherd's understanding of the relationship between baptism and regeneration: "Perhaps, in view of the originality which the author is obviously seeking to inject into an important area of discussion, it is inevitable that he has not, apparently, thought through some of the implications of his teaching."[10] Ferguson concluded: "It would be our hope that, for the welfare of the Reformed churches, Professor Shepherd would return to the drawing board, and come again, so that we may hear him further on these matters."[11] Sound advice, to be sure. *The Call of Grace* is Shepherd's reply to Ferguson and others among his critics. Has Shepherd been listening responsibly to the questions and criticisms which have been raised? Has he made a sincere attempt to answer them in a direct and forthright manner? We contend that he has not.

In an open letter (dated May 19, 1981) Professor Richard Gaffin, Shepherd's ardent defender and the co-father of the new, anti-Reformational teaching at Westminster Seminary, accused a specific group of critics, known as the "Committee of Forty-Five" (signers of a letter sent to a wider segment of Westminster's constituency), of espousing nothing more than "loosely supported allegations of serious doctrinal error."[12] Gaffin wrote of the "inherent implausibility of the position taken by the signers."[13] In addition, Gaffin accused the opposition of procedural misconduct – accusation "without due process." The truth is, there was ample opportunity for Professor Shepherd to clarify his position at every level of discussion both within the Seminary and the Orthodox Presbyterian Church, of which he was a member at that time. Due process was given. (Of course, there are times when the courts of the church fail in their duty to uphold biblical truth, for whatever reasons. Luther was correct in rejecting the "wisdom" of the church court in his day and in challenging the doctrinal error of the Magisterium.) The history of the controversy at Westminster in the early years was complicated and convoluted. The "Committee of Forty-Five" was convinced that the time had come for exposing the error of Shepherd's teaching in the wider Seminary/church arena. Gaffin in his letter defended the view of his friend and theological collaborator that sinners are justified by faith and (non-meritorious) works. Citing Reformed dogmatician Herman Bavinck, Gaffin disputed the view maintained by some theologians which distinguishes between two justifications, the first being the "justification of the sinner" (attributed to the teaching of the Apostle Paul) and the second the "justification of the just" (attributed to the teaching of James). Gaffin contended that there is but one justification, combining all that is found in the writings of Paul and James. The problem here is *how* Gaffin and Shepherd treat the Biblical data in their formulation of the doctrine of justification by faith (*sola fide*), one which incorporates the teaching of Paul and James.[14] Gaffin concluded his letter by noting that the issue in this dispute does not only concern how we expound this singular doctrine, but also the question whether or not the "theological structure and doctrinal formulations" of the Reformation are true to the whole counsel of God – this issue, he noted, involves "something more than what we imagine we already have under our control and have already mastered."[15] Simply put, Gaffin and Shepherd are convinced that the Protestant-Reformed tradition is in need of correction and modification in its understanding of the biblical doctrine of justification by faith.¹⁶ (The underlying dispute concerning Scripture's teaching on the covenants does not surface here in Gaffin's letter. He and others were skillful in avoiding that subject. But what is clear is the denial of the traditional formulation of justification by faith alone on the part of Shepherd and Gaffin.)

    It was not until Shepherd presented his lectures on "Life in Covenant with God" at the French Creek Bible Conference at Sandy Cove, Maryland, in the summer of 1981 that the debate over the doctrine of the covenants finally moved out into the open. Many were convinced (some for the first time) that these lectures served to clarify the underlying error in Shepherd's theologizing. More significantly, these lectures provided the occasion for then-President Edmund Clowney to reassess the Seminary situation. It was at this juncture that Clowney made a complete reversal in his position and proceeded to take the steps necessary to remove Shepherd from the faculty. On November 20, 1981, the Board of Trustees of Westminster Seminary called for Shepherd's dismissal. With the input of many individuals, including my own analysis of Shepherd's Sandy Cove lectures (requested by and submitted to those assigned the task of writing the document titled "Reason and Specifications Supporting the Action of the Board of Trustees in Removing Professor Shepherd Approved by the Executive Committee of the Board [February 26, 1982]"), the evaluation of Shepherd's theology given by his leading critics, now including President Clowney and Robert Strimple, Dean of the Faculty, was recognized and adopted by the Board of Trustees. The eighteen-page document "Reason and Specifications" summarized briefly the history of the controversy and offered a fair and balanced critique of Shepherd's teaching on such doctrines as justification, the covenants of God, election, and the assurance of salvation. Parenthetically, Shepherd had opportunity to respond to this evaluation, but instead decided to withdraw himself from the hearing process afforded him. Shortly thereafter he transferred his membership into the Christian Reformed Church, where his views were certain to find safe harbor. In summation of the early history of the theological controversy at Westminster, both the error of Shepherd's teaching and the evasive responses supplied by Shepherd throughout the course of the controversy persuaded a growing number of theologians and pastors – some previously supportive of Shepherd's teaching – to support the decision of President Clowney calling for Shepherd's removal.

"Reason and Specifications," the official document of the governing board of the Seminary, stated the following as the theological basis for Shepherd's dismissal:

> The Board has come to the decision that Prof. Shepherd's removal is necessary for the best interests of the Seminary with great regret, and only after seven years of earnest study and debate, because it has become convinced that Mr. Shepherd's teaching regarding justification, the covenant of works and the covenant of grace, and related themes is *not clearly in accord* with the teaching of Scripture as it is summarized in the system of doctrine contained in the Westminster Standards.[17]

In the historical sketch of the controversy at Westminster Seminary, the reader is informed that after admitting theological ambiguity and in an effort to distance himself from all earlier formulations, Shepherd at one point in time wished to be judged in light of two particular writings: (1) his "Thirty-four Theses on Justification in Relation to Faith, Repentance and Good Works," submitted in November 1978 for discussion in the Philadelphia Presbytery of the Orthodox Presbyterian Church; and (2) a paper titled "The Grace of Justification." Both of these were rather carefully crafted in the attempt to convince concerned parties that Shepherd's theology was indeed faithful to Scripture and to the Reformed faith.[18] At this juncture these formulations did succeed in gaining some additional support for Shepherd's position and in bringing about a temporary closure to the Seminary dispute. It was not until the circulation of the letter signed by forty-five theologians, including both scholars and pastors (dated May 4, 1981), that the case reopened. "Reason and Specifications" takes note of the following: "The President [Edmund Clowney] deplored the mailing of this letter to the general public rather than to the Board and Faculty."[19] This latest development, to be sure, added further conflict to an exceedingly tense situation within the Seminary community. (It should be noted here, however, that the controversy had moved beyond the faculty and the board long before this point in time. It was widely debated in the Orthodox Presbyterian Church and in other ecclesiastical circles.)

Here are some of the conclusions reached in "Reason and Specifications" with regard to Shepherd's theology:

> In spite of modifications that Mr. Shepherd has made in his expressions, the Board finds that the problems in his teaching are not resolved, and that they are inherent in his view of the "covenant dynamic." Although Mr. Shepherd appeals to the history of Reformed covenantal theology to support his position, the Board finds that Mr. Shepherd's construction is distinctive. It is in the distinctive elements and emphases of his theology of the covenant that the problem appears.[20]
>
> In his "covenant dynamic" Mr. Shepherd develops a formula that permits him to join good works to faith as the characteristic and qualifying response to grace. Obedience is the proper, full, and comprehensive term for all covenantal response, and specifically for our response in the covenant of grace.[21]

The "covenant dynamic" of Mr. Shepherd makes the function of our obedience in the covenant to be the same as the function of the obedience of Adam in the covenant before the fall ("Life in Covenant with God," Tapes 1, 2). Mr. Shepherd finds one covenantal pattern in all of Scripture. The pattern joins God's free grace and our response in faithful obedience.[22]

The omission of any clear treatment of Christ as the covenant Head, of his active obedience, of the imputation of his righteousness in the fulfillment of the covenant command, of his probation in our place (this in a treatment of the covenant that professes to be distinctively Reformed, after years of discussion) evidence a lack of clarity that cannot but cause concern.[23]

Mr. Shepherd insists that the threat of the curse is a necessary part of the covenant structure for Adam, for Israel, and for us. It promises blessing for the faithful and curse for the unfaithful. He has described the reservation that the threat of eternal death does not apply to believers as a "moral influence" theology of the warnings of Scripture (Faculty conference, October 26, 1981). He urged before the Board that just as Adam's posterity would not be "off the hook" if Adam had obeyed, but would be bound to fulfill the condition of obedience, so the posterity of Christ are not "off the hook."[24]

By rejecting the distinction between the covenant of works and the covenant of grace as defined in the Westminster Standards, and by failing to take account in the structure of the "covenant dynamic" of Christ's fulfillment of the covenant by his active obedience as well as by his satisfaction of its curse, Mr. Shepherd develops a uniform concept of covenant faithfulness for Adam, for Israel, and for the New Covenant people. The danger is that both the distinctiveness of the covenant of grace and of the new covenant fullness of the covenant of grace will be lost from view and that obedience as the way of Salvation will swallow up the distinct and primary function of faith.[25]

How does Shepherd answer his critics? *The Call of Grace* demonstrates conclusively that Shepherd has no intention of reformulating his views to bring them into accord with orthodox Reformed dogmatics. Modifications previously made were merely temporary in nature, and disingenuous at that.

The dispute does not end here. Presently, Gaffin continues to promote vigorously and aggressively the new theology at Westminster Seminary, all the more so in Shepherd's absence. Gaffin sees himself carrying on the work he and Shepherd began in the 1970s and earlier.[26] In a letter dated March 7, 1983, addressed to the "Committee of Forty-Five" and written by three members of this "Committee," attention was directed to several recent events that had then transpired. Among the several concerns expressed in this communication was the following:

> in its most recent communication to us [the faculty of Westminster Seminary] has totally ignored the existence of this paper ["Reason and Specifications"]. Their position is tantamount to a continuing support of the theology of Norman Shepherd, and a defense of its own position that his theological formulations were not in error.
>
> This attitude must be treated with the seriousness it deserves. If the assessment of Mr. Shepherd's theology in the paper specifying the reasons for his dismissal is correct, he has departed from the system of theology in the Westminster standards in the areas of justification, the covenant and assurance. For the faculty now to ignore these findings could have the gravest consequences for the Seminary.[27]

That fear has now become reality. Unquestionably, the Shepherd-Gaffin dispute has become the watershed for

Westminster Seminary in Philadelphia. Gaffin, who remains the most dominant member of the faculty, and the current President, Samuel Logan, have succeeded in removing all opposition from within the Philadelphia faculty, even though the Seminary denies barring Shepherd's critics from faculty appointments.[28] This falsification of the facts is challenged in the letter of March 7, 1983 (and elsewhere). Members of the faculty, administration and board of the Seminary have for many years attempted to mislead the public about what is being taught at the Seminary. As one former member of the Philadelphia faculty commented, the problem at Westminster is theological *and* moral. And in the estimation of another, the well at Westminster has been contaminated. The pernicious, insidious teaching of the Shepherd school is now intrenched in the Seminary and in some of the churches it serves. From all appearances, there is little hope of seeing a return of Westminster to its original position and role in the propagation and defense of historic Calvinism. Westminster in Philadelphia no longer is the bastion of Reformed orthodoxy it once was (see endnote 26).

Those familiar with changes taking place in contemporary "evangelical" theology more broadly understand that the Shepherd-Gaffin teaching is by no means novel. In *A New Systematic Theology of the Christian Faith* author Robert Reymond observes how

> a view that insists upon "grace" everywhere winds up with true grace nowhere and a kind of works principle everywhere, with [Daniel Fuller's] representation of the relation of works to justification coming perilously close to what late medieval theologians would have called works having not condign but congruent merit. One thing is certainly clear from Fuller's representation of this whole matter: He has departed from the *sola fide* principle of the Protestant Reformation.[29]

(In this section of his systematics Reymond relies heavily upon the work of Meredith G. Kline, leading Old Testament scholar and Reformed theologian of our day.) Since the time of Shepherd's dismissal from Westminster, exchanges between both sides in this debate have not abated. Kline remains one of the principal defenders of covenant theology within the Reformed community. In the latest edition of his *Kingdom Prologue*, the *magnum opus* of his teaching and writing career, Kline draws together the major lines of refutation to be made against the Shepherd-Gaffin theology.[30] The fruit of ongoing debate can be seen in these summarizing remarks:

> Since the works principle is thus foundational to the Gospel, the repudiation of that principle – in particular, the denial of the possibility of meritorious works where paternal love is involved (as it certainly is in the relation of the Father and the Son [in the "Covenant of Redemption" established in eternity]) – stands condemned as subversive of that Gospel. What begins as a rejection of works ends up as an attack, however unintentional, on the biblical message of saving grace.[31]
>
> . . .[at creation] man's hope of realizing the state of glorification and of attaining to the Sabbath-consummation belonged to him by virtue of his very nature as created in the image of the God of glory. This expectation was an in-created earnest of fullness, to be denied which would have frustrated him to the depths of his spirit's longing for God and God-likeness. Whatever he might have been granted short of that for his obedience would be no blessing at all, but a curse.[32]
>
> The distinctive meaning of grace in its biblical-theological usage is a divine response of favor and blessing in the face of human violation of obligation. Gospel grace takes account of man in his responsibility under the demands of the covenant and specifically as a

covenant breaker, a sinner against covenant law. Accordingly, the grace of Christ comes to expression in his active and passive obedience, together constituting a vicarious satisfaction for the obligations and liabilities of his people, who through failure and transgression are debtors before the covenant Lord, the Judge of all the earth. Gospel grace emerges in a forensic framework as a response of mercy to demerit.[33]

One of the major issues of debate brought to the fore in discussions at the *Covenant Roundtable*, convened at Westminster Seminary for the purpose of resolving differences among some of the principal disputants, was the question of proportionality or disproportionality respecting the covenantal reward of life everlasting promised to Adam upon successful completion of the probationary test. Speaking to this issue, Kline remarks:

> Another form of the attack on the Covenant of Works doctrine (and thus on the classic law-gospel contrast) asserts that even if it is allowed that Adam's obedience would have earned something, the disproportion between the value of that act of service and the value of the proffered blessing forbids us to speak here of simple equity or justice. The contention is that Adam's ontological status limited the value or weight of his acts. More specifically his act of obedience would not have eternal value or significance; it could not earn a reward of eternal, confirmed life. In the offer of eternal life, so we are told, we must therefore recognize an element of "grace" in the pre-redemptive covenant. But belying this assessment of the situation is the fact that if it were true that Adam's act of obedience could not have eternal significance then neither could or did his actual act of disobedience have eternal significance. It did not deserve the punishment of everlasting death. Consistency would compel us to judge God guilty of imposing punishment beyond the demands of justice, pure and simple.[34]

> Refusing to accept God's covenant word as the definer of justice, the disproportionality view exalts above God's Word a standard of justice of its own making. Assigning ontological values to Adam's obedience and God's reward it finds that weighed on its judicial scales they are drastically out of balance. In effect that conclusion imputes an imperfection in justice to the Lord of the covenant. The attempt to hide this affront against the majesty of the Judge of all the Earth by condescending to assess the relation of Adam's act to God's reward as one of congruent merit is no more successful than Adam's attempt to manufacture a covering to conceal his nakedness. It succeeds only in exposing the roots of this opposition to Reformed theology in the theology of Rome.[35]

Gaffin counters this argument by pressing the case for scholastic federalism's use of the nature/grace dichotomy (that is, the imposition of the covenant arrangement upon an assumed, prior order of nature). This construct, Gaffin maintains, ameliorates the notion of "meritorious reward" suggested by the familiar terminology of the "Covenant of Works." According to Gaffin, the creation covenant in the Reformed theological tradition is best construed as a *gracious* disposition of God, the Lord of the covenant. Grace, in Gaffin's view, nullifies all talk of human "merit." That is to say, all that Adam has and receives is a matter of "sovereign grace and promise." No works, no merit. The final verdict concerning this dispute at Westminster and within the broader evangelical-Reformed community is not yet in. Those standing within the tradition of historic Protestant-Reformed orthodoxy have sounded the alert concerning clear and present dangers facing contemporary evangelicalism.[36]

## 5. Closing Evaluation: Ambiguities in the Shepherd(-Gaffin) theology

Returning to the focus of this evaluation of current teaching at Westminster Seminary, a critical look at Shepherd's book *The Call of Grace*, it is clear that Shepherd's theological formulations are deeply flawed. The summation of historic Calvinism offered by Shepherd is largely a caricature; his reading of the Reformed theological tradition lacks careful documentation and analysis. (Interaction with the current literature is entirely lacking. Only the names of Charles Hodge and Karl Barth are mentioned.) Shepherd assumes that his readers will simply accept his reading of the history of doctrine and acknowledge in Calvinism the underlying problem as he sees it. The two principal theses made by Shepherd are these: First, God never relates to his image-bearers in terms of a covenant-of-works arrangement, wherein reward is contingent upon meritorious obedience on the part of the creature; second, the doctrine of the covenant(s) rather than the doctrine of election and regeneration is determinative in the church's evangelistic outreach. The author's "covenant evangelism" is presented as the remedy for Calvinism's alleged inability to make a *genuine offer of grace* to needy sinners. The way of the covenant is the way of faith *and* good works. This view stands in opposition to the traditional Protestant-Reformed doctrines of justification by faith alone and sovereign election.

In his distinctive style of writing, Shepherd claims: "Christ did not die for inanimate objects or preternatural beings, not did he die for abstractions. He died for people, for sinners, for you and for me" (85). This assertion stands in flat contradiction to the Reformed doctrine of the definite atonement, that is, the teaching that Christ died for the elect, for them only, and that he actually acquired their salvation. Shepherd's exegesis of Ephesians 1:1-14 up-ends the Reformed (and biblical) teaching concerning the relationship between redemptive covenant and election. Rather than looking at "election from the perspective of covenant," as Shepherd would have us do, Reformed theology has – in different ways, to be sure – understood election to be the "proper purpose" of redemptive covenant. That is to say, *covenant is broader than election*. On this subject, Shepherd's interpretation is an Arminian hybrid, an attempt to extract what Shepherd sees as the best of these two diverse theological traditions, all the while paying lip-service to the Reformed doctrine of sovereign, decretive election. Shepherd concludes his chapter on covenant and election with this thought: "In light of the covenant, we learn that the particularistic doctrines of Calvinism are pure grace and not a mixture of blessing and curse" (91). What precisely is he saying here? What might strike one at first as insightful and helpful is actually ambiguous and ill-conceived. *The root of Shepherd's misformulation is his unease with the Reformed doctrine of predestination – including election and reprobation – especially when it comes to working out the implications of covenant theology for evangelism and Christian living.*[37]

    Not only does Shepherd's teaching undermine the Reformed doctrine of the assurance of salvation, at the same time his views undercut the decisive nature of (true) conversion, including the once-for-all declaration of the sinner *saved* by grace, by virtue of the believer's justification and union with Christ in his death and resurrection. The divine act of justification rests upon the *finished* work of Christ. According to Shepherd, "evangelism does not end with regeneration, but *continues* as long as a person lives" (100, emphasis mine). Coordinate with this understanding of conversion, Shepherd stresses the need for obedience (that is, good works) in the way of salvation *as an ongoing process*. As cited previously, Shepherd maintains: "When the call to faith is isolated from the call to obedience, as it frequently is, the effect is to make good works a supplement to salvation or simply the evidence of salvation. According to the Great Commission, however, they belong to the essence of salvation" (104). In connection with his erroneous exegesis of Leviticus 18:5 (and its New Testament citations), Shepherd contends that God's salvation is to be received "with a living and active faith." Faith and works are the means of justification. Shepherd takes exception to both Rome and the Protestant Reformation, specifically their employment of the "merit" idea in connection with the doctrine of justification and the covenants. (Unlike the theology of Rome, Protestant theology maintains that Christ's obedience is the *exclusive* meritorious ground of salvation.)

Joining other voices in contemporary "evangelical" theology – surfacing as early as the 1950s – Shepherd's work exemplifies the renewed interest in Barth's teaching on covenant and justification. His teaching, like Barth's, is anti-Reformational theology in the guise of authentic Calvinism. What we actually uncover in the pages of *The Call of Grace* is one more variation on neoorthodox themes. The controversy surrounding this book is of singular import today for Westminster Seminary and the churches it serves. The guard at Westminster in Philadelphia is radically different from that of its early days. Since its founding in 1929, Westminster Seminary saw itself as the conveyer of Old Princeton theology; today it is caught up in the winds of change. No longer does Westminster stand in the stream of confessional Reformed orthodoxy. That day has passed. What remains for those standing true to Scripture and the historic Reformed faith at the turn of this new millennium is the increasingly more difficult task of defending the Gospel against *every* assault, both within and without the halls of the academy and the church.[38]

## ENDNOTES

\* This essay was first published by The Trinity Foundation (Unicoi, TN, 2001); also published as issues 193 and 194 of *The Trinity Review*. Available online, with additional documents posted on the publisher's website: www.trinityfoundation.org.

¹ For a historical sketch of Westminster Seminary's formation and its ties to Old Princeton, see Mark Noll, "The Princeton Theology," *Reformed Theology in America: A History of its Modern Development* (ed. D. F. Wells; Grand Rapids: Eerdmans, 1985) 15-35; and his "The Spirit of Old Princeton and the Spirit of the OPC," *Pressing Toward the Mark: Essays Commemorating Fifty Years of the Orthodox Presbyterian Church* (eds. C. G. Dennison and R. C. Gamble; Philadelphia: The Committee for the Historian of the Orthodox Presbyterian Church, 1986) 235-246.

² Presbyterian and Reformed, 2000. Page references from this book are provided in the text.

³ "Reason and Specifications Supporting the Action of the Board of Trustees in Removing Professor Shepherd Approved by the Executive Committee of the Board (February 26, 1982)," 1. (Available online at http://www.covopc.org/Shepherd_Contents.html.)

⁴ See the argument in Hans Küng, *Justification: The Doctrine of Karl Barth and a Catholic Reflection* (trans. T. Collins, E. Tolk, and D. Granskou; New York: Nelson, 1964), which contains "A Letter to the Author" written by Barth.

⁵ Compare the similar sentiments of G. C. Berkouwer, *Sin* (Studies in Dogmatics; Grand Rapids: Eerdmans, 1971), 208-209; the entire chapter is highly formative in Shepherd's thinking. To be sure, Berkouwer earns greater respect for his command of exegetical and historical theology. He is, at the same time, clearer (and more open) with respect to his own philosophico-theological commitments.

⁶ On the contrary, see, for example, the several articles in *Modern Reformation* (July/August 2000). To complicate matters, the founder and president of the *Alliance of Confessing Evangelicals*, the late James Montgomery Boice, wavered in his thinking on the biblical doctrine of the covenants, specifically the Reformed doctrine of the "Covenant of Works." Having moved from his earlier dispensational leanings, Boice was influenced to some degree by the teachings of Westminster Seminary (several of the faculty members attended Tenth Presbyterian Church where Boice preached). Boice developed an especially close relationship with Sinclair Ferguson, frequent speaker at the Philadelphia Conference on Reformed Theology. It is also the case that the composition of the *Alliance* has been theologically eclectic, and that creates problems of its own.

⁷ See my review of Michael Thomas' *The Extent of the Atonement: A Dilemma for Reformed Theology from Calvin to the Consensus*, in *Trinity Journal* 20 NS (1999) 116-119, republished in my *Covenant Theology in Reformed Perspective: Collected Essays and Book Reviews in Historical, Biblical, and Systematic Theology* (Eugene, OR: Wipf and Stock, 2000) 147-150.

⁸ In the Fall of 1997 Ferguson was installed as the Charles Krahe Professor of Systematic Theology (funded by those sympathetic to his views); the following Spring (1998) Ferguson resigned, returning to Scotland where the covenant theology of the Torrance school prevails. Ferguson himself studied covenant theology under the feet of James Torrance, his doctoral supervisor. (The Torrance school is commonly, though incorrectly, viewed as evangelical both here in the States and in Britain; actually, this school of thought is Barthian.) See further my paper, "Current Theological Trends in Reformed Seminaries: The Dilemma in Ministerial Education," paper read at the Eastern regional meeting of the Evangelical Theological Society in Lancaster, PA (April 3, 1998). Extracts from this paper are included in the present writing.

⁹ Sinclair Ferguson, book review in *The Banner of Truth* 166-167 (July-August 1977) 61-62.

[10] Ferguson, 63.

[11] Ferguson, 63. For an insightful and helpful discussion of the biblical teaching on baptism, see most notably Meredith G. Kline, *By Oath Consigned* (Grand Rapids: Eerdmans, 1968). The Reformed doctrine of church and sacraments differs sharply from "baptistic" interpretations which place a premium upon personal faith at the expense of the confessor's corporate standing in the church, the holy institution established by Christ. Those who preach and administer the Word have been granted the "keys of the kingdom," the authority to exercise church discipline within the household of faith.

[12] Open letter of Richard B. Gaffin, Jr. (May 19, 1981), 1. Gaffin's endorsement of *The Call of Grace* on the back cover reads: "This lucid and highly readable study provides valuable instruction on what it means to live in covenant with God. God's covenant is the only way of life that fully honors both the absolute, all-embracing sovereignty of his saving grace and the full, uninhibited activity of his people. *The Call of Grace* should benefit anyone concerned about biblical growth in Christian life and witness."

[13] Gaffin's open letter, 2.

[14] See my "Justification in Redemptive History," *The Westminster Theological Journal* 43 (1981) 213-246, republished in my *Covenant Theology in Reformed Perspective* 157-180. Here I restate the biblical-Reformed teaching on justification by faith in terms of its two distinct aspects – the constitutive and the demonstrative.

[15] Gaffin's open letter, 7.

[16] At no point in the controversy, from the beginning to the present, has Gaffin taken exception to Shepherd's formulations. He has vigorously defended Shepherd thesis by thesis, point by point, adamantly insisting upon the soundness of Shepherd's views.

[17] "Reason and Specifications" 2, emphasis mine.

18 In the paper, "The Grace of Justification," J. Gresham Machen is misinterpreted by Shepherd at the place where Machen contrasts works of merit with works of faith. Machen is not suggesting that the works of faith which New Testament authors commend are *instrumental* in justification, as Shepherd is proposing.

    In a shrewd and calculated move, Shepherd's "Thirty-four Theses on Justification," which served as the basis for discussion and debate in the hearing conducted by the Philadelphia Presbytery of the Orthodox Presbyterian Church (what Shepherd himself had requested of his presbytery), skillfully avoided the weightier, more controversial aspects of his teaching. Over the course of the many days of this hearing Gaffin frequently answered for Shepherd, all in the effort to mislead further the church court concerning the critical issues in the Seminary dispute. (To reiterate, all discussion of the doctrine of the covenants was deliberately circumscribed during the initial phase of the controversy. Fortunately, Shepherd could not contain himself on that subject. Subsequent airing of his views on the covenants resulted in his swift removal from the Seminary faculty.) At the conclusion of his hearing, the Presbytery of Philadelphia neither affirmed Shepherd's teaching as being in accord with the confessional standards of the Orthodox Presbyterian Church, nor ruled it out of accord – it simply ended in a deadlock. A few years later Shepherd withdrew from the denomination.

19 "Reason and Specifications" 9. In response to this situation, Westminster's administration and faculty expressed their desire to censure the signers in the church courts for violation of the Ninth Commandment (respecting Shepherd's good name – and that of the Seminary). That wish was never realized, though the accusation lingers on. Westminster continues to maintain this same posture in the face of ongoing criticism. See, for example, *Presbyterian and Reformed News* 6:1 (January-February 200) 12-13; and Samuel Logan's response posted in the following issue of this publication, *Presbyterian and Reformed News* 6:2 (March-April 2000) 8. By insisting that all criticism against faculty members be presented as charges in the courts of the church, President Logan thinks he is free to ignore the critics.

[20] "Reason and Specifications" 11.

[21] "Reason and Specifications" 11.

[22] "Reason and Specifications" 12.

[23] "Reason and Specifications" 14.

[24] "Reason and Specifications" 15.

[25] "Reason and Specifications" 15.

[26] John M. Frame speaks of the injustice of Shepherd's dismissal, in view of the fact that Gaffin, who holds the same views, remains on the Seminary faculty – a rather surprising comment on the part of Frame who also sympathizes with Shepherd's teaching (see Frame's unpublished paper, "Let's Keep the Picture Fuzzy" [Westminster Theological Seminary, June 5, 1985], 5). Compare further Frame's comments in his *Cornelius Van Til: An Analysis of His Thought* (Presbyterian and Reformed: 1995) 393, and my critique of Frame on Shepherd (including Frame's perspectival methodology) in "John Frame and the Recasting of Van Tilian Apologetics: A Review Article," *Mid-America Journal of Theology* 9 (1993) 279-296 [note: this issue of the *Journal* was published in the Spring of 1998]. I have been informed that Frame makes another attempt to answer my criticisms and those of others in his forthcoming book, *The Doctrine of God* (Phillipsburg: Presbyterian and Reformed, 2001). The first appears in the same issue of *Mid-America Journal of Theology* cited above.

Westminster Theological Seminary in California, where Frame taught for many years after teaching at the Philadelphia campus, does not – for the most part – recognize Gaffin's theology as being at odds with historic Reformed doctrine, even though most of the California faculty regard Shepherd's theology to be outside the bounds of confessional orthodoxy. Robert Strimple, who eventually came to oppose Shepherd's theology, finds no problems in Gaffin's teaching. Illustrative also of this institutional dilemma is Michael Horton's misleading remark that theologians Geerhardus Vos, Herman Ridderbos, Meredith Kline, and Richard

Gaffin all "find their roots in classical Reformed (covenant) theology" (in "Eschatology after Nietzsche: Apollonian, Dionysian or Pauline," *International Journal of Systematic Theology* 2 [2000] 42, n. 49). As long as the Shepherd theology prevails at Westminster East, the failure of Westminster West to distance herself unequivocally from the new theology places her in a very unstable and precarious position. In some measure, Shepherd's teaching marks a great divide between East and West. But that line becomes fuzzy when we weigh the approval given to Gaffin's teaching. (Note again, Gaffin's endorsement of Shepherd's formulations on the back cover of *The Call of Grace*.) Clearly, Shepherd's dismissal did not succeed in removing the insidious, heterodox teaching from Westminster Seminary. Frame's point concerning the injustice of the situation is well taken (see endnote 38 below). Frame, unhappy with developments on the California campus, recently left Westminster; he is currently teaching at Reformed Theological Seminary in Orlando, Florida.

A strange irony of history, Sinclair Ferguson, called to Westminster in Philadelphia as Shepherd's replacement, has also been critical of the traditional Reformed doctrine of the "Covenant of Works." Teaching alongside Gaffin in the Systematics Department, Ferguson has continued to move further in the direction of the Shepherd-Gaffin theology, including a rethinking and reformulation of his understanding of the doctrines of justification and election. See my review of Ferguson's *The Holy Spirit* in the *Journal of the Evangelical Theological Society* 42 (1999) 529-531, included in my *Covenant Theology in Reformed Perspective* 334-336.

[27] Letter of March 7, 1983, 1.

[28] Gaffin wields wide influence within the Orthodox Presbyterian Church, including its denominational publication (*New Horizons*), at Presbyterian and Reformed Publishing (which from the beginning had committed itself largely to publishing writings of Westminster Seminary's faculty and constituents), and the Seminary's own journal (*The Westminster Theological Journal*). Lee Irons laments one incidence of editorial heavy-handedness: "In his article 'Covenant Theology Under Attack,' a critical evaluation of these trends [within the Reformed community], Professor Meredith G.

Kline has raised a clarion call to all sons of the Reformation to rise up and repudiate such developments." For the record, Irons notes: "Several remarks were edited out contrary to Kline's intentions. The unexpurgated version has been published privately [by the congregation of the Park Woods Orthodox Presbyterian Church in Kansas City, Mo.]" ("Redefining Merit: An Examination of Medieval Presuppositions in Covenant Theology," in *Creator, Redeemer, Consummator: A Festschrift for Meredith G. Kline* [eds. H. Griffith and J. R. Muether; Greenville, S.C.: Reformed Academic Press, 2000] 254, also n. 4).

Curiously, in *Fighting the Good Faith: A Brief History of the Orthodox Presbyterian Church* (Philadelphia: The Committee on Christian Education and the Committee for the Historian of the Orthodox Presbyterian Church, 1995) no reference to the Shepherd controversy is to be found. It is a chapter in the history of the denomination and the Seminary some would prefer to forget – or possibly erase from the historical record, were that possible. For further study of this debate, see Robert M. Zens, "Professor Norman Shepherd on Justification: A Critique" (Th.M. thesis, Dallas Theological Seminary, 1981); and O. Palmer Robertson, *The Current Justification Controversy* (Unicoi: The Trinity Foundation, 2003).

[29] Robert L. Reymond, *A New Systematic Theology of the Christian Faith* (Nashville: Nelson, 1998) 431-432. For the similar teaching of John Piper, see my *John Piper on the Christian Life: An Examination of His Controversial View of 'Faith Alone' in Future Grace* (Great Bromley: CRN [Christian Research Network], 1999).

[30] *Kingdom Prologue* 107-117.

[31] *Kingdom Prologue* 109.

[32] *Kingdom Prologue* 111-112.

[33] *Kingdom Prologue* 112-113.

[34] *Kingdom Prologue* 114.

[35] *Kingdom Prologue* 115.

³⁶ See especially my "The Original State of Adam: Tensions in Reformed Theology," *The Evangelical Quarterly* 59 (1987) 291-309; and "The Search for an Evangelical Consensus on Paul and the Law," *Journal of the Evangelical Theological Society* 40 (1997) 563-579, both republished in *Covenant Theology in Reformed Perspective* 95-110 and 209-226. This collection of writings contains a wide-ranging discussion of covenant theology, Reformation and modern, with special attention to the Westminster school. Gaffin's reading of traditional covenant theology is wide of the mark; it is a serious distortion of the clear testimony of Reformed orthodoxy, past and present.

³⁷ See my remarks concerning Sinclair Ferguson's recent thinking on these issues in *The Holy Spirit* cited above in endnote 26.

³⁸ See Meredith G. Kline's "Covenant Theology Under Attack," *New Horizons* 15 (February 1994) 3-5, discussed above in endnote 28. In the controversy spilling over into the Presbytery of Philadelphia of the Presbyterian Church in America, it was the opinion of William Barker, Westminster's Dean of Faculty, that the Barthian view might prove to be the correct one in the minds of the Seminary faculty. What Barker was also saying is that Gaffin's views had received the faculty's support. (The current Board of Trustees is satisfied with Gaffin's work. The newest additions to the faculty, including Carl Trueman and David McWilliams, are of the same theological persuasion. And long-standing adjunct professors Robert Letham and Peter Lillback are outspoken proponents of the Shepherd-Gaffin theology.)

On the opposite side, Robert Godfrey has written: "[T. F.] Torrance's neoorthodox theology wants to eliminate the Covenant of Works and identify creation with the Covenant of Grace. This position fits well with a Barthian christomonism and quasi-universalism, but is far from the fullness of the biblical revelation. The two-covenant theology of Westminster is the best understanding of the structure of biblical revelation and the best key to understanding the work of Christ" ("The Westminster Larger Catechism," *To Glorify and Enjoy God: A Commemoration of the 350th Anniversary of the Westminster Assembly* [eds. J. L. Carson and D. W. Hall; Carlisle: The Banner of Truth Trust, 1994] 139-140). Godfrey wondered, however, what direction the Westminster school will take in the coming years. Responding to analyses by Richard Lints and Vern Poythress regarding developments within Reformed theology, including an evaluation of developments at Westminster Seminary (East and West), Godfrey acknowledged the prominence that John Murray's teaching on the covenants has had at the theological institution. He suggested that "This [resultant] change in 'biblical theology' may have significant systematic and confessional implications. A relational metaphor is used as the controlling metaphor with profound systematic results in the theology of the Council of Trent, Karl Barth, Daniel Fuller, and Norman Shepherd. Is Murray conceding something important to any of those theological positions? Surely that is a question that must be raised" ("Developments in Reformed Theology in the Twentieth Century: A Response," paper presented at the 45th annual meeting of the Evangelical Theological Society in Washington, D.C. [November 18-20, 1993], 4). In this paper Godfrey also questioned the compatibility of John Frame's perspectivalism with confessional Reformed interpretation. Clearly, the Westminster faculties have not reached anything close to consensus of opinion regarding issues currently in dispute. Whether differences will ultimately lead to a division between the two campuses remains highly uncertain. Godfrey claims that "Westminster is now actually two schools" ("Developments in Reformed Theology" 1). The case for this claim, however, is not at all convincing. Agreeably, there are at present two faculties, but not two schools. Surely there is work to be done in bringing clarity to the pressing issues of the day and in exercising courage within the wider Seminary community. The future of Westminster West depends upon such action. For a thorough analysis of Murray's theology of the covenants and related doctrines, see my essay "Paul's Letter to the Romans in the *New International Commentary on the New Testament* and in Contemporary Reformed Thought," *Evangelical Quarterly* 71 (1999) 3-24, republished in my *Covenant Theology in Reformed Perspective* 227-245.

**SELECTED BIBLIOGRAPHY: On the Shepherd Controversy (Available from Westminster Seminary's Montgomery Library)**

**By Norman Shepherd:**
"Debates on Justification," Orthodox Presbyterian Church, Presbytery of Philadelphia (sound recording; Philadelphia: Westminster Media, 1979). 17 sound cassettes. These debates concern the theological views of Norman Shepherd as presented in 34 theses on justification.

"Doctrine of the Holy Spirit; a course in systematic theology" (sound recording; Philadelphia: Westminster Media, 1980). 43 sound cassettes. Lectures for the course ST311, Doctrine of the Holy Spirit taught at Westminster Theological Seminary.

"The Biblical Doctrine of Reprobation: Part 1," *The Banner* (March 21, 1980), 16-17; "The Biblical Doctrine of Reprobation: Part 2," *The Banner* (March 28, 1980), 18-19.

"The Grace of Justification," typescript, Westminster Theological Seminary, 1979.

"Life in Covenant with God" (sound recording; Philadelphia: Westminster Media, 1981). Series of lectures given during the French Creek Bible Conference at Sandy Cove, Maryland, 1981.

**By the Faculty:**
"Westminster Statement on Justification," Philadelphia, May 27, 1980

**Other:**
Zens, Robert M. "Professor Norman Shepherd on Justification: A Critique (Th.M. thesis, Dallas Theological Seminary, 1981).

**For additional resources, consult:**
Robertson, O. Palmer. *The Current Justification Controversy* (St. Louis, 1983; Unicoi, TN: The Trinity Foundation, 2003).

Robbins, John. *A Companion to the Current Justification Controversy* (Unicoi, TN: The Trinity Foundation, 2003).

See also, http://www.covopc.org/Shepherd_Contents.html (the website of OPC pastor Robert Lotzer).

"Historic Documents of American Presbyterianism: The Justification Controversy" (PCA Historical Center: www.pcanet.org/history/documents/shepherd/justification.html).

Chapter 7

# The Impact of Norman Shepherd's Teaching within Westminster Theological Seminary *

This year's annual meeting addresses issues relating to the boundaries – the broad parameters – of evangelical doctrine. The pivotal doctrine which distinguishes Protestant evangelicalism from all other expressions of religious faith is justification by faith alone, what Martin Luther and all the Protestant reformers correctly identified as the article of the standing or falling church. Two things are to be noted here: (1) the church is defined by her adherence to the biblical doctrine of salvation, specifically, justification by faith. Apart from the proclamation of this gospel, the one and only gospel, there can be no true church. God has promised that he will indeed preserve a remnant for himself down through the ages, within or without the institutional church, a remnant that faithfully adheres to the good news of Jesus Christ, the only savior of the world. No other religion is worthy of obeisance. No other religion can claim credence in its offer of salvation. Christ alone offers hope and assurance concerning redemption from sin. The fact that other religions of the world espouse partial truths – truths which come through the "light of nature," what God has freely granted humankind by virtue of its creation in God's own image, now damaged by the Fall – does not validate those religious faiths as sources of redemptive revelation. (2) If we take seriously Luther's dictum respecting that article of the Christian faith upon which the church stands or falls, then we are at the same time acknowledging that only the teaching of Protestant evangelicalism concerning the nature and means of salvation is expressive of Christian orthodoxy. The Apostles' Creed, one of several early ecumenical creeds, makes reference to the "forgiveness of sins," an integral aspect of the biblical doctrine of justification by faith. By definition, creedal orthodoxy must distinguish between truth and error. In so doing, we are obliged to distinguish between three branches of Christianity – Protestant, Roman, and Greek. For the Protestant, the early creeds of the church necessitate the fuller, more explicit statements of faith produced in the age of the Reformation and thereafter, statements which are themselves the product of the church's apologetic defense of the Christian faith. Needless to say, the Protestant self-understanding does not sit well in an age of secularism and religious equality. Secular dogma claims that all religions are to be regarded as valid; all roads lead to the same supreme being.

The documents arising out of discussions between leading Protestant evangelicals and Roman Catholics in recent years are illustrative of the changes now taking place in evangelicalism in general. (The assaults on biblical truth are striking ever close to home – the duty to remain vigilant has only intensified.) These documents reflect the current mood of theological interpreters. Norman Shepherd is one of many who have offered proposals how to achieve the reconciliation between Catholics and Protestants on the doctrine of salvation. In his book *The Call of Grace: How the Covenant Illuminates Salvation and Evangelism*, Shepherd abandons the Protestant doctrine of justification by faith and adopts a Barthian formulation on covenant and election. I have critiqued this book in the Spring 2001 issue of *Trinity Journal* and in my fuller exposé *The Changing of the Guard: Westminster Theological Seminary in Philadelphia*, an analysis which places Shepherd's theology in the context of the dispute within the Westminster community, a dispute that has extended over a quarter-century. The issues in this controversy, however, are issues more widely debated in contemporary scholarly circles. The Evangelical Theological Society in timely fashion raises the question, What are the boundaries of evangelical doctrine? The twofold query I bring today is this: How did the teaching of Shepherd gain a foothold within Westminster Seminary, once the bastion of Reformed-Protestant orthodoxy? And what is the extent of this teaching within the institution and within the wider community served by Westminster?

Back in the late 1960s differences over the interpretation of the divine covenants first began to surface among members of the faculty. Prior to this time, John Murray, long-time professor and systematician, was already engaged in a reformulation of this critical element within the system of Reformed doctrine. It would be many years, however, before Murray's ideas would begin to jell in his own thinking and in the thinking of his students. Parenthetically, Murray's faculty colleagues, perhaps with the exception of one or two, were not alert to or cognizant of the changes taking place in Murray's thinking. Further background to Murray's own preoccupation with the subject of the covenants was the situation in his own homeland of Scotland. The Scotch Presbyterians never fully recovered from the divisions that occurred during the Marrow controversy in the eighteenth century. In the thinking of Murray and the Torrance clan the root of the problem lay in the Reformed orthodox doctrine of the covenants. According to Murray, what was needed was a "recasting" of the doctrine. Murray moved in a direction that was similar to – yet fundamentally different from – the neoorthodox school of Karl Barth and Thomas Torrance. That is not the case, however, for Murray's student and successor in the systematics department of Westminster, Norman Shepherd. Sinclair Ferguson, Shepherd's replacement upon his dismissal from the faculty, likewise adheres to Barth's mono-covenantalism. The travesty in all of this is that while Shepherd went out the front door, Ferguson came in the back. But that takes us well ahead of our story.

What follows is a thumbnail sketch of Murray's theology of the covenants in its most mature form. (Further analysis is provided in my book *Covenant Theology in Reformed Perspective*.) Much of Murray's theology reflects standard Reformed teaching. Adam was originally placed on probation: it was required of him to render full and perfect obedience in order to receive God's gift of eternal life, including confirmation in righteousness. Adam was federal head – his one act of righteousness or disobedience would be imputed to the account of the entire human race. So long as Adam rendered obedience to God he was counted worthy of life and blessing. Adam's obedience was meritorious of life and communion with God; reward was based upon Adam's own works. The principle informing the natural relationship between the Creator and the creature was, in Murray's words, one of "perfect legal reciprocity" (merit). Justification was a matter of works-obedience (in contrast to the principle of grace informing the covenant of reconciliation between God and the redeemed). Adam's transgression required the making of a second covenant, traditionally called the Covenant of Grace, spanning the entire redemptive epoch, from the fall of Adam to the return of Christ at the close of the age, the consummation of history. This latter covenant was established on the merits of Christ's obedience. Christ, as Second Adam, fulfilled the legal demand of perfect righteousness and thus inherited the reward of a redeemed people, those numbering among the elect of God.

We now turn to some of the distinctive peculiarities of Murray's formulation. According to Murray, the gift of eternal life proffered to Adam at the beginning of history was something more than he could rightly earn for himself. Utilizing the familiar and widely adopted nature/grace – nature/covenant – dichotomy, forged in the fires of medieval scholasticism, Murray distinguished between Adam's initial state of nature and the subsequent order of probation, what Murray termed the "Adamic administration." He was reluctant to identify this probationary arrangement as a covenant, since in the Bible explicit covenant terminology appears only in connection with divine-human relationships in the redemptive epoch, and that beginning with Noah. Murray defined the covenant idea in terms of sovereign grace and redemptive promise. In doing so, Murray rejected the notion of a covenant of works, what he considered to be a contradiction in terms and a source of grave misconception in the history of Reformed interpretation. All that Adam could have merited on the grounds of his own righteousness was momentary life and fellowship with God, life that was ever contingent upon man's inherent righteousness which could be lost by moral failure. Confirmation in righteousness was one of the benefits of successful completion of probation, the special situation associated with the Adamic administration, the arrangement that was superimposed upon the initial order of nature. Such blessing, according to Murray, was a gift of God's unmerited grace and favor lavished upon the undeserving creature of dust. Significantly for Murray, what was required for this higher blessing was a "God-righteousness," as opposed to a "human righteousness." Here Murray enters the murky waters of theological obfuscation. In what sense does Murray employ the notion of God-righteousness, antithetical to human-righteousness, as requisite for the creature's glorification even before the entrance of sin into the world? According to the apostle Paul, what distinguishes the two biblical orders, that of Law and that of Grace, is human-righteousness versus God-righteousness (see, for example, Rom 3:21-31 and Phil 3:1-11). The seeds for later mischief were laid here in Murray's writings.

In a second, related instance Murray's objection to the idea of meritorious reward in the covenant relationship appears in connection with his interpretation of the Mosaic economy. Contrary to mainstream Reformed thought, Murray contends that the Mosaic dispensation was wholly and exclusively one of grace and promise, having no element of works-inheritance. Whereas the apostle Paul identifies a legal principle antithetical to the principle of grace within the Mosaic administration, Murray equates the principle of "do this and live" (Lev 18:5) with the Pauline concept of the "obedience of faith" (Rom 1:5). Accordingly, law is compatible with grace, not antithetical. It is precisely here that Murray undercuts the classic Protestant teaching on Law and Gospel, opening the door to yet more serious doctrinal error to follow in his wake. It must be noted here, however, that Murray did not jettison the Law/Gospel contrast altogether in his theological system. As a consequence, his theology falls within the parameters of Reformed orthodoxy. (Some historians of doctrine falsely allege that the Reformed tradition emphasizes the normative or "third use" of the law, virtually to the exclusion of Luther's "second use," the pedagogical. In this reading of Reformation theology, only the Lutheran tradition is seen to uphold the radical antithesis between Law and Gospel.)

Whatever the differences between Murray and Murray's OT colleague Meredith G. Kline on the doctrine of the covenants, the Westminster faculty at that time was unified in its understanding of justification by faith, at least until the controversy over Shepherd's teachings surfaced in 1975. Temporary resolution of the dispute on the seminary campus meant the dismissal of Shepherd from the faculty in 1982. However, the same deviant teaching, more skillfully camouflaged, continues to be advanced by Richard Gaffin, co-father of Westminster's new theology. After Shepherd's departure Gaffin moved from the department of New Testament to the department of systematics in order to carry on more effectively the program and agenda he and Shepherd had devised. Recent publication of Shepherd's *The Call of Grace*, which bears Gaffin's full endorsement, has occasioned renewed conflict within the seminary community. Robert Strimple of Westminster West has expressed his utter dismay and consternation over this latest move on Gaffin's part. Scott Clark, also of Westminster West, asserts in no uncertain terms: "Shepherd's views are outside the pale." In the publication *Christian Renewal* Clark is reported as saying that with respect to the young denomination to which Clark belongs, the United Reformed Church, "he would not be willing to stay under one federative roof with men holding such views."[1] The central issue in this debate cuts to the heart of what it means to be Protestant and evangelical. Grave doctrinal error continues to parade as truth in the corridors of Westminster.

With the exception of the views of apologist Cornelius Van Til, the old Westminster school has not been known for novelty, but rather for fidelity to the teaching of Scripture and the Reformed faith.[2] Geerhardus Vos, who never taught at Westminster and who died in relative obscurity, and Meredith Kline are the leading theologians to have contributed to the ongoing elucidation of covenant theology within the tradition of historic Reformed orthodoxy. Since the time of Shepherd and now through the efforts of Gaffin, Westminster in Philadelphia is charting a radically different course. For the most part, the faculty at

Westminster West stands opposed to the teachings of Shepherd. At the same time, however, it regards Gaffin's theology as falling within the bounds of orthodoxy. If nothing else, Gaffin's recent endorsement of Shepherd's theology should serve as a wake-up call. Just how diligent and resolute the faculty of Westminster West will be in the defense of Reformed orthodoxy remains to be seen. This much is certain: there can be no mixture of truth and error; this is now Westminster West's defining moment.[3]

Throughout the controversy at Westminster the presentation of Gaffin's own thinking, like Shepherd's, has suffered greatly from obfuscation and misformulation.[4] In a two-part lecture entitled "Ordo Salutis and Historia Salutis," delivered August 2001 at the Kerux Biblical Theology Conference in Lynnwood (outside Seattle, WA), Gaffin places his interpretation of the gospel over against that of Karl Barth.[5] Gaffin locates the vortex of biblical theology in the exposition of the death and resurrection of Jesus Christ, the climatic event-complex of redemptive history and revelation. At the eye of this confluence of redemptive events accomplished in the fullness of times is the humiliation/exaltation of the Servant of the covenant. In Gaffin's opinion it is precisely this event-complex which properly defines the article of the standing or falling church, not the doctrine of justification by faith as identified by the Protestant reformers. The death, resurrection and glorification of Christ mark the transition from wrath to grace in history. This is the great Before and After of redemptive history, the "irreducible" of biblical theology rightly formulated.[6] This interpretation, notes Gaffin, stands diametrically opposed to the teaching of Barth, whose doctrinal system makes no allowance for the transition from wrath to grace in history. The entire human race stands under the wrath of God as a consequence of Adam's transgression in the Garden. God's grace and favor is extended to sinners on the basis of the Second Adam's substitutionary atonement for sin. According to Barth, it is a misconception to regard Christ's submission to God's wrath as something having taken place wholly in the past, namely, at the cross. What one finds in Barth's theology is a commingling of redemption accomplished and applied, a "timeless above and below" of divine grace and human sinfulness.[7] In all of this Gaffin understands his teaching to be fully in line with the teaching of John Calvin, teaching that, in Gaffin's opinion, has been obscured in the subsequent history of Calvinist theology. In the period after Calvin, we are told, the redemptive-historical character of biblical revelation begins to blur, only to be regained in the work of Geerhardus Vos, the father of Reformed biblical theology, and in the work of G. C. Berkouwer and Herman Ridderbos (to name only three modern-day exponents).[8]

Turning to the second part of his lecture, Gaffin takes up the topic of *ordo salutis*, the application of Christ's redemptive work begun at the cross and now continuing in his high-priestly ministry in heaven at the right hand of God the Father. Here the vortex of redemption applied is experiential or existential union with Christ. This conceptualization of union with Christ, according to Gaffin, differs from decretive election, that is, predestinarian union with God before the foundation of the world. Existential union with Christ is effectuated by Christ himself as life-giving Spirit and is appropriated by the individual through faith.[9] From where does such faith come? Gaffin rightly acknowledges that it is the Holy Spirit who is the source of true, saving faith – the faith which unites the believer to the *exalted* Christ. Union with the glorified Christ is a distinctly and uniquely new covenant experience. *Ordo salutis* contemplates the believer's union with Christ as resurrected Lord in oneness with the Spirit of Pentecost. Gaffin reiterates a point made earlier: Reformed theology after Calvin lost sight of his doctrine on union with Christ. In the later period of theological ossification (that is, scholastic Protestant-Reformed orthodoxy extending from the seventeenth century into the present century), Christ fades into the background. Christ is replaced by logical schematizations of the application of redemption.[10] Gaffin claims that the *Westminster Confession of Faith* and *Catechisms* do not provide us an explicitly articulated *ordo*. These confessional statements do not set forth a clearly delineated arrangement of benefits accruing to the believer who is united to Christ by faith. In this regard Gaffin finds the teachings of Westminster to be true to the teaching of Calvin.[11]

The Kerux conference provides Gaffin the occasion to respond to his critics. And this response comes by way of an exposition of Calvin's theology in his *Institutes of the Christian Religion*. Gaffin begins by asking the question: Why does Calvin treat the doctrine of sanctification before the doctrine of justification (the reverse of the order found in traditional Protestant dogmatics). Gaffin concedes that the reformers were correct in placing justification before sanctification in terms of their challenge to Rome. But more important for Gaffin is Calvin's emphasis on the nature of justifying faith *as manifested in its sanctifying power*.[12] In Gaffin's own words, "faith entails a disposition toward holiness." This leads Gaffin to speak of the *relative priority* of justification to sanctification. Actually, the question of priority for Gaffin – as well as for Calvin, we are told – is "indifferent theologically."[13] What needs emphasis, contends Gaffin, is the priority of union with Christ to justification and sanctification.[14] Calvin's formulation is judged to be superior to that of later Reformed dogmatics. (Gaffin states that Calvin does not address the question of logical, causal, or temporal sequence in the *ordo*.) *In brief, union with Christ is the context of justification.* This insight, suggests Gaffin, is obscured in the subsequent Calvinist tradition, resulting in a *de*-eschatologizing of biblical theology. The tendency in traditional dogmatics is to focus on logical, causal, and temporal aspects in a way that obscures Christ's mediation of redemptive blessings. The test, Gaffin suggests, is what to do with union with Christ. "The question of what to do with the benefit of union with Christ in the traditional *ordo* becomes [and remains] a real conundrum." (Gaffin refers to John Murray's wrestling with this very question.) More significantly, the already/not yet structure of redemptive revelation, according to Gaffin, is not given its due. Christ is reduced to being a facilitator, rather than consummator of redemption applied. Gaffin stresses that it is Christ's present ministry of intercession which "secures" the justification of God's elect, not merely his prior work on the cross. In light of Romans 8, observes Gaffin, the idea of the *finished* work of Christ is only "relatively true." There is more for the exalted Christ to do. The effect of Gaffin's formulation is to minimize the value and the merit of Christ's atoning work on the cross; it is to destroy the biblical distinction between redemption accomplished and applied. In fact, Gaffin argues that the biblical-theological distinction between *historia salutis* and *ordo salutis* properly begins to blur in Calvin's thinking. The accent now falls on the present, ongoing ministry of Christ. (The believer is secure in Christ *so long as* he/she exhibits the fruits of union with Christ. As Gaffin has taught, justification is in the mode of perseverance; or, union with Christ is the context for justification.)

The way to maintain the forensic/renovative distinction, Gaffin tells us, is to give full credence to the "already/not yet" contrast in Pauline theology. He illustrates this twofold appropriation of Christ's redemption by reference to the benefit of adoption. The believer is already adopted into the family of God by virtue of experiential union with Christ. This initial installment in the application of redemption bears a decidedly forensic connotation. In union with Christ the believer is *legally* a child of God. Future adoption awaits the redemption of the body. Justification, reasons Gaffin, is both already and not yet. The future actualization of soteric justification is final judgment according to works – and here Gaffin's proof-text is Rom 2:6ff., the text which deals "most substantially" with future justification. Once more, Gaffin claims support for his interpretation by referring to Calvin, specifically, to the chapter in the *Institutes* entitled "The Beginning of Justification and Its Continual Progress." (In this connection, Gaffin prefers to speak of the believer's "progress in justification," a notion that is not found in Calvin.) What stands out in bold relief in Gaffin's reading of Calvin is the notion that something deeper than the forgiveness of sins, something deeper than the imputation of Christ's righteousness determines the believer's identity. That something deeper is union with Christ. Thus, explains Gaffin, justification depends not only on what Christ has done (redemption accomplished), but also on what he is doing (redemption as presently applied by the Spirit of Christ). Justification depends on union with Christ – not just on what he has done in the past, but also on "who he is and continues to be" for us (viewing Christ as life-giving Spirit and eternal Highpriest). The accent clearly falls on sanctification. All of this leads Gaffin to conclude that the believer's justification is still future. The consummation of justification presently enjoyed by the believer is contingent upon future, open acquittal on the Last Day (judgment according to works).[15] In the final analysis, Gaffin's teaching on union with Christ has a leveling effect with regard to the several and distinct benefits in the application of redemption. This being the case, Gaffin's criticism of traditional Reformed teaching on *ordo salutis* does not come as any surprise.

Gaffin brings his lectures to a close by addressing that "most mettlesome issue," the question of the relationship between old and new covenants. Gaffin contends that what is most basic and fundamental is just this: The redemptive-historical contrast between the old and new covenants finds its explanation strictly in terms of radical discontinuity. What Gaffin has in view here pertains exclusively to *historial salutis*. From the standpoint of *ordo salutis*, however, there is essential continuity. How does all of this translate with respect to redemption accomplished and applied? Gaffin contends that the uniqueness of Pentecost is wholly a matter of *historia salutis*, not *ordo salutis*. The profound, existential difference between old and new covenants is union with the exalted Christ. Prior to Christ's resurrection from the dead, the saints of God were merely "friends with God." They were not united with the glorified Christ. They did not yet experience the "something better" spoken of by the writer to the Hebrews (11:40). Spiritual union with the resurrected Lord of Glory awaits the eschatological age, life in the Spirit. What this means precisely with regard to personal, individual appropriation of saving grace, however, lies beyond the purview of Scripture. In other words, the question of the difference between the two covenants lies on the periphery of biblical teaching. Scripture permits us to speak only of a fuller, clearer revelation under the new covenant – and in conjunction with that a deeper, fuller experience of union with (the exalted) Christ. Beyond this, the differences cannot be quantified.[16]

Gaffin maintains that the law of God has the same *ordo salutis* function under both covenants. "Faith and works sustain the same positive relationship to each other." More expressly, the way of salvation – wherein faith and good works are the means of justification (so Gaffin understands Rom 2:6ff.)[17] – is identical in the time of the Mosaic law and in the time of Christ. To allay misunderstanding, Gaffin seeks to explain the difference between the teaching of Romanism and Protestantism in terms of conflicting interpretations of the nature of saving faith. For Protestants the nature of true, justifying faith is defined in terms of union with Christ. What precisely does this mean? No further explanation is given. Gaffin's assessment of the differences between these two ecclesiastical traditions concerning the way of salvation offers little, if any, help. (On the differences between the Roman Catholic and Protestant doctrine of justification and the covenants Shepherd is more forthright in his book, *The Call of Grace*.) The point I made earlier bears repeating: Gaffin's thinking at critical points obscures, rather than illuminates.[18]

In the final place, what does Gaffin make of the Pauline contrast between the ministration of death and condemnation, that is, the old covenant, and the ministration of life and righteousness, the new covenant (as expounded in 2 Cor 3)? He tells us that the contrast is a relative one. More ultimately, the law of the old covenant is one with the law of the new covenant. It is sin that kills, not the law. Sin having entered the human race makes the law a facilitator of disobedience. (Gaffin construes the Pauline antithesis between "letter" and "Spirit" in terms of the external writing of the law upon tablets of stone, the law of Moses delivered to Israel on Mount Sinai, and the internal writing of the law upon the hearts of believers, what is effectuated by the Spirit of Pentecost.) Paul's negative assessment of the Mosaic law, therefore, is "targeted," to use Gaffin's word. The redemptive-historical contrast between old and new covenants pertains exclusively to outward appearance; it does not bring into view the actual substance or essence of the matter, what Gaffin sees as Paul's positive reading of the law. From this latter point of view, obedience to the law of Moses is the reflex of saving grace. (The legal requirement of the covenant under Moses is seen as a gracious summons to the obedience which is of faith.)

According to Gaffin's understanding of the history of Christian doctrine, the theology of law in the Reformed tradition is sharply different from that of the Lutheran tradition with its radical "absolutizing" of Law and Gospel.[19] The question remains: Is there a genuine difference between the two covenants, the old and the new? Is the scriptural contrast between a principle of faith and a principle of works descriptive of two antithetical principles of inheritance operating within the covenant of law established by God with ancient, theocratic Israel? Reformed theology correctly maintains that the Spirit of Christ was active (proleptically) within the hearts of believers under the old economy of redemption, since apart from the Spirit's regenerating and renovating work no saint in the old covenant could participate in the spiritual blessings of life with God (that is, eternal salvation). The view that the letter/Spirit contrast is to be explained wholly in terms of an external/internal writing of the law does not satisfy the total witness of Scripture. *What is paramount in Reformed theology is the covenantal contrast between two principles of inheritance, between the way of law-righteousness and the way of faith-righteousness.* In these Kerux lectures we find Gaffin guilty of misrepresenting and misinterpreting Calvin's doctrine. Gaffin's participationist understanding of union with Christ obscures or significantly minimizes the forensic aspect of the believer's standing before God (justification in the "here and now").[20]

Another recent excursion in Reformed covenant theology comes from the pen of Peter Lillback, adjunct professor at Westminster in Philadelphia, in his book *The Binding of God: Calvin's Role in the Development of Covenant Theology*,[21] what is essentially his 1986 Westminster dissertation. Like numerous other historians of doctrine in the current literature, this author attempts to rewrite history and reinterpret the Reformed tradition. Lillback is a protégé of Shepherd and Gaffin. Like his teachers, he has produced a study that is marred by theological confusion and contradiction. His analysis is flawed, seriously flawed. Contrary to Lillback's assertion, the Law/Gospel antithesis was employed by Lutheran and Reformed theologians alike. In the teaching of the new Westminster school, justification is attained in the way of faith and works. Curiously, Lillback locates the origin of this particular theological formulation in medieval nominalism, in the doctrine of congruent merit (slightly nuanced). This old/new school theology teaches that man's obedience does not in strict justice merit God's blessing and favor – not in the order of creation, and not in the order of redemption. The source of all creaturely blessing is divine grace.[22] Here again is the mono-covenantalism of Barth and the neoorthodox school. Edmund Clowney, former president of Westminster in Philadelphia, rightly considers Lillback's views as "dangerous." It is in fact a restatement of Shepherd's heterodox teaching on justification and the covenants.

Westminster in Philadelphia regards itself as "the doyen of intellectually rigorous Reformed seminaries worldwide."[23] That estimate aside, we can agree that Westminster exercises a profound influence upon Reformed theological education. Sadly, her doctrinal error extends far beyond the Philadelphia campus – to the new Dallas campus (where the newly-appointed systematician David McWilliams teaches [see "Introduction," endnote 14]), to the fledging Northwest Theological Seminary outside Seattle (headed up by James Dennison, past librarian and instructor at Westminster West), and to Reformed Theological Seminary in Orlando (where dissident voice John Frame is heard). These are only some of the places where the Shepherd-Gaffin theology is having a great impact. If Reformed-Protestant orthodoxy is to remain true to her confession, this doctrinal error must be rooted out. The question has frequently been asked: Is Shepherd's theology to be branded as "heretical?" Was Shepherd's dismissal from Westminster Seminary in 1982 on grounds of doctrinal error? The message that went out at the time was unclear and ambiguous, and remains so to this day.

The correct answer to the question is the following: In the judgment of then President Edmund Clowney – and of those who wrote "Reason and Specifications Supporting the Action of the Board of Trustees in Removing Professor Shepherd Approved by the Executive Committee of the Board (February 26, 1982)" – Shepherd's teaching was found to be contrary to the teachings of Scripture and the Reformed faith. Although his teaching obscured the gospel of sovereign grace, Shepherd was dismissed from the seminary not on grounds of the doctrinal error laid out in full detail in the document, but in the hope of bringing closure to the dispute within the faculty and within the broader community. The pronouncement of heresy was left to the courts of the church. (The judgment of grave error was clearly articulated in the pages of "Reason and Specifications.") Shepherd's hearing in the Presbytery of Philadelphia of the Orthodox Presbyterian Church in 1978 and 1979 produced no final resolution of the matter at that juncture. Shepherd's subsequent departure from the Orthodox Presbyterian Church prevented further ecclesiastical review and discipline.[24] And there the matter stands.

In the meantime, Shepherd's theology on justification and the covenants continues to be widely received in the Orthodox Presbyterian Church, in the Presbyterian Church in America, in the United Reformed Church, as well as in the Christian Reformed Church where Shepherd now holds his membership. These communions have proven unwilling or unable to condemn the teaching found in *The Call of Grace*. Regrettably, Gaffin has succeeded in keeping Shepherd's theology before the Orthodox Presbyterian Church, where he wields great influence. What makes for the widespread appeal of the new anti-reformational theology? One must not only take account of the influence of the prominent theological institutions of our day, but account must also be taken of the popular teaching of preachers and churchmen like Sinclair Ferguson and John Piper. Ted Dorman in his article in the current issue of the *Journal of the Evangelical Theological Society* would have evangelical Protestants reach out to Roman Catholics precisely in terms of the new consensus he sees arising in contemporary Christian thought. He writes:

> Further progress will be made when attempts to reconcile two very different languages of salvation via verbal compromise give way to the sort of Biblical theology advocated by [Paul] Stuhlmacher and like-minded theologians. In the meantime, whatever significant differences remain between Protestants and Catholics regarding the doctrine of justification might be mitigated, if not fully resolved, by the following affirmation set forth by a number of Protestants and Catholics seeking reconciliation with the body of Christ: "Justification by grace alone through a faith that is never alone" (cf. Eph 2:8-10)."[25]

Dorman favors Stuhlmacher's teaching of justification as a *process*. This position spells disaster for evangelical theology. How do we preserve the integrity of the one, true gospel to be preached in pulpits across America and around the world? I suggest that we study afresh the theology of our Protestant forebears. They had recovered the purity of the gospel in their day. The traditional Law/Gospel contrast was deemed essential to the system of orthodox doctrine. The same needs to be (re)affirmed in our day.

**ENDNOTES**

* This paper was read at the 2001 national meeting of the Evangelical Theological Society in Colorado Springs, CO.

¹ *Christian Renewal* (March 26, 2001) 7. In this connection Clark also takes exception to the teaching of Timothy Trumper and David McWilliams, both of whom serve on Westminster's faculty. Compare the (mildly) critical review of Shepherd's book by David VanDrunen, who now replaces Strimple upon his retirement, in *New Horizons* (July 2001) 23-24 and Shepherd's response, *New Horizons* (November 2001) 26-27. Despite these criticisms of Shepherd's theology, the faculty of Westminster West has not been able to deal adequately with the doctrinal error currently being disseminated on the Westminster campuses. Although John Frame presently teaches at Reformed Seminary in Orlando, he continues to take his stand with Shepherd's teaching, including espousal of the erroneous notion that faith and works are instrumental in justification. (Frame has reiterated his position to me in a letter dated May 30, 2001.) All the while, President Sam Logan actively promotes the new theological stance of the Philadelphia school. For a representative sampling of the exchanges that have ensued since the appearance of *The Changing of the Guard: Westminster Theological Seminary in Philadelphia* see Trinity Foundation's web-site (www.trinityfoundation.org); this material appears on the website following my essay. See Chapter 6.

² To be sure, Van Til's work, both as dogmatician and as apologist, had exercised a decisive role in giving shape and direction to the Westminster school in its formative years. For the most part, that is no longer the case today. See my critique of Frame's *Cornelius Van Til: An Analysis of His Thought* in "John Frame and the Recasting of Van Tilian Apologetics: A Review Article," *Mid-America Journal of Theology* 9 (1993) 279-296. (This essay was published in the Spring of 1998.) A second attempt to respond to my criticisms appears in an appendix to Frame's *The Doctrine of God* (Phillipsburg: Presbyterian and Reformed, 2002). See my Appendix D in this volume.

³ The citation from Paul van Buren appearing in an earlier writing of mine bears repeating: "In recent years, there have also appeared some Christians who, having learned something about Judaism and its teachings, and having assumed that Paul knew at least as much about it as they did, have also begun to reject the church's traditional picture of Paul and this traditional other 'gospel.' Some have, but certainly not the majority. The church is presently engaged in a debate, conducted largely among biblical scholars and generally ignored by most of the church, as to which is the real Paul. Much is at stake in this debate, including ecclesiastical traditions, beloved teachers, and esteemed fathers. Indeed, the debate is ultimately about which is the real gospel!" See Mark W. Karlberg, *Covenant Theology in Reformed Perspective* (Eugene, OR: Wipf and Stock, 2000) 289. Whether or not one sides with van Buren's (mis)interpretation, the author rightly sees this dispute as centering upon the question how one understands Paul on the Mosaic law. That certainly is *the critical issue* in evangelical theology today.

⁴ Gaffin's criticism of the argumentation of N. T. Wright and James Dunn are telling. Gaffin castigates these theologians – both of whom regard themselves as "evangelical" – for having "overstated" their case and for making assertions "without adequate qualification." Gaffin finds them guilty of "a certain vagueness," "beg[ging] certain issues," as well as exhibiting "considerable confusion," Their argument at times is "unclear," "ambiguous," "subject to misunderstanding." Gaffin concludes that their "overall construction is problematic." In a word, the theology of Wright and Dunn betrays a "dis-ease" with the teaching of traditional Protestant orthodoxy, for which Gaffin presumes to speak. But Gaffin has no right to assume this posture, when he himself is not only guilty of the very same evasiveness in theological formulation, but also, and more significantly, is guilty of *radically* reinterpreting the Protestant-Reformed tradition along similar lines. See Richard B. Gaffin, Jr., "Paul the Theologian: Review Essay," *WTJ* 62 (2000) 121-41.

⁵ This critique, based on sound recordings of the Kerux conference, is in addition to what I have analyzed elsewhere in Gaffin's writ-

ings. Consult further *Covenant Theology in Reformed Perspective* and *The Changing of the Guard* (here as Chapter 6).

⁶ Gaffin draws the following paired contrasts, all of which "are not equally helpful:"

| **Historia salutis** | **Ordo salutis** |
|---|---|
| Redemption accomplished | Redemption applied |
| Objective | Subjective |
| Indicative | Imperative |

Of these four, Gaffin prefers the first two. From the standpoint of this schematization, Gaffin applies his interpretation of the "second use of the law" to the category of *historia salutis*, not *ordo salutis*. The "third use of the law" – that emphasized by Calvin and the Reformed tradition – pertains exclusively to *ordo salutis*. Accordingly, the law at Sinai appears as "bare command," as imperative. Gaffin understands this external writing of the law upon tables of stone to refer to the "letter" of the law, that which is distinct from the work of the Spirit inscribing the law upon tables of flesh. The law of Moses is mere demand; the law of Christ is spiritual empowerment. Gaffin rejects the classic Protestant doctrine on the second use of the law (as well as the traditional Law/Gospel antithesis). See *Covenant Theology in Reformed Perspective* 223, n. 23.

For Gaffin, the apostle Paul's negative reading of the law pertains exclusively to *historia salutis*, his positive reading of the law to *ordo salutis*. Two observations by way of a critique of Gaffin's position: (1) the law/gospel antithesis is relevant to both aspects of Christ's redemption, its accomplishment and its application; and (2) Gaffin's theology of law does not take into account the crucial feature of probation associated with the covenant of creation and the covenant between the Father and the Son, which covenant was fulfilled by Christ in his work at the cross. The First Adam had a particular task to perform, the outcome of which would have been imputed to the account of the entire human race. This "one act of righteousness," were Adam to pass probation, would have been the basis – the just and legal ground – of confirmation in righteousness and eventual glorification after the completion of humankind's historical mission in carrying out the cultural mandate. According to the Scriptures, the principle of inheritance in this initial covenantal arrangement is that of works, not grace. By virtue of Christ's work of reconciliation and atonement the salvation of God's elect has been secured by the merits of Christ's obedience, active and passive. For this reason, the Protestant reformers well understood the necessity of stressing the sole instrumentality of faith in receiving the righteousness of Christ in justification. In no sense is justification a process. (With respect to the demonstrative aspect of forensic justification – in the letter of James, for example – the believer is *shown to be just* in his good works. This declarative state is altogether distinct from the believer's sanctification in its twofold signification, definitive and progressive. Sanctification as God's renovative work in the believer is progressive; justification is not.)

7 What Gaffin does not tell his audience is that he shares Barth's doctrine of mono-covenantalism. Gaffin's reference to Van Til's searching critique of Barthianism hides the fact that Gaffin parts company with Van Til's theology of the covenants. Although Gaffin maintains the historicity of the Fall, his mono-covenantalism forbides him to prioritize Law over Gospel. Like Barth, Gaffin sees only continuity between the two. The Barthian "slogan" is this: *law in grace* or *grace in law*. (This substitutes for the classic Protestant-Reformed Law/Gospel contrast and the doctrine of *sola fide*.)

8 Gaffin writes: the *historia salutis/ordo salutis* distinction "also serves to correct an undeniable tendency within the Reformation tradition to be excessively preoccupied with questions of *ordo salutis* and so inadequately appreciate or miss entirely Paul's overarching redemptive-historical orientation" (in "Paul the Theologian" 126).

9 Why introduce a disjuncture here between decretive election (that is, union with Christ in eternity past) and effectual ingrafting (that is, union with Christ in historical time)? Not only is this not helpful, it exposes a fundamental misconception of the biblical doctrine of individual election unto salvation. In Gaffin's thinking, individual election also partakes of the "already/not yet" structure of Pauline eschatology, as he construes it. By way of criticism of Gaffin's formulation, existential union with Christ must not be abstracted from what Gaffin calls "predestinarian union" and "re-

demptive-historical union." Calvin is careful to relate all three "moments" together in his exposition of union with Christ.

[10] On the question of the relationship between Reformed orthodoxy and scholasticism see the recent collection of essays in *Reformation and Scholasticism: An Ecumenical Enterprise*, ed. W. J. van Asselt and E. Dekker (Grand Rapids: Baker Academic, 2001).

[11] Gaffin is not interested in the question of sequence or ordering of benefits, other than to accent the priority of union with Christ. (Here again Gaffin claims to follow Calvin.) The question of order is "left open." The category of *ordo salutis* pertains to the appropriation of salvation "in whatever time or place since the Fall." (In my judgment, the precise order in the application of redemption is inconsequential in certain respects. Some relationships among the various benefits, however, are crucial and determinative in the exposition of the theology of grace.)

[12] This is a misconception on Gaffin's part. The sanctifying power is the Spirit of Christ, not faith. (It is clear that Gaffin is not here using the term "faith" as a metonomy for Christ, what is certainly appropriate in certain contexts.)

[13] Again, the priority for Gaffin is union with Christ, what is the "absolutely necessary, indispensable context for justification." In these lectures Gaffin contends that union with Christ must be kept central and controlling. In Gaffin's doctrine of justification by faith the biblical teaching on the two aspects of forensic justification, the constitutive and the demonstrative, has been lost. (Rather, Gaffin substitutes the already/not yet structure of New Testament eschatology.) The constitutive aspect of justification has in view God's definitive and decisive declaration of the believer's righteous standing before the divine bar of justice (on grounds of Christ's "alien" righteousness imputed to those who believe). Contrary to Gaffin's teaching, justification is not contingent upon sanctification, perseverance in holiness, or any of the other benefits accruing from union with Christ. The reformers were right in speaking of good works as the fruit of saving faith. Justification rests exclusively on the *finished work of Christ*. See my "Justification in Redemptive

History," *WTJ* 43 (1981) 213-46; reprinted in *Covenant Theology in Reformed Perspective* 157-180.

Gaffin prefers to speak of the ongoing work of Christ. For someone to rely wholly on Christ's finished work at the cross, Gaffin warns, he has then cut himself off from the "whole Christ," from the Christ who now is working out the benefits of atonement. What is obscured in Gaffin's formulation is the fact that the application of salvation has already and completely been secured by Christ in his work of reconciliation. There is nothing future to be attained by Christ. This is the mystery of the union between Christ and the Spirit in the economy of redemption.

[14] Gaffin speaks repeatedly of the "irreducible" benefits of union with Christ. What does this mean? I take it that the point Gaffin is wanting to make is this: We are not to isolate (that is, discriminate) one benefit among others, nor are we to give one benefit special weight in the application of redemption. (Of course, Gaffin does give special weight to the benefit of union with Christ. And he is free to do so because matters of *ordo* – that is, logical arrangement and sequence – is "indifferent theologically" to him. All of the discrete benefits are solidified, as it were, in union with Christ.) The implication here is that the Protestant reformers were wrong to emphasize the doctrine of justification by faith and to turn it into the doctrine of the standing or falling church.

[15] In the "already/not yet" pattern of application, the latter brings to view the consummative realization of redemption in Christ, what is a distinctly future hope. Present benefits are eschatological. Once again, Gaffin informs us that there is a definite de-eschatologizing tendency in the traditional *ordo salutis* approach, one which lacks proper focus on union with Christ. Gaffin describes this as the *prevailing tendency* in Protestant dogmatics; here there is the danger that Christ fades more or less into the background of theologizing. (Gaffin does concede, however, that the future aspect of forensic benefits he is seeking to accent is difficult to explain; it is, he says, a "puzzling" feature of the believer's union with Christ that must be explained by the systematician. He remarks that his entire two hours of lecturing might easily been given to an elucidation of future justification. For so controversial a subject,

Gaffin left insufficient time for himself. Poor planning, I say, and poor instruction. But that was quite deliberate on Gaffin's part. This omission did not escape the attention of his audience at the Kerux conference.)

[16] As I see it, the difference is better described in terms of servanthood and sonship for the people of God, and in terms of shadows and reality. Life under the new covenant entails fuller revelation, fuller "possession" and assurance of salvation (see my citation from Vos in *Covenant Theology in Reformed Perspective* 199-200).

[17] The question is not whether Paul contemplates two real groups of people in this passage – I concur with Gaffin and Shepherd that Paul is doing precisely that – but whether this text in Romans tells us *how* one is justified and made an heir of life eternal. Paul addresses the *how* of justification elsewhere in the epistle to the Romans. Those who fall into the category of the "doers of the law" are those who are sanctified and justified – justified by faith apart from the works of the law (apart from good works). Where Gaffin and Shepherd err is in their contention that Rom 2:6ff., their key text to unlock the Pauline teaching, supports their peculiar doctrine of *future justification*. Bringing all facets of Gaffin's teaching together, he is saying that present and future justification are summed up together – as the single act of justification – in the notion of justification as a *process*. This, according to Gaffin, is the heart of Paul's understanding of the gospel in the letter to the Romans. See Gaffin's problematic exposition in "The Obedience of Faith," in *Israel and the Church: Essays in Honour of Allan Macdonald Harman on his 65th Birthday and Retirement,* ed. D. J. W. Milne (Melbourne: The Theological Education Committee of the Presbyterian Church of Victoria, 2001) 71-85. In Gaffin's thinking the obedience of faith (justification as process) takes precedence over the doctrine of the righteousness of God as gift – as the *imputed* righteousness of Christ which avails to the believer's justification. Gaffin's formulation is virtually identical to that of Don Garlington in *Faith, Obedience and Preserverance: Aspects of Paul's Letter to the Romans* (Tübingen: J. C. B. Mohr [Paul Siebeck] 1994). My review of this

work is found in *TrinJ* 18 NS (1997) 254-258; republished in *Covenant Theology in Reformed Perspective* 263-267.

[18] Actually, the question of the priority of justification to sanctification (Protestantism) or sanctification to justification (Romanism) has simply produced, in Gaffin's opinion, "another conundrum." What distinguishes these two theological traditions is their differing interpretations of the nature of faith. Protestantism, according to Gaffin, sees faith as focused on Christ (that is, union with Christ). But says Gaffin, he does not want to exaggerate the problem. He concedes that the Protestant reformers were right in emphasizing the role of faith as the alone instrument of justification. This justifying faith, he notes, is always accompanied by all other saving graces. Here again, the way of salvation for Gaffin and Shepherd includes faith *and* good works. The expression "faith alone" in their formulation is meant only to exclude works of a meritorious character. Throughout his lectures Gaffin stresses the "irreducibility" of all the benefits accruing to the believer by virtue of union with Christ. Together justifying faith and good works are the way/means of salvation. Good works are the fruit of union with Christ, rather than the fruit of justification. Good works must not be reduced to being merely the expression of gratitude for God's justification of the sinner saved by grace (as uniformly taught in Reformed theology, past and present). Faith all too often has been viewed as "purely reflexive," as merely a "cognitive act." There is more to the exercise of justifying faith in receiving the righteousness of Christ for justification. That more is good works, that is, the obedience of faith. Let's be clear on this: Gaffin's formulation on the way of salvation is surely not Calvin's. Gaffin has distorted Calvin's teaching. (As much as it is needed, a rebuttal of Gaffin's reading of Calvin cannot be provided here.)

[19] Gaffin notes that in later Lutheran dogmatics union with Christ follows justification in the *ordo*. This too is attributed to Lutheranism's polarizing of Law and Gospel. The Reformed tradition, in Gaffin's estimation, is free of this charge. At the same time, Gaffin sees a tendency in Reformed interpretation to develop a whole theology of the law out of Paul's negative statements, especially in present-day discussions on Paul and the law. Gaffin states: "Paul's

negative statements do not represent his entire theology of the law" – which being translated means an endorsement of Barth's law/gospel construct (= *law in grace*).

[20] In Gaffin's critique of Wright and Dunn on the subject of Paul and the Mosaic law one looks in vain for a clear, unambiguous presentation of orthodox Reformed teaching. In this review essay, as in other writings by Gaffin, the federalist doctrine of the imputation of Christ's meritorious righteousness through the sole instrumentality of faith – *apart from all other graces which flow from true, justifying faith* – is obscured. What is clear is Gaffin's exclusive emphasis upon the Second Adam's satisfaction of divine wrath against sin – sin that was introduced into the human race by the First Adam's one act of disobedience. In this formulation Gaffin ignores the vicarious substitution of Christ's active obedience, whereby Christ fulfilled all righteousness on behalf of God's elect. Reformation theology maintains that the sinner redeemed in Christ does not return to the position of Adam respecting legal obedience (a requirement Gaffin does not recognize in the first covenant made by God with Adam in Eden). In refuting the teaching on condign/congruent merit in Roman Catholic theology, Gaffin abandons the Protestant doctrine of merit altogether. Gaffin's formulation of the "righteousness of Christ" as the ground of salvation for God's elect is, as noted above, truncated. Gaffin vaguely defines the righteousness of Christ in terms of God's faithfulness to his covenant promises, rather than in forensic terms. Such a view denies that both the active and the passive obedience of Christ is the exclusive meritorious ground of life and salvation. See Lee Irons, "Redefining Merit: An Examination of Medieval Presuppositions in Covenant Theology," in *Creator, Redeemer, Consummator: A Festschrift for Meredith G. Kline* (ed. H. Griffith and J. R. Muether; Greenville, SC: Reformed Academic, 2000) 253-269; and Irons, "The Case for Merit in the Covenant of Works," *Always Reformed* (ed. D. G. Hagopian; Phillipsburg, NJ: Presbyterian and Reformed, forthcoming).

    Michael S. Horton of Westminster West, like several of his faculty colleagues, has taken a strong stand against the Shepherd theology. In this he has been countered by Canadian Reformed theologian N. H. Gootjes in "Doctrinal stumbling blocks?" *Clarion*

50/15 (July 20, 2001) 350-352. Gootjes erroneously posits a discontinuity between Dutch Reformed theology and the theology of the Westminster standards. From yet another ecclesiastical quarter, Donald G. Bloesch takes exception to Horton's formulation of what he calls "a wholly extrinsic justification and a wholly objective revelation" (in *The Holy Spirit: Works and Gifts* [Christian Foundations; Downers Grove, IL: InterVarsity, 2000] 338). Bloesch reasons that in so doing Horton "fails to do justice to the mystical dimension in the theologies of both Calvin and Luther to which the Pietists appealed in their struggle against Protestant orthodoxy. . . . Horton rightly upholds the polarity of law and gospel, which was indeed significant in the preaching and ministry of the Reformers and their followers. Yet he tends to make this polarity too stringent [compare the similar charge against traditional covenant theology by Sinclair Ferguson; see my *Covenant Theology in Reformed Perspective* 126-127, n. 21 and 23; also 212-213] and fails to recognize with the Reformed that there is an underlying unity between law and gospel, though it is not immediately perceptible. Calvin referred to the gospel as 'the soul of the law.' For both Reformers the law is always God's gracious law (though this is more apparent in Calvin than in Luther) and is not to be associated exclusively with God's judgment and wrath. . . . Horton could learn from Karl Barth that law and gospel belong together in a paradoxical unity" (*The Holy Spirit* 338-339).

[21] Grand Rapids: Baker Academic, 2001.

[22] Without any sense of modesty, Lillback (falsely) claims, "this is the first study that has taken seriously the historical context in which the early Reformed covenant thought was given life." (*The Binding of God* 485). What is lacking in Lillback's study is substantive interaction with the scholarly literature.

[23] Westminster's website, www.wts.edu (August 2001).

[24] See further, Chapter 6. Currently, the seminary administration in Philadelphia will not release upon request material relating to the Shepherd controversy– at least not without close screening.

[25] Ted M. Dorman writes "as a confessional Reformed Protestant with pronounced Lutheran leanings" ("The Joint Declaration on the Doctrine of Justification: Retrospect and Prospects," *JETS* 44 [September 2001] 422). Equally as befuddled as Gaffin on the subject of Paul, the law and justification is Thomas Schreiner. Even in his latest work, *Paul, Apostle of God's Glory in Christ* (Downers Grove, IL: InterVarsity, 2001), Schreiner shows that he is still working through the basic issues in this contemporary debate. Starting out as a proponent of the Protestant reformers, Schreiner, like Gaffin, now finds himself in a mediating position somewhere between the Reformation teaching and that of the "new perspective." Curiously, the views of Schreiner and those of Gaffin are strikingly similar. Compare my remarks on Schreiner in *Covenant Theology in Reformed Perspective* 254-55, n. 9 and 256-57, n. 22.

# Chapter 8

# Covenant and Imputation: The Federal System of Doctrine *

Christian doctrine is the product of the church's ongoing elucidation of the inscripturated Word of God. Various ages of church history have devoted concentrated attention to particular doctrines contained in the Bible. The early church, for example, addressed matters relating to the triunity of the Godhead and the divine and human natures of Christ; in the time of the Protestant Reformation consideration was given to the primacy of Scripture over church tradition (that is, the teaching magisterium) and to the pivotal doctrine of justification by faith alone (the article of the standing or falling church).[1]

Today the church of Christ returns once again to the doctrine of soteric justification and, most directly, to the doctrine of the imputation of Christ's righteousness through the sole instrumentality of justifying, saving faith, God's gift to sinners chosen in Christ (the elect of God). The focal elements in this modern-day reformulation of doctrine are these: the covenants of God, sovereign election, and justification by faith apart from good works (what some equate with the Pauline expression "obedience of faith"). To be sure, on any interpretation of the Bible we are obliged to come to terms with the system of doctrine contained in the Bible. No interpreter can operate apart from a systematic restatement of Christian theology. Specific doctrinal statements aside, the systematic reformulations of the teaching of the Bible associated with various schools of interpretation (what is termed systematic or dogmatic theology) – will and do differ from one another both in the degree of consistency and in comprehensiveness. This writer regards Reformed theology to be the most consistent and comprehensive restatement of divine revelation. This does not mean that Reformed interpreters do not have much to learn from other traditions, whether by way of sharpening our critical tools or by re-evaluating and reformulating the dogmas of the Reformed churches.

The subject before us in this paper – divine imputation – relates to doctrine that was once peculiar to the Reformed tradition. It has gradually become something of a commonplace in evangelical theology in recent decades, largely due to awakened interest in the doctrine of the covenants of God. Needless to say, one today cannot neatly categorize all the varied and competing interpretations within precise theological camps. There is much overlap and borrowing of ideas in the theological marketplace today. In this regard, complicating matters in the assessment of evangelical theology as a whole is the impact that Barthianism has had in the last several decades. But Barthianism, as Cornelius Van Til (twentieth-century's most incisive Reformed apologist) has rightly contended, is modernist theology in orthodox Christian garb. The insidious effect of this unwelcome development in contemporary theology will be noted in the following analysis.

One final comment by way of introduction: the doctrines of the Bible are unified and mutually interpretive of one another. We cannot isolate any single doctrine from the totality of divine revelation. Likewise, exegesis and theological interpretation complement each other in such a way that neither has priority over the other. The circularity of biblical hermeneutics is itself governed by the Spirit of God who is the ultimate interpreter of the Word. It is God who provides illumination and understanding to those who hear with humble, contrite faith. Common confession among Christian interpreters is the byproduct of the Spirit's work in the midst of the seven churches – the inter-advental, pentecostal church of Christ. It is the goal to which all true believers aspire and for which they earnestly pray.

## Reformed (Covenant, or Federal) Theology

### 1. The federal headship of the two Adams

In the opening years of the Protestant Reformation it was Ulrich Zwingli, the father of the Reformed tradition, who grasped the importance of the Pauline teaching on the First and Second Adams.[2] The history of humankind and the history of redemption had to be understood against the backdrop of the two Adams. The failure of the first Adam to observe the prohibition against eating of the tree of the knowledge of good and evil resulted in the entrance of death into the human race and the spiritual estrangement between God and God's image-bearer, Adam (man-kind). God's love, mercy, and grace were the motivation for the sending of his only-begotten Son to offer up atonement for sin by the sacrifice of his own body on the cross, what secured once-for-all the reconciliation between God and (redeemed) humanity.

The doctrine of the imputation of sin (the sin of the First Adam being reckoned as the sin of the entire human race) and the imputation of Christ's righteousness (the active and passive obedience of the Second Adam being the meritorious ground of life and salvation, what is an "alien" righteousness) would find explicit formulation within the Reformed theological tradition over the course of many decades. One of the baffling questions addressed by this tradition relates to the manner of sin's transmission (whether mediate or immediate). Differences aside on this question, all were agreed that fallen humankind was guilty before God, having a depraved nature incapable of pleasing God spiritually. Apart from God's work of grace, no one could be declared righteous before the Judge of the living and the dead. Essential to this interpretation of humanity in the early years of its history (from creation to the fall into sin) is adherence to the theological contrast taught in both the Lutheran and Reformed systems of doctrine, namely, the contrast between the "Law" and the "Gospel." The law of God requires full and perfect obedience for the sustaining of life and fellowship with the holy God, Creator of heaven and earth. The gospel proclaims the forgiveness of sins and the imputation of Christ's righteousness to all who believe. In the pre-Fall order, in the time of probation, Adam was obliged to obey God fully; the blessing of the covenant was contingent upon meritorious observance of the law of God. (The express doctrine of the Covenant of Works would become a staple of international Reformed theology by the late sixteenth and early seventeenth centuries.) The Law/Gospel antithesis, essential to Protestant evangelical faith, is vital to the biblical exposition of the doctrine of justification by faith alone.

Adam did not act on his own behalf, but rather on behalf of the entire human race, of which he was appointed the federal or representative head. Adam's transgression did not merely provide a bad example for all those who followed him, but rather was reckoned to the account of each and every human being who comes into the world. Such is the justice and good pleasure of God, sovereign Lord of the covenant made with Adam when he was created in the image of God. Here lies a crucial difference between the creation of humankind and the creation of the angels: the former was created as a race, the latter as a heavenly host. Each good angel would stand in the integrity of his own obedience to the will and revelation of God; disobedient angels would suffer eternal punishment without mercy. Their final, eschatological destiny – like that of humankind – awaits the reappearance of the Son of God when he sums up of all things in heaven and on earth.

    The Second Adam, Jesus Christ, acted on behalf of the elect seed, those chosen in Christ before the foundation of the world. According to Reformed teaching, the death of Christ was sufficient to save all humankind, but (by divine design) efficient only for the elect. The Spirit, who is one with Christ in the economy of redemption, grants life and salvation to all those for whom Christ died. Christ as representative head of the elect of God accomplishes redemption. He does not merely make salvation possible or effective only if one place his or her faith in Jesus Christ. The Spirit of God effectually applies the benefits of Christ's death and resurrection to the elect. These benefits include justification, sanctification, and final glorification. Christ fully bore the wrath of God on behalf of the elect. Spiritual regeneration marks the historical point of transition from wrath to grace for all those who are granted the gift of saving faith. Christ's fulfillment of all righteousness results in the removal of the curse of the Law against transgressors. Apart from the grace of God, the Law always and only works wrath and condemnation. The grace of God in Christ Jesus attains favor and pardon for all those who are in Christ, justified by faith. This is the Gospel.

## 2. Probation

The command not to eat from the tree of the knowledge of good and evil was not arbitrary on the Creator's part. Rather it was reflective of the deepest intent of the covenant relationship (the creature's duty to love, honor, and obey God perfectly) in the presence of the worldly enticements of the flesh (self-gratification), sin (disobedience to the will and word of the Lord), and the devil (Lucifer, the Prince of Darkness). Sin was already present in the angelic world. At some point in the distant past, before the creation of our first parents in the image of the angelic council,[3] the angels found themselves under probation. They too, as creatures of God, had to prove what was good and right and holy. They too had to discern between good and evil. Nothing mysterious or esoteric about the tree of knowledge in the Garden of God, the place of special, supernatural revelation.

The eighth Psalm tells us that Adam was made a little lower than the (good) angels, those now confirmed in righteousness. Adam's confirmation in righteousness – and that of the entire human race represented in the First Adam – had to await the outcome of probationary testing, specifically, successful guardianship of the Garden against the wiles of the Serpent. Rather than protecting the holy sanctuary of God, however, Adam and Eve were cast out of Eden by the angel-protectors of God wielding fiery sword. Keeping the covenant would have resulted in the barring of Satan forever from humanity's earthly abode, her place of habitation prior to the eschatological, consummate new heavens and new earth brought about by a supernatural, cataclysmic event at the close of history (what was the original goal of creation). Christ at his first advent has attained the eternal reward on behalf of the elect of God, those justified, sanctified, and glorified in spiritual (mystical) union with Christ in his death and resurrection. This eternal kingdom of priests and kings, the inheritance promised to Christ upon completion of the task assigned to him in the Covenant of Redemption (or the Counsel of Peace) would be realized in time by means of Christ's successful completion of probation under law, under a covenant of works.[4]

### 3. Imputation (the "one act" of righteousness)

In the covenant of creation there was a specific task given to Adam as representative head of humanity, namely, to guard and protect the sanctity of the Garden of God. The outcome of that test would be reckoned to humanity in all its individuality. (Had God not extended mercy and forbearance to our first parents, the number of humanity would have numbered only two.) Imputation is forensic and it is covenantal. The application of this principle in the covenant between God and Adam is what distinguishes the human race from the angels when they were created a host. Adam's "one act of righteousness," had that been rendered, would have supplied the meritorious ground upon which the promised inheritance would have been granted. It would have secured an eternal kingdom of priests and kings. Initially, humanity would have experienced confirmation in righteousness at the successful close of Adam's probation. Glorification would await the consummation of history.

In the fifth chapter of Romans the apostle Paul draws upon the parallel between the First and Second Adams in their representative capacity as federal heads, specifically, their "one act" to be performed in accordance with the stipulations and sanctions of the covenant established by God, the Covenant of Works with Adam in creation and the Covenant of Law (instituted under Moses) to which Christ made full satisfaction as Adam's substitute and Israel's messiah. The universality of death in the human race is to be attributed to the imputation of sin to all, whereas reconciliation and redemption are grounded upon the meritorious obedience of Christ imputed to all who believe (the elect in Christ). A full-orbed biblical theology requires the explication of these aspects of the early history of humanity, notably, the first covenant with Adam as federal head, including the features of probation and imputation. Nothing less will do justice to the eschatological design and teleological goal of history. Redemptive covenant resumes the program and purpose of God in the new creation, the new order of things.

## 4. The twofold covenants

Distinctive to the Reformed theological tradition is the doctrine of the covenants, hence the synonymity of the nomenclature "Reformed theology" and "covenant theology." The chief element in this teaching is the contrast between two specific covenants established by God with humanity, the Covenant of Works at creation and the Covenant of Grace in recreation. All covenants between God and his people in the history of redemption fall under the rubric of the Covenant of Grace. What this implies, among other things, is that there is only one path to salvation, one way to God. In the nature of the case sinners are alienated from God – by virtue of Adam's representative sin (imputed to every human being) and personal, individual sin (disobedience arising out of a nature that is totally depraved). The free gift of grace includes the removal of guilt and freedom from the dominion of sin by way of union with the resurrected Christ.

Prior to the doctrinal elucidation of the twofold covenants, Protestant reformers (Lutheran and Reformed alike) repeatedly drew attention to the two, antithetical principles summed up in the terms "Law" and "Gospel." It was the distinctive contribution of the Reformed tradition to give articulation to the twofold covenants, expressive of these same contrasting principles of inheritance, faith versus works, (gospel-)grace versus law. Evangelical theology has in recent years come to acknowledge – to one degree or another – the importance of the biblical doctrine of the covenants in its exposition of the history of redemption and in the system of doctrine contained in the Bible. Nevertheless, substantive differences remain in the formulation of the doctrine of the covenants, both with respect to the eschatological design of the covenants (including the matter of the relationship between Israel and the church in the history of the Covenant of Grace) and the role of probation and imputation at the opening of human history.

     Contrary to the teaching of classic dispensationalism, there is an underlying continuity in the history of redemption. God relates in a singular way to his redeemed people down the corridors of history, from the Fall to the Consummation. There is only one way of salvation – faith in Jesus Christ – and only one people of God (the true church of Christ spanning all ages of redemptive history). The biblical doctrine of the single, unfolding Covenant of Grace decisively calls into question the defining element in dispensationalism (as suggested in its nomenclature). Happily, progressive dispensationalism in recent years has certainly proved itself progressive in its reformulation of doctrine. Further work, however, needs to be done. Among other elements requiring elucidation are the covenant at creation (the covenant with Adam as federal head of humanity) and the peculiar function of the law of Moses in the covenant God made with Israel at Sinai. Here we meet up once again with the question of the relationship between Israel and the church and the important subject of covenant typology (including biblical eschatology and symbolism).

## 5. The Mosaic economy (under the "Law")

No aspect of covenant theology has been more perplexing than the subject of the relationship between the two economies of redemption, the old and the new. The old economy is temporary, coming to an end with the establishment of the new covenant in Christ Jesus, who is himself the end of the law. According to the great interpreter of the history of redemption, the apostle Paul recognizes the principle of works-inheritance (opposite to faith-inheritance) as uniquely characteristic of the Mosaic covenant. To be under Law is to be under divine wrath and condemnation. This ministration of condemnation, the Mosaic economy as a whole, is nevertheless glorious, though far less glorious in comparison with the new ministration of life and righteousness. The old is "letter," the new is "Spirit." The term "letter" refers to the outward administration/manifestation of the old covenant. It highlights the external writing of the law on tablets of stone versus the internal writing on tablets of flesh, characteristic of the new covenant in the (semi-)eschatological age of the Spirit. Additionally, the letter/Spirit contrast brings into view two distinct covenantal functions of the law: first, as means of inheriting the promised blessing of God (reward based upon meritorious accomplishment at the successful close of probationary testing); and second, as empowerment of the Spirit enabling those united to Christ by grace through faith to fulfill the law of righteousness – that is, to manifest the life of holiness and sanctification, wherein good works are evidential of true, justifying faith (what has been dubbed the "third use" of the law of God).

The Reformed theological tradition has attained broad consensus with regard to its interpretation of the Mosaic covenant. Firstly, and most importantly, the Mosaic covenant is understood to be a realization of the Abrahamic promise. The covenant previously established by God with Abraham was thoroughly gracious, that is, *unconditional* (reward based not on human works, but on the work of Christ exclusively). The blessing of God is unconditional, in the sense that God himself would in due time provide the full and final sacrifice for sin. God himself would provide all that was necessary for the redemption of Abraham and his faithful seed. Of course, God's promise itself was conditioned upon the Son's fulfillment of all righteousness in the Covenant of Law – as vicarious sacrifice and substitute (hence Christ's submission to the Covenant of Works broken by Adam.) Secondly, Reformed expositors recognize universally – in accordance with the teaching of the apostle Paul – that the works-principle (antithetical to the faith-principle) is uniquely descriptive of the Mosaic administration of the Covenant of Grace. The precise way in which these two contrary principles function within the old economy of redemption, however, has been explained in a variety of ways.[5]

Over the years debates among Reformed interpreters have generated strong opposition and contention, but such has proved necessary and beneficial in the ongoing elucidation of the theology of the covenants. That debate has not ended. In fact, it has been revived in recent decades, especially in response to the so-called "new perspective" on Paul and the law, what is the greatest challenge today to the teaching of the Protestant reformers. Issues now raised call into question some of the most fundamental elements within the theological system of Reformed federalism in particular, and Protestantism in general. Common to the new thinking is repudiation of the vital and essential Reformed doctrine of the Covenant of Works. Those holding this line of interpretation follow the lead of Karl Barth, whom many mistakenly regard as the greatest Reformed thinker of the twentieth century.[6] Repudiation of the doctrine of the Covenant of Works inevitably undermines the teaching of Protestant orthodoxy, specifically the traditional Law/Gospel antithesis.[7] The time has now come to affirm the truth of this Protestant teaching.

## 6. The Law and the Gospel

Largely through the efforts of Barth and his disciples, Reformed theology has been in the process of being recast since the middle of the last century. At the opening of this third millennium the Reformed tradition has the challenge – and obligation – to reclaim its heritage in accordance with the teaching of Scripture. According to Barthian interpretation, there is no contrast – no antithesis – between the Law and the Gospel. Barthians speak of law in grace, or grace in law. They point to the Pauline expression "the obedience of faith" in support of their understanding of the correlativity between faith and works in the article of justification. The Pauline expression substitutes for the Reformation slogan "faith alone" (*sola fide*).[8] The ramifications of this theological change are seismic. The success of Barth and his school lay in subtlety and in the skillful use of traditional theological and biblical terminology. Superficial reading of Barth has led many to view him as a faithful exponent of Reformed theology. That estimation could not be further from the truth.[9]

Contrary to the teaching of neoorthodoxy, the Law enunciates the way of blessing and communion with God in terms of perfect law-keeping. The creature's duty is to obey God with his or her whole heart unswervingly. Nothing less than perfect obedience is required for fellowship with God. It is the way of works, the opposite of grace (saving faith). The Gospel proclaims the forgiveness of sins and the gift of life everlasting to those who believe in Jesus Christ, whose perfect obedience is the exclusive, meritorious ground of life and salvation. (Good) works do not contribute to the sinner's justification before God or to the granting of life in the kingdom of Christ. Faith is the alone instrument which receives the righteousness of Christ imputed to all who believe (those spiritually united to Christ in his death and resurrection). For those outside of Christ and under Law (whether the law of creation or the law of Moses) they are children of wrath, objects of God's holy displeasure. Where there is sin, Law works wrath and condemnation. Where there is (gospel-)grace, there is freedom – Law no longer condemns. Christ delivers the sons and daughters of God from bondage to sin and the Law. Christ's deliverance is complete and irreversible; such is the power and efficacy of his atoning death. The resurrected Christ has sent his Spirit – the Spirit of Pentecost – into the world as demonstration of his once-for-all accomplishment of redemption in the fullness of times. This Spirit – the Spirit of Christ – effectually applies all the benefits of Christ's work on the cross to those chosen in him before the foundation of the world. There can be no admixture of the Law and the Gospel. These are two contrary ways to the promised inheritance – life in the eternal, consummate kingdom. The Protestant reformers were precisely right in their affirmation of justification by faith alone and the corresponding Law/Gospel contrast. Denial of the latter undermines the article of faith upon which the church stands or falls.

## 7. Election and reprobation

By way of concluding our summary of the Reformed system of doctrine – selective as it is – two remaining elements within that system require comment. History is the process of differentiation between the seed of Christ and the seed of the Serpent, between the elect and the reprobate. With the introduction of common grace in the period from the Fall to the Consummation (at which point

God's common grace will be withdrawn) and the free, universal offer of the Gospel to all indiscriminately (notably in the economy of redemption that dawned with the first appearing of Christ), the Gospel calls upon all to repent and believe in Christ and his redemption. There is but one way of salvation and one people of God. Chapters nine through eleven of Romans consider the historical outworking of God's predestinating purpose in the salvation of the elect and the condemnation of the reprobate. Israel's national calling is illustrative of God's purpose in predestination. Believing gentiles are grafted into the olive tree (true Israel); the dead branches of the natural tree are lopped off. God's judgment against disobedient Israel resulted in her exile. Her expulsion from the land was a pointer to the final Day of judgment at the return of Christ at the end of the age. Until that Day, those of ethnic Israel have the opportunity (along with the gentile nations) to repent and turn to God, to be grafted into the ancient tree of life, representative of the true Israel of God, the seed of Abraham, the father of all believers.

Election is according to grace – election is in Christ, the fountain of salvation. As it turns out, the first covenant, the Covenant of Works established by God with Adam as federal head of all humanity, is prelude to the manifestation of God's redeeming love and grace revealed in Jesus Christ, whose atoning death is requisite for the salvation of the elect. (Paul speaks of Adam as a type of the one to come.) Reprobation has two components: (1) the passing by of those not chosen as recipients of God's predestinating love and favor (salvation is all of grace); and (2) the condemnation of the reprobate on grounds of sin (personal and imputed). God is just and true in all his ways. The salvation of sinners is grounded upon the merits of Christ's obedience; the condemnation of the ungodly is their just recompense.

## 8. Particular atonement

According to the teaching of the Bible and the Reformed faith, the atonement of Christ is particular and wholly efficacious. Christ died for the elect, and the elect alone. In the history of Christian doctrine there are those who erroneously contend that Christ's death is intended for all indiscriminately. Some holding this view argue that the Spirit of Christ (the Holy Spirit) alone enables one to respond savingly to the offer of salvation (hence the Spirit's work of regeneration is particularistic). This interpretation, however, creates a disconnect between the work of Christ and the work of the Spirit in the economy of redemption. Then there are the Arminians who teach that the individual is entirely free to accept or reject the offer to come to Christ by the exercise of his or her own will. Both of these interpretations undermine the efficacy of Christ's atoning death.

Christ is the one, true sacrifice for sin, the representative substitute for all the elect. Christ has made full and complete atonement, obtaining reconciliation between God and sinners saved by grace. Nothing has been left to human ingenuity, strength, or self-determination. All is of grace, from start to finish. Such is the nature of Christ's salvation. The righteousness that saves is an alien righteousness – a perfect righteousness imputed to the account of each believer. Christ, the Second Adam, is our righteousness.

### John Piper's Doctrine of Imputation: Another gospel

Piper appreciates the Reformed theological tradition, but does not buy into it hook, line, and sinker. If there is just cause to challenge the confessional statements of the Reformed churches, I say, let us listen carefully to the reasons furnished. In response to my criticisms and those of others regarding Piper's interpretation of the doctrine of justification and the covenants Piper offers his readers a reconsideration of his position. In *Counted Righteous in Christ* we are now provided with a passionate appeal for the Reformed (federal) doctrine of the imputation, both the sin of Adam to each member of human race and the righteousness of Christ to those united to him by grace through faith. The crucial question, however, is this: Is Piper's doctrine of imputation true to Bible and historic Reformed orthodoxy? In a word, the answer is No. The changes that Piper has made are superficial and cosmetic, not substantive and systemic. His theological work continues to mark a radical departure from Protestant orthodoxy. What is required is nothing less than a thoroughgoing reworking of Piper's system of doctrine.

The author is to be commended for recognizing the importance of the doctrine of imputation, as one critical element in the system of biblical truth. I would only add – by way of emphasis – that the current dispute addresses a doctrine of greatest theological import. It is a doctrinal controversy of the first order in contemporary evangelical theology. Piper's response to my critique of his theology (though he nowhere cites my work) is wholly inadequate, by virtue of the fact that his theology is built on a radically different framework than that set forth in covenant theology. As a disciple of Daniel Fuller, Piper's teaching nullifies the classic Protestant Law/Gospel antithesis. Having done so, his theological formulation in this book, as elsewhere, is destructive of the Gospel of grace.[10]

The most significant change in Piper's theology is twofold: (1) his application of the term "merit" with reference to Christ's perfect obedience, that alien righteousness which is imputed to all who believe; and (2) his insistence upon the sole instrumentality of faith in justification. What precisely does Piper mean by these doctrinal affirmations? Before turning to this question, we call attention to the many, well-known endorsers who have praised this book. Included in this number are theologians who embrace and defend Norman Shepherd's reformulation of Calvinistic doctrine.[11] As for others endorsing Piper's teaching, one can only conclude how easily misled are Piper's readers. To be sure, this group represents a wide spectrum of thinking within contemporary evangelicalism. Those on the right side of the spectrum – those of Calvinist pedigree – apparently have not done their homework with respect to the controversy that looms so large in our day, and to Piper's teaching specifically.

Piper begins with an apology for the theological exercise undertaken. He explains at some length why in the busy life of a pastor he has taken time to write this book. What we have in the opening pages is a pious homily from the pen of a busy pastor. One of his principal contenders is Robert Gundry. The author expresses no animosity between himself and Gundry. Would that we all understood well the necessity to engage theological opponents in polemical debate – without accusation of personal attack and mean-spiritedness.[12] Contention for the faith is a necessity for the defense of the Gospel throughout the ages of the Christian church. The present is no different from the past. With regard to the Gospel of grace, there can be no compromise.

Succinctly stated, Piper's doctrine of imputation is based upon a speculative notion of divine gratuity as that characterizes all God's acts in creation and in redemption. Piper's view is comparable to the medieval, scholastic nature/grace conceptualization. Accordingly, grace (the *donum superadditum* of the medieval scholastics) is requisite to supplement the efforts of the earthly pilgrim on his way to the heavenly, eternal kingdom. The gifts of nature are insufficient. At creation Adam's perfection in knowledge, righteousness, and holiness – the Thomists tell us – was not adequate to the task. The creature was and is dependent upon the unmerited, unearned grace of God in order to attain life everlasting – what constitutes the beatific vision of God in glory. It is a matter of nature and grace cooperating together (a divine-human synergism).[13] In Piper's view Adam as a creature of the dust was not in a position to merit the promised blessing of God (namely, confirmation in righteousness and glorification at the consummation of history). There is no works-inheritance principle with respect to human achievement. Not in the pristine order of creation, and not in the subsequent order of redemption. Divine grace precedes and undergirds human ability. Additionally, there is no doctrine of probation in Piper's theology, and no doctrine of the (twofold) covenants, which the author finds especially repugnant.[14] Here Piper adopts the Barthian construct of "law in grace," which he learned from his mentor Daniel Fuller.

Why, according to Piper, is imputation necessary for salvation? What exactly is imputed? What is the nature and the significance of that which is imputed to believers? Piper explains that the imputation of Christ's righteousness is necessitated by Adam's one, representative sin at the opening stage of human history. It is needed to erase the slate, to give humankind a fresh, new start in pursuit of the life of true faith and obedience. Faith (in distinction from obedience) is the human response to divine gratuity – *whether before or after the Fall*. Works of obedience arise out of gratitude to God for all his good and gracious gifts – *whether before or after the Fall*. Piper flatly denies all human merit. Perfect obedience does not provide grounds for divine blessing and reward. At the same time, however, Piper wishes to avoid any and all conflating of faith and works with respect to the reception of blessing and inheritance from God. As regards the situation after the Fall, the righteousness of imputation (Christ's righteousness), that which is essential for salvation from sin, is an "alien" righteousness. It is, Piper informs us, the sole, meritorious ground of salvation.[15] The problem is that Piper's doctrine does not square with that of the apostle Paul when he draws an explicit parallel between the "one act" of the First Adam (by whose demerit sin and death entered the world of humanity) and the "one act" of the Second Adam (which brought righteousness and immortality). Had Adam fulfilled the law of the covenant in his time of probation he would have obtained the promised blessing of God for himself and all his posterity. This is the merit-principle. It is a matter of meritorious accomplishment in the case of both representative heads. To say otherwise is to destroy the comparison enunciated so clearly and so unambiguously by the apostle. The principle of works informs the first covenant with Adam, the principle of grace informs redemptive covenant. This is the Law/Gospel contrast. And Piper will have none of it.

As already indicated, Piper does insist that faith is the alone instrument of justification – *before and after the Fall*. The faith of which Piper speaks is humble faith, trust in God for who he is and what he has done, is doing, and will do for his creation. All God's blessings are bestowed by grace. They are manifestations of divine gratuity, never a reward earned by creatures of the dust. Saving faith is merely faith of the second order (a gift of second-order grace). Piper's emphasis upon the sole instrumentality of faith in justification is meant to ensure that the accent is placed on divine gratuity. This is not the Protestant doctrine of justification by faith alone. In *John Piper on the Christian Life* I wrote:

> Piper has no doctrine of the Covenant of Works and his system of doctrine makes no allowance for the classic Protestant law/gospel antithesis. The Fuller-Piper reformulation of Christian theology transforms the older dog-

> matic distinctions into something radically different. The *sola fide* formulation is understood in vastly different ways. On the surface, the two schools of theology give the appearance of saying the same thing. But that is so only on the surface.[16]

That assessment of an earlier book by Piper equally pertains to the present work. Whatever statements of Piper appear to reflect the teachings of Protestant-Reformed theology – statements that are good as far as they go – are (on the surface) merely borrowed capital from Protestant orthodoxy and Reformed covenant theology, specifically.

Piper attempts to make a sustained, exegetical case for the doctrine of imputation. He fails, however, to provide a faithful account of the apostle Paul's teaching on the Mosaic law and, most importantly, Paul's handling of one of the crucial OT texts, Leviticus 18:5, what is absolutely vital to Paul's explication of God's revelation of justification in redemptive history. (Piper notes that this critical debate in contemporary theology falls outside the parameters of his book, but is one requiring separate treatment sometime in the future. The sooner he gives concentrated attention to this subject, the better. I must add, however, that I do not expect to find there a reliable handling of the Word of God, given the direction of Piper's theologizing.) Protestant-Reformed teaching unanimously identifies the works-inheritance principle as operative within the old economy of redemption. To be sure, there are widely differing interpretations in formulation, but all within the bounds of orthodoxy. What unifies the varied doctrinal and confessional formulations is adherence to the Law/Gospel antithesis. And this is what is lacking in Piper's interpretation of the Mosaic economy of redemption and in his theology as a whole. The theological contrast between the Gospel and the Law, between faith and works, is absolutely essential. It is a nonnegotiable element in the system of biblical truth.

Leviticus 18:5 enunciates the principle of works, antithetical to the principle of faith (gospel grace, the only grace that saves sinners). Grace is God's sole remedy for covenant-transgression. It is the grace of the Lord Jesus Christ who was sacrificed for sinners. This grace of God is not operative in the period before the Fall. Our theological terminology must be true to the teaching of Scripture. Grace is redemptive in nature. God is good, but he does not manifest grace to humankind in creation. There is no need for grace at this stage of biblical history.[17] God declared all created things good (see Gen 1), and he is just in rewarding Adam's faithfulness to his command(s), as he is just in condemning the disobedient. God was not and is not obliged to favor the unrighteous, except for what he has promised his own Son by way of the eternal Counsel of peace, namely, the salvation of the elect (here is the doctrine of the consequent, absolute necessity of the atonement). The favor that the elect enjoy is all of grace, not human merit or human praise-worthiness. To God be all thanks and all glory.

### The Achilles' Heel of the New Westminster School

When one thinks of historic Reformed orthodoxy and the ongoing dissemination of Calvinistic teaching, one immediately thinks of Westminster Theological Seminary, founded by J. Gresham Machen in 1929. That movement led to the establishment of not one, but two main campuses, one outside Philadelphia and the other outside San Diego. Ironically, it was the controversy over the heterodox teaching of Norman Shepherd in the mid 1970s to early 1980s – teaching that is virtually identical to that found in the writings of John Piper – that prompted the formation of a faculty in exile (other factors also played a role). Expansion out to the West Coast was made in an effort to alleviate the tension and rancor that arose within the Philadelphia faculty. Allegations and false charges of personal animosity (including the breaking of the Ninth Commandment[18]) on the part of some or all critics of the seminary only serves to obscure the doctrinal focus of this dispute.[19] The controversy has reached a new level, now that two ecclesiastical courts of the Orthodox Presbyterian Church have – at long last – declared the new doctrine on justification by faith and works to be heretical. The focus in this round of ecclesiastical debate is the teaching of OPC elder John Kinnaird.[20]

I will not take the time to repeat what I have written elsewhere,[21] except to say that the faculties of Westminster (East and West) have not succeeded in freeing either campus from the insidious error and corruption (both moral and theological) so deeply embedded in the institution.[22] Talk of Christ's active obedience as meritorious ground – expressed, for example, in the teaching of Richard Gaffin (now echoed by Piper) – is negated by denial of the historic Reformed doctrine of the Covenant of Works and, more fundamentally, the classic Protestant Law/Gospel antithesis. The one affirmation cancels out the other. In terms of the system of doctrine mention of the active and passive obedience of Christ as meritorious ground of justification and life everlasting (imputed to all who believe) is meaningless – or perhaps we should say bears an altogether different meaning from that found in the writings of Protestant-Reformed orthodoxy. By way of analogy, it is like affirming the doctrine of the inerrancy of Scripture, while arguing that the apostle Paul was mistaken in his prohibition of women from ordained office.[23] Returning to the teaching under examination, the affirmation of faith as the sole instrument receiving the righteousness of Christ in justification is, likewise, meaningless – meaningless apart from the biblical doctrine of (meritorious) works, works performed by the servant/son of the covenant in accordance with the probationary command explicitly laid out in the covenant arrangement. Otherwise, the works of justifying faith become the subordinate (if not the coordinate) means of justification.[24]

Timothy Trumper, one of the newer members of the Philadelphia faculty, has taken upon himself the role of advocate for the seminary. (In 2002, however, he announced his resignation from the faculty.[25]) In the Fall 2002 issue of *The Westminster Theological Journal* Trumper addresses the situation the faculty now faces. Let the reader be clear: Trumper's article is the work of the faculty, whole or in part – and that, most especially, the thinking of Gaffin, Westminster's senior systematician.[26] What we are addressing in this section of the essay, then, is not the thinking of one or two individuals, but a school of thought – that of New Westminster. Despite the input of the faculty, the essay is marked by shoddy scholarship and a deliberate unwillingness or inability to engage the broader debate (the relevant literature is voluminous). Can we then regard Trumper as an able crusader for the New Westminster School? I do not think so. The essay is neither straightforward nor honest about the facts of the dispute. And as we will see in the following, what Trumper gives with the right hand, he takes away with the left.

As a means of evaluating Westminster's new doctrine on justification and the covenants (including the doctrine of the imputation of Christ's righteousness), we identify three objectives or traits in Trumper's essay: (1) a defense of what the author misleadingly calls "constructive Calvinism;" (2) strident criticism of the theology of Meredith G. Kline, whom I regard to be Old Westminster's leading scholar and biblical theologian; and (3) the deception used to (re)state the faculty's theological position, including misrepresentation of the views of her opponents and falsification of the facts of the controversy. As one more attempt to malign the character of the critics of the New Westminster School and to call into question their motivations in exposing this moral and doctrinal error, Trumper freely resorts to innuendo and snide comment.

(1) The "constructive Calvinisim," for which Trumper crusades, is in some ways peculiar to the Westminster School, at least one strand of it – that arising out of the teachings of Westminster's first systematician, the late John Murray. The setting for Trumper's case is a review and evaluation of Jeong Koo Jeon's book *Covenant Theology: John Murray's and Meredith Kline's Response to the Historical Development of Federal Theology in Reformed Thought* (1999).[27] Essentially, this publication is Jeon's doctoral dissertation written under the supervision of Clair Davis and Sinclair Ferguson, previous occupant of the Charles Krahe chair in systematics (now held by Gaffin). Both sides in the dispute are agreed that Murray's theology falls within the parameters of Reformed orthodoxy. At the same time we differ in the significance of Murray's recasting of Reformed covenant theology and the effect that teaching has had upon the later systematizing of doctrine by Murray's closest disciples (Shepherd, Gaffin, Ferguson, Trumper, and others) – what has produced the New Westminster School. Trumper regards Murray's teaching as more faithful to Scripture, in contrast to the teaching of Kline. And he calls for a "sympathetic-critical reading" of the Reformed tradition, past and present. He mistakenly and anachronistically equates Murray's thinking on the inappropriateness of the terminology "Covenant of Works" as descriptive of the original Adamic administration prior to the Fall with John Calvin's theology of the covenants. Here he commends to his readers the study of Peter Lillback, a work that grossly distorts and misrepresents Calvin's theology (including his doctrine of justification by faith alone).[28]

With the stroke of his pen Trumper dupes his readers into believing that he (like Murray) affirms the classic Protestant Law/Gospel contrast. "It is Murray's unmodified retention of the unsuffused antithesis that leaves untouched his Protestant understanding of justification as well as his Reformed perspective on the third use of the Law."[29] By slight of hand, Trumper later suggests that Murray was "keen to maintain the credibility of the tradition's theology by debunking more scholastic aspects of its form."[30] We have to ask: What aspects did Murray deplore? Trumper does not tell his readers. What he does say is that Kline weaves "into his biblico-theological reflections nuances more reminiscent of the traditional scholastic methodological structure of the theology of Westminster Calvinism."[31] Readers note: Westminster Calvinism differs from the "constructive Calvinism" advocated by Trumper. What this crusader trumpets here – and throughout the review article – is the erroneous and deceptive claim that the difference between these two schools of thought is merely "methodological" and "attitudinal". Contrary to Trumper's contention, the difference between Old and New Westminster is substantive and fundamental. It goes to the roots of the system of doctrine. In a subsequent footnote Trumper observes: "Later Calvinistic federal theologians, shaped by the moderate Protestant Scholasticism of the seventeenth century, have assumed that [the doctrine of the Covenant of Works] was [a 'non-negotiable of federal theology']." He goes on to assert that "the contemporary challenges of biblical theology and the renaissance of Calvin studies reopens the question."[32] How so? Trumper does not explain. In the opinion of Trumper just how important is an answer to this question? Trumper opines: "the future of Westminster Calvinism very much hangs on a fresh approach that takes into account the methodological alternative to the moderate scholasticism of the Westminster Standards that the biblical theology of Calvin presents."³³ Trumper would have us believe that only the "constructive Calvinists," among whom he is numbered, hold the answer to this all-important question. And in his judgment Murray is "the Father of constructive Calvinism."³⁴ Not true. Trumper deceives his readers.

(2) The reader must understand that the criticisms leveled against Kline's theology are equally applicable to the Reformed tradition as a whole. It is certainly the case that Kline's interpretation of the original covenant with Adam and the covenant with Moses is more fairly representative of mainstream, historic Reformed theology than is Murray's.³⁵ The view of the New Westminster School (post-Murray) lies altogether outside the bounds of Protestant-Reformed orthodoxy, notably, in its interpretation of the doctrine of covenant and justification by faith (apart from the works of the law). It is also the case that virtually every Reformed dogmatician has recognized that the interpretation of the Mosaic covenant – as a peculiar manifestation of the overarching Covenant of Grace extending from the Fall to the Consummation – is one of the most difficult subjects, if not the most difficult subject, to expound. The new "constructive Calvinists" (those sharing Trumper's mindset) claim that the interpretation of the Klinians (those Trumper deems to be out of step with the Calvinistic tradition) is too complicated, too dogmatic (alleging that Kline's formulation has become in the eyes of some the measure of true orthodoxy), dispensational in its leaning (despite repeated outcries of the Klinians), and utterly confusing. Trumper pens these words all in the spirit of conciliation!

Apologetically justifying his urge (or rather the faculty's urge) to respond to the Klinians – whom they would prefer to ignore altogether – Trumper asserts that this debate is nothing more than a parochial skirmish within the Westminster community, one that originated within the seminary faculty.³⁶ Nonsense. This opinion betrays either

Trumper's failure to understand and master the current theological literature or the deliberate, willful distortion of truth advocated by the seminary faculty, board, and administrators. Trumper is more intent upon misleading his readers into thinking that the villains in this local skirmish are none other than the Klinians. Trumper faults Professor Kline himself for not setting the record straight – for not correcting the "slur" against Murray's theology, whom the "constructive Calvinists" regards not only as the father of the movement, but as impeccably orthodox, Calvin's truest disciple. For the record, Kline has stated his position clearly regarding the pernicious teaching of the Shepherd-Gaffin school. If anyone bears responsibility for obstruction and obfuscation, it is Gaffin and his cohorts who have prevented Kline from publishing his views unedited and unexplicated in the pages of *The Westminster Theological Journal* and in the OPC's denominational publication *New Horizons*.[37]

Trumper takes Kline to task for foisting his understanding of the theological term "grace" upon the Reformed tradition, despite the fact that this term has commonly been (mis)applied by the federalists in their formulations of the pre-Fall order at creation. On this score, if there is to be an accurate use of the label "constructive Calvinist," that belongs to Kline and his disciples. The views advanced by New Westminster are deconstructive; they are the result of the *deformation* – not the reformation – of doctrine. It is New Westminster that has betrayed the Reformed faith. At the same time, it is entirely wrong to suggest that Kline "made orthodoxy to hang so definitely on the assumed correctness of his particular understanding of grace."[38] It is true that Reformed theology must yet free itself fully and consistently from the misappropriation of the medieval, Thomistic nature/grace dichotomy, if its theology is to be reformed and reforming according to the Word of God. But this is altogether different from saying that the Reformed scholastics destroyed the Gospel of grace in their doctrinal formulations, taken as a whole.[39]

(3) Here we highlight specifically Trumper's use of calculated deception, duplicity, and falsification of facts in his reading of the controversial Shepherd-Gaffin theology, that which stands over against the teaching of historic Reformed covenant theology (as advocated and advanced by Kline). The faculty of New Westminster is not the defender of federal theology, as falsely claimed.[40] The grandest deception of all is the contention that Trumper and certain other faculty colleagues knew little – nor did they care to know – about the views of Norman Shepherd, Murray's hand-picked successor in systematics, who was dismissed from the faculty in 1982 in an attempt to bring a measure of closure to the controversy raging on campus (what President Edmund P. Clowney misleadingly called at the time a "tempest in a teapot").[41] Truth be told, Shepherd's teaching provides the immediate context for New Westminster's theology. On the one hand, Trumper dissociates himself from the Barthian school. On the other, he embraces its reinterpretation of the Reformed tradition (concerning the doctrines here being discussed). Trumper reiterates this very point in the conclusion of his review article. He writes: "Calvinists who follow Murray's example nevertheless often discern justification for some of the neo-orthodox concerns."[42] What precisely are *these* concerns?

We have already noted that what Trumper gives with the right hand, he takes away with the left. Such is the case with respect to the traditional Protestant Law/Gospel antithesis. It is precisely here that Trumper takes explicit exception to the Protestant-Reformed tradition. "A mere repetitive banging of the forensic drum," he writes, "is proving ineffective in persuading multitudes of the reformers' understanding of justification. This cardinal doctrine is set firmly in the biblical context of paternal grace and love, as it is in Calvin. . . . Accordingly, we cannot but infer that Kline's setting of grace in the context of law is the perpetuation of a reactionary mindset shaped by the Reformation and post-Reformation need to defend the forensic nature of justification. . . . In this [Kline] but continues the apologetic inadequacies of the later Calvinism of the preceding centuries."[43] New Westminster adopts the Barthian Gospel-Law construct, "the kernel of truth [that] may be the very means of resuscitating the credibility of federal theology in the mainstream of Reformed thought," reasons Trumper.[44] What Trumper advocates is a theology of grace that undergirds his doctrine of God's paternal love. Leading the way to a fuller appreciation of what Trumper regards to be Calvin's teaching on adoption, Trumper urges "constructive Calvinists" "to reflect more proportionately the biblical profile of the paternal grace and love of God. . . . [W]e ought not to expect a diminishing of the criticisms leveled against Westminster Calvinists until we begin to do justice to the familial, gracious and loving nature of the gospel"[45] – something that has allegedly been lost in federal scholasticism (that is, Reformed Orthodoxy). New Westminster has made it her mission to furrow a new path, one that leads away from the theology of the Protestant reformers – notably in her exposition of the doctrine of justification and the covenants. This trek has proven unsuccessful, judged in light of the Bible and the great creeds and confessions of orthodox Christianity. Repudiation of the classic Protestant Law/Gospel antithesis in the Shepherd-Gaffin theology is Westminster's Achilles' heel. The "constructive Calvinism," for which Westminster now champions, results in the deformation of doctrine and the destruction of the Gospel of sovereign grace.

In the end Trumper finds Jeon's study to be of limited usefulness. It is, he judges, too narrowly focused. On this point, compare the assessment of W. Robert Godfrey,

President of Westminster West, in the "Foreword" to Jeon's book. It truly is a matter of theological perspective – one Reformed, the other neoorthodox.[46] Tongue in cheek, Trumper closes with these words: "What criticisms I have made of Kline have been intended to reduce the level of acrimony among Westminster Calvinists and not to aggravate it. But there can only be genuine unity in the defense of federal theology if it is made to rest on the Law-Gospel antithesis itself and not on a covenant of works *in se*. Therein lies the issue."[47] Here is our retort: the understanding and employment of the antithesis between the Law and the Gospel in the New Westminster School are radically different from that found in Protestant-Reformed orthodoxy. There can be no compromise or accommodation of views destructive of the Gospel. Michael S. Horton is partly correct when he writes: "A revisionary perspective of a covenant theology antithetical to the law-gospel distinction may turn out to be more biblical, in which case we would have to dissent from our [Reformed] tradition. Nevertheless, we hope to have shown that it is inaccurate to identify this perspective as 'Reformed' in any sense that is identifiable with the tradition that goes by that name. As far as the law-gospel distinction is concerned, it is as integral to Reformed theology (embedded in federalism) as it is to Lutheranism."[48] In entertaining the possibility that the traditional Protestant Law/Gospel contrast is unscriptural, Horton leaves open the door to neoorthodox teaching, meaning that his predecessor in apologetics, Cornelius Van Til, did not read this modernist doctrine aright. For the Klinians and Van Tilians, those numbered among modern-day exponents of historic Reformed covenant theology, this theological construct is a nonnegotiable. Trumper scores on this astute observation.

## Conclusion

The issue in this contemporary dispute does not devolve on the forensic, theological term "merit" *per se,* but rather on the appropriateness and usefulness of the Protestant Law/Grace construct in its system of doctrine. The grace of which we speak here is *gospel grace*. And the focal issue in Reformed theology is not scholastic federalism's restatement of the doctrine of the covenants and justification. But having said that, historians of doctrine and biblical interpreters cannot simply leave the matter there. Ongoing reformulation of Christian doctrine in the light of Scripture's teaching remains the task of systematico-exegetical theologians in every age of the history of the church. What Piper and the New Westminster school propose does not contribute to the reformation of churchly dogma, but rather to the devolution, the deformation, of doctrine. Along the way, New Westminster's attempt to trace Murray's covenant theology back to Calvin himself (what some naively regard as the pristine age of "pure" Reformed teaching) is misguided and erroneous.

It is inconceivable to view the angels or humanity apart from the initial circumstance of probationary testing. And it is precisely in connection with probation that we are obliged to speak of "meritorious" attainment and reward. Successful completion of the "one act of righteousness" – performed by angels individually or by Adam representatively as head of the human race – results in confirmation in righteousness. And once there is confirmation in righteousness it is no longer appropriate to speak of righteous works done in compliance with the will of God as meritorious, not now and not in the kingdom of consummate glory. Adam's transgression made requisite the imputation of Christ's perfect obedience – his one act of righteousness – in order that sinners united to Christ by grace through faith might enjoy fellowship with God and life everlasting. The doctrine of Christ's imputation is essential in the biblical interpretation of justification by faith alone. The Reformed doctrine of the covenants offers the best system of doctrine to accommodate all the biblical data.

## ENDNOTES

\* This paper was read at the 2003 Eastern regional meeting of the Evangelical Theologicl Society in Lancaster, PA.

[1] See my "Doctrinal Development in Scripture and Tradition: A Reformed Assessment of the Church's Theological Task," *CTJ* 30 (1995) 401-418; republished in my *Covenant Theology in Reformed Perspective: Collected Essays and Book Reviews in Historical, Biblical, and Systematic Theology* (Eugene, OR: Wipf and Stock, 2000) 341-355.

[2] See my "Reformed Interpretation of the Mosaic Covenant," *WTJ* 43 (1980) 1-57; republished in *Covenant Theology in Reformed Perspective* 17-57.

[3] Consult further, Meredith G. Kline, *Images of the Spirit* (Grand Rapids: Baker, 1980).

[4] Christ was born under the law. The principle governing this covenant was that of works, the legal principle identical with that operative in the original covenant with Adam at the beginning. While under law, Christ was on probation in order to secure the inheritance of an eternal kingdom of sons and daughters. The writer to the Hebrews informs us that Christ in his human nature had to learn obedience through his sufferings. This pertains to what theologians have called the "active" and "passive" obedience of Christ.

[5] See endnote 2 above.

[6] Barth is the father of neoorthodoxy, that brand of theology that has the appearance of orthodoxy, but is radically different. It is misleading to label Barth as a "Reformed" theologian. The modern-day school of thought identified with the "new perspective on Paul and the law" converges closely with that of the Barthians on the subject of justification and the covenants, especially in its anti-juridical posture.

7 John Murray's views are an exception to what is generally the case. Daniel Fuller and Norman Shepherd hold opinions representative of the anti-reformational slant so commonplace in contemporary theology.

8 Some interpreters are more subtle in their recasting of traditional Reformed theology. As we will see, John Piper and Richard Gaffin claim to hold passionately to the Reformation theology of *sola fide*. They do so at the expense of fidelity to orthodox formulation. Their writings require close, careful reading. Such is the subtlety used by these writers.

9 See Cornelius Van Til's critique of Barth in *The New Modernism: An appraisal of the theology of Barth and Brunner* (Philadelphia: Presbyterian and Reformed, 1947; and *Christianity and Barthianism* (Philadelphia: Presbyterian and Reformed, 1965. Consult also Richard A. Muller, "Karl Barth and the Path of Theology into the Twentieth Century: Historical Observations," *WTJ* 51 (1989) 25-50.

10 John Piper, *Counted Righteous in Christ: Should We Abandon the Imputation of Christ's Righteousness?* (Wheaton, IL: Crossway Books, 2002). See my review article of Piper's earlier work, *John Piper on the Christian Life: An Examination of His Controversial View of 'Faith Alone' in* Future Grace (Great Bromley: Christian Research Network, 1999). This essay is republished here as Chapter 5.

11 The many endorsements are provided in the opening pages of *Counted Righteous in Christ*.

12 John Frame has falsely accused me of this very thing. See endnote 40 below and Appendix D.

13 See my "The Original State of Adam: Tensions in Reformed Theology," *EvQ* 59 (1987) 291-309; republished in *Covenant Theology in Reformed Perspective* 95-110.

14 Compare the views of Scott J. Hafemann, who relies heavily upon Piper's theology, in *The God of Promise and the Life of Faith: Understanding the heart of the Bible* (Wheaton, IL: Crossway, 2001.

# Covenant and Imputation

I am most grateful and appreciative to Hafemann for his kind invitation to participate in the Biblical Theology Study Group held during the 2001 annual meeting of the Evangelical Theological Society in Colorado Springs to address the subject of Law and Gospel. I can only hope and pray that his spiritual fervor will result in the reclamation of the Protestant-Reformed teaching. See Chapter 4.

[15] The "merit" of Christ, in this view, merely parallels the "demerit" of Adam. Piper expressly states that no human creature, including Adam, could have merited anything from God. The issue here is far more than semantics.

[16] *John Piper on the Christian Life* 11.

[17] In the popular misinterpretation view of Paul and the law, the principle of works in Lev 18:5 is understood to be consistent with the principle of faith (thus the reading on the Pauline expression "obedience of faith," according to this argument). What this view clearly evinces, however, is antipathy for the works-inheritance principle so plainly and consistently expounded in Protestant orthodoxy. It is true that Protestant-Reformed scholasticism has been guilty at times – within certain *loci* of doctrinal formulation – of employing speculative dichotomies, such as the Thomistic nature/grace dualism. Contemporary Reformed theology has the obligation to reassess these alien, unbiblical constructs in its corpus of doctrine. (See endnote 13 above.) In this regard, it bears pointing out that Cornelius Van Til deserves credit for identifying the deficiencies in classical apologetics with respect to its propensity for rationalistic argumentation in defense of the truths of the Bible. Van Til stood virtually alone in his thoroughgoing criticisms of rationalism in all its guises and in his rejection of evidentialism in all its forms. His solitary stand does not in any way invalidate his understanding concerning the first principles of Reformed theology and hermeneutics.

[18] The strategy on the part of the seminary administration has been to accuse (falsely) critics of Shepherd, on grounds that no court of the church had yet declared his teaching heretical. (There is more to the history than this.) To be sure, it takes courage and tenacity

to confront the onslaughts of error in the church and in the academy. In terms of the confessional teaching of the Reformed churches, the Shepherd theology clearly falls outside the bounds of orthodoxy. Those who endorse Shepherd's theology are the ones who wish to reinterpret the Reformed tradition. For the record, Shepherd was dismissed from Westminster on grounds of expediency, even though the official document of the seminary explicitly declares his teaching to be outside the bounds of Scripture and confession. For more on this, see my account in *The Changing of the Guard* and in its sequel, "The Impact of Norman Shepherd's Teaching in Westminster Seminary," included in this volume as Chapters 6 and 7. (See also endnote 41 below.) The latter contains a detailed analysis of Gaffin's lectures first presented at the Kerux Conference in Lynnwood, Washington in August 2001. The content of these lectures has been presented in several other settings; it provided the substance of Gaffin's inaugural lecture as Charles Krahe Professor of Biblical and Systematic Theology on October 16, 2002. Another version appears in *The Practical Calvinist: An Introduction to the Presbyterian and Reformed Heritage* (ed. P. A. Lillback; Ross-shire: Christian Focus, 2002) 425-442. Gaffin's thinking is echoed in Craig B. Carpenter's essay "A Question of Union with Christ? Calvin and Trent on Justification," WTJ 64 (2002) 363-386, what amounts to a strange mix of orthodox and heterodox formulation.

[19] In addition to the struggles over the Shepherd theology in the Orthodox Presbyterian Church, the controversy looms large in the United Reformed Church, the Presbyterian Church in America, and, to a lesser extent, in the Christian Reformed Church.

[20] Kinnaird, a long-time supporter of Westminster Seminary in Philadelphia and ardent follower of Norman Shepherd, had appealed his case to the highest judicatory of the church, the General Assembly (OPC). During that round of debate in the courts of the OPC Kinnaird's teaching had been endorsed by Professor Richard Gaffin (one of the co-authors of the new theology at Westminster and one of the driving forces in the OPC, as well as in the seminary) and Samuel Logan, president of Westminster East. Other signers included Peter Lillback, a pastor in the Presbyterian Church

in America. For many years Lillback served as an adjunct professor on the Philadelphia campus aggressively promoting the Shepherd-Gaffin theology. The John Kinnaird case is only the latest chapter in the ongoing history of the controversy at Westminster, now well into its third decade. Professor Robert Strimple, recently retired from Westminster West, has taken his stand in opposition to the teaching of Kinnaird. This is a step in the right direction. (See my opening "Preface" for the outcome of the OPC's 2003 General Assembly.)

[21] See references in endnote 18 above.

[22] Many other seminary faculties have also been adversely effected by this heresy to one degree or another (such is the case at Covenant, Reformed, Mid-America Reformed, and Calvin Seminaries). The situation is mirrored in other parts of the globe – among evangelical-Reformed churches and institutions in Canada, Great Britain, South America, Australia, and elsewhere. The controversial subject that Trumper addresses in this review article is far from provincial. Nothing could be further from the truth. See Doug Barnes' reporting on Gaffin's lectures at Mid-America Reformed Seminary in *Christian Renewal* (December 16, 2002). In answer to the question "Has the Reformation misunderstood Paul?" – the subject of Gaffin's address – Gaffin argues that Reformed theology has "room to grow and improve, particularly in discussing how the finished act of justification by faith relates to the on-going application of salvation to believers" (p. 4). Barnes makes mention of the complex debates over the relationship of faith and works in the procurement of justification. He summarizes (quoting Gaffin): "'works are the integral fruit and evidence of faith,' wherein sanctification is an aspect of the on-going application of our justification which will culminate that last great day, in 'an open manifestation of what has been there all along – that Christ's righteousness has been imputed to me'" (p. 4). Note also the article by John P. Elliott, "Mid-America [Reformed Seminary] at 20+," which refers to the theological "clash" between Westminster West and Mid-America Reformed Seminary over the doctrine of the covenants, especially the views of Norman Shepherd (pp. 9, 18).

[23] Some would base Paul's teaching on changing cultural mores. This is a different hermeneutical approach, though equally unpersuasive.

[24] In Shepherd's view, works function coordinately with faith as the way or means of justification/salvation. In the view of Gaffin and Piper, they serve a subordinate role. The difference between these two opinions is wholly inconsequential. See my "Justification in Redemptive History," *WTJ* 43 (1981) 213-246; republished in *Covenant Theology in Reformed Perspective* 157-180.

[25] A degree of mystery surrounds Trumper's resignation, coinciding as it does with the ecclesiastical examination of the teaching of John Kinnaird (what is only a variation on the Shepherd-Gaffin theology) in the Orthodox Presbyterian Church, the denomination where Gaffin serves as an ordained minister of the Word and to which denomination the seminary has had very close ties since its founding. David McWilliams, systematician on the Dallas campus, has also resigned recently. It is quite apparent that Westminster East (which includes the Dallas campus) has difficulty holding its systematicians (ever since the departure of Norman Shepherd).

[26] It is Gaffin's *modus operandi* to employ the penmanship of others – in this case, Trumper – for the advancement of his thinking (in some instances as trial-balloons). This has enabled Gaffin to distance himself somewhat from direct criticism. The history of the seminary controversy, however, firmly establishes Gaffin as co-author of the Shepherd theology, and now the principal architect of the New Westminster School. That the faculty is fixated on this new theology of the covenants and justification is evident from recent issues of *The Westminster Theological Journal* (the Fall 2002 issue only being the latest in a series). Further indication of the theological trend can be gleaned from the doctoral dissertations written under the Westminster professors.

[27] Lanham, MD: University Press of America.

[28] *The Binding of God: Calvin's Role in the Development of Covenant Theology* (Grand Rapids: Baker, 2001), a reworking of his 1985 Westminster dissertation.

[29] Tim J. R. Trumper, "Covenant Theology and Constructive Calvinism," *WTJ* 63 (2002) 389.

[30] *Ibid.* 394.

[31] *Ibid.*

[32] *Ibid.* 396 n. 12.

[33] *Ibid.* 396 n. 13.

[34] *Ibid.* 403.

[35] Such was the conclusion reached in my doctoral study "The Mosaic Covenant and the Concept of Works in Reformed Hermeneutics: A Historical-Critical Analysis with Particular Attention to Early Covenant Eschatology" (Th.D. dissertation, Westminster Theological Seminary, 1980). See also my article "Paul's Letter to the Romans in the *New International Commentary on the New Testament* and in Contemporary Reformed Thought," *EvQ* 71 (1999) 3-24; republished in *Covenant Theology in Reformed Perspective* 227-245.

[36] Trumper writes: "the contemporary preoccupation among Westminster Calvinists with a covenant of works (notably the Murray-Kline debate) is myopic. . . . [It] has created unnecessarily a tension among those who really ought to be standing shoulder to shoulder in defense of federal theology" ("Constructive Calvinism" 387). Trumper's thinking is a delusion of the most virulent kind. There can be no admixture of truth and error in the proclamation and exposition of the Gospel of grace in Christ Jesus. The chasm between the two points of view could not be wider. Until the time when Gaffin gave endorsement to Shepherd's book *The Call of Grace* (published in 2000), it was Gaffin's strategy to promote Shepherd's theology at Westminster and elsewhere without mention of his name. Times have changed.

[37] There can be no doubt where Kline stands on the insidious and pernicious teaching of Shepherd and Gaffin. He has made himself clear. Trumper and his colleagues know and understand it – they simply cannot or will not accept it.

[38] "Constructive Calvinist" 395.

[39] See endnote 13 above.

[40] John M. Frame has knighted me *Defensor Fidei,* a title upon which I lay no special claim. I humbly, yet proudly, stand in a long line of confessionalists. For those who are Reformed in persuasion and theologically discerning we say "good night," "lights out" to perspectivalism. Frame's claim to orthodoxy is specious, his allegiance to the Reformation doctrine of justification by faith alone duplicitous – but such is the genius of multi-perspectivalism, by Frame's own design. See below "Appendix D," written prior to the appearance of Frame's *The Doctrine of God: A Theology of Lordship* (Phillipsburg: Presbyterian and Reformed, 2002), which contains two appendices attempting to interact with the substance of my critique of his work. No additional word need be sounded.

[41] See Kline's "Covenant Theology Under Attack," *New Horizons* 15 (February 1994) 3-5. The unedited version of this essay was widely disseminated by the congregation of Park Woods Orthodox Presbyterian Church in Kansas City, MO. President Clowney did finally come to denounce the teachings of Shepherd – along with the Board of Trustees – as contrary to the teaching of Scripture and the Reformed confessions. In the convoluted course of events the seminary trustees produced its "Reason and Specifications Supporting the Action of the Board of Trustees in Removing Professor Shepherd Approved by the Executive Committee of the Board (February 26, 1982)" to explain the action it had already taken. This document addressed the doctrinal errors, but agreement was reached to hide this evaluation as best as possible, thus obscuring the true state of affairs in reports to the seminary community and to the public at large. Statements issued through the media and elsewhere were to the effect that Shepherd had been dismissed

merely as a way for the seminary to put this controversy behind her. That prospect was never realized.

Trumper falsely and mischievously posits: "the Shepherd controversy of twenty years past has provided a convenient foil by which to attack Westminster Seminary" ("Constructive Calvinist" 389). In a later footnote he adds: "In this context it ought to be said that those intent on keeping alive the controversy surrounding Norman Shepherd do so precisely because that sad episode in the seminary's history appears to provide plausibility to what is otherwise a weak argument. . . . [I]t reflects more directly and more negatively on the credibility of the apologetic orientation of Kline's theology" (p. 402 n. 17). Gaffin's endorsement of Shepherd's recent book *The Call of Grace* (published in 2000 by Westminster's unofficial press, Presbyterian and Reformed) apparently does not factor in at all! Gaffin cannot disassociate himself from Shepherd's work – not without renouncing his own heterodox views. (Of course, Gaffin does not care to disassociate himself from his own views which coincide with Shepherd's.) By appeal to the opinion of James B. Torrance, Trumper attempts to lay down the line of demarcation between orthodoxy and neoorthodoxy quite narrowly, wanting his readers to think that "the critical issue is the extent of the atonement" (p. 394 n. 7). Granted that is one critical issue, there are others as well – most notably, the Law/Gospel antithesis. The Shepherd controversy was brought to Trumper's attention when he candidated at Westminster for the teaching post. He had the responsibility and duty to grapple with Shepherd's teaching as he worked alongside Gaffin, his senior in the systematics department.

[42] "Constructive Calvinism" 404.

[43] *Ibid.* 397-98. Concerning the classic Law/Gospel distinction, Trumper adds: "A uniform definition and a convincing warrant for its hermeneutical usefulness is particularly requisite if the Protestant community is to remain persuaded that the antithesis is indeed a yardstick of orthodoxy. In short, Jeon's volume would have proven more useful had he not assumed so many first principles which, while acceptable to Murray and Kline and their admirers, are not necessarily so to the contemporary reader" (p. 398). Obviously, the

Law/Gospel contrast is a negotiable element for Trumper and the New School. Quoting from his doctoral dissertation, "it was the ongoing necessity to defend the doctrine of Justification that kept Protestants preoccupied with the forensic elements of the faith, with the result that the emphasis on law came increasingly to predominate over grace (especially a familial portrayer of grace)" (p. 398 n. 15). Trumper and his colleagues are convinced they know a better way to elucidate Reformed, biblical theology.

[44] *Ibid.* 399.

[45] *Ibid.* Trumper maintains that "a portrayal of the gospel that does not leave us overwhelmed by the superlative love of God in providing us with a meritorious Savior, is tantamount to a heresy of silence" (400). He speaks of "the past and present failure of the persistent one-dimensional approach to the defense of Reformed orthodoxy" – what is the "exclusive pre-occupation with the forensic aspects of the gospel" (p. 401). He repeatedly accuses the traditionalists (whom he labels the "orthodox Calvinists" – a nomenclature with which I am proud to be identified!) – of the "glib manner" in which they employ the Law/Gospel antithesis. There is nothing of substance in this charge; it is mere rhetoric on the part of Trumper.

[46] See, for example, W. Robert Godfrey's essay "The Westminster Larger Catechism" in *To Glorify and Enjoy God: A Commemoration of the 350th Anniversary of the Westminster Assembly* (ed. J. L. Carson and D. W. Hall; Carlisle [Edinburgh]: The Banner of Truth Trust, 1994) 127-142. Countering the evaluation of Godfrey, staunch opponent of the Shepherd theology, Trumper snidely dubs the subject of Jeon's doctoral study "a side-show in the context of the broader Reformed tradition" ("Constructive Calvinist" 398). To be sure, the faculty of Westminster East has made a circus of this theological crisis, what actually is the watershed in the history of the seminary.

[47] "Constructive Calvinist" 404.

[48] "Law, Gospel, and Covenant: Reassessing Some Emerging Antitheses," *WTJ* 64 (2002) 287. It is inexplicable to me how Horton,

President of the Alliance of Confessing Evangelicals (ACE), can reduce this long-standing dispute to an "internecine controversy" (279) when he knows better. ACE, what is a disparate group of evangelical leaders, has been unable to find common ground in recent years in addressing the current scene, notably in regards to this highly controversial dispute concerning the Law and the Gospel. See Appendix B.

# Appendix A

# Richard Gaffin's Teaching on Justification and the Covenants: A Summary and Critique[1]

### 1. Summary Statement

Sinners are justified by grace through faith on the grounds of Christ's righteousness, including both his obedience to the law of God and his death on the cross (Christ's active and passive obedience). Good works are necessary for salvation and are inseparable from true, saving faith. The way of salvation, that is, justification, is the way of faith and works. These (good) works are not meritorious; they are a fruit of the Spirit's work in the believer's life. Justification is present and future – the believer united to Christ in his death and resurrection is already justified; at the same time, (final) justification awaits the end of the age. On the Last Day, believers will be justified consummately. Only the doers of the law will be justified on that Day. In summation, the believer is justified by faith and works. Faith alone cannot justify, for without good works (that is, personal holiness) no one will see the Lord. "Justification is in the mode of perseverance."

The "ground" of life and salvation is exclusively the righteousness of Christ. That righteousness is both imputed to the believer and inwrought in the believer. Justification, as God's present and future declaration, is contingent upon the believer's exercise of faith and obedience. The "merit" or credit goes to Jesus Christ alone, but human response – expressed through the exercise of faith and obedience – is also requisite. On the basis of Christ's substitutionary work on the cross and by means of the Spirit's inworking the believer is placed in a position analogous to that of Adam prior to his fall into sin. Once again, the sons and daughters of God have the obligation to produce works that are pleasing to him. Just as the believer's good works in the post-Fall age are not meritorious, so also Adam's obedience in the pre-Fall age would not have been meritorious of God's blessing and reward. *God's grace informs every covenant relationship, from the creation of the world to the end of age.* The only exception is the covenant between the Father and the Son: Because he is the Son of God, Christ merits the promised reward, specifically, a people redeemed by the blood of the Lamb.

The first covenant with Adam (the so-called Covenant of Works) and every subsequent covenant between God and his people in the history of redemption (the so-called Covenant of Grace) are expressions of divine grace to those who are mere creatures of the dust. The creature never earns anything from God – every blessing is a gift of free, unmerited grace. Man ever remains an unprofitable servant. God is never obliged to bless or reward him for any accomplishment. Had Adam sustained the time of probation, he would not have earned anything at all from God. All is a gift of God's grace, including life eternal. Adam simply rendered what was his due. So also, in the Covenant of Grace the believer produces good works, what is merely his due. Before and after the Fall, the creature is justified in God's sight, that is, "right" with God, on condition of faith (dependence upon God) and obedience (working faith). What was required of Adam at the beginning was perfect obedience. Subsequent to the Fall, however, God accepts imperfect obedience from sinners.

## 2. The View of Norman Shepherd

Shepherd flatly denies the doctrine of the "Covenant of Works."[2] According to him, there is only one creaturely relationship in covenant with God. That relationship or bond is established and maintained by God – by grace alone. Reward and blessing from God are never merited by creatures of the dust. Even in the Father-Son relationship, blessing is never a matter of meritorious attainment. What distinguishes God covenantal grace is his paternal love for his sons and daughters. Justification – or righteous-ness – in the sight of God is always and only by grace through faith. That was true for Adam prior to his transgression of God's commandment not to eat from the tree of the knowledge of good and evil, as it was true for Adam after his disobedience. So also with regard to the Second Adam, Jesus Christ: He lived his perfect life in faith, sustained by the Spirit of God. Obedience always yields divine blessing, received by grace alone. After the Fall, the promise of salvation – granted to those who keep covenant with God – offers hope to sinners who turn from their sins and cleave to Christ. In so doing, the grace of justification restores sinners to their right-standing before God, wherein they are empowered to fulfill the law – as required of Adam before the Fall. There is pure continuity respecting the keeping of the law before and after the Fall, just as there is one divine-human covenant before and after the Fall. The doers of the law are those who keep covenant with God, obeying God sincerely and without personal gain (or human "merit").

The covenant relationship is always a matter of divine promise and command. Promise refers to the God's bestowal of grace to obedient covenant-keepers; command refers to that obedience which is necessary to preserve and sustain the covenant relationship on the part of the children of God. The event of the Fall does not alter this fundamental, covenantal continuum. Works as an expression of faith are necessary for justification (so Shepherd interprets James); accordingly, the keepers of the covenant are justified by faith and works (both are the "instrumental" means to justification). That is to say, faith and works are correlative in the way of salvation. Election and final justification are attained only in the way of persevering faith and good works. Salvation is contingent upon human perseverance, faith working through love.

### 3. Comparison and Critique

Firstly, Gaffin's formulation obscures the sole instrumentality of faith in receiving the imputed righteousness of Christ for life and salvation secured for those redeemed by his shed blood. (The imputation of Christ's righteousness as legal "grounds" of justification plays no significant or meaningful role in Gaffin's interpretation.) According to the Bible, Christ merits the reward by fulfilling the law of God on behalf of the ungodly (God's elect). The apostle Paul draws an explicit parallel between the First and the Second Adams. The "one act of righteousness" is the *meritorious* ground of life and blessing. Contrary to Gaffin's teaching, had Adam passed probation, his "one act of righteousness" would have earned (merited) for him and for all his posterity the reward promised to him in the first covenant. Secondly, Gaffin confounds the imputed and inwrought righteousness of Christ (the latter being personal holiness/sanctification) in the procurement of the justification of sinners. According to Gaffin and Shepherd, the way of salvation is faith *and* works. Thirdly, it is misleading and confusing on the part of Gaffin to speak of justification as future. To be sure, there is a future aspect to the justification of the ungodly, namely, open acquittal and final vindication of what has already been fixed and established in the life of God's elect.

According to orthodox Reformed-Protestant theology, the principle of inheritance in the first covenant with Adam at creation is that of works ("law"). The principle of inheritance in the covenant renewed with God's people after the Fall is that of saving faith. (The term "grace" in the Bible is synonymous with "gospel," the good news of salvation by grace through faith, freedom from the demand for perfect, personal obedience as grounds of reward.) Gaffin denies the classic Protestant law/gospel contrast. God's requirement that the creature be obedient and walk in covenant-faithfulness as the way to blessing, according to Gaffin, is wholly *gracious*. Accordingly, God's law is a manifestation of his grace. If grace is everywhere present in the covenant relationship, what guarantee is there that the believer – now under the new covenant – is *secure* in Christ? According to the teaching of Scripture, "grace" is God's remedy for sin and disobedience. God's grace secures the promised inheritance. It cannot fail. The implication of Gaffin's teaching is that God's grace (which he insists was operative before the Fall) was insufficient. It could not deliver on its promise. Why was perfect obedience required of the covenant-keeper under the Covenant of Works, but not required of the covenant-keeper under the Covenant of Grace? The answer is that Jesus Christ has fully and completely satisfied the requirement of God's law on the behalf of sinners. In accordance with the holiness and justice of God perfect obedience pleases him, and is worthy of blessing and reward. Would God be just to curse or destroy Adam even if he had rendered perfect obedience to his covenant

Lord during his time of probation? Of course not. Expressly in terms of the divine covenant (and the circumstance of probation), God would have been unjust in not rewarding Adam for obedience. According to the probationary terms of the first covenant before the Fall, Adam's representative obedience would, indeed, have been meritorious.

Fidelity to Scripture requires us to maintain these points of doctrine: (1) good works, though not the instrument of justification (whereby believers receive the righteousness of Christ), are nevertheless the necessary fruit or evidence of justifying faith; (2) the final vindication of the saints is not contingent upon good works (their standing is already secure in Christ by grace through faith); (3) the theological term "grace" is applicable only to the post-Fall situation (application of this term to the pre-Fall epoch only leads to confusion and error); (4) the meritorious ground of salvation is the righteousness of Christ (including his active and passive obedience), which satisfies the legal demand of the first covenant made with Adam in the Garden; (5) the principle of law-inheritance is antithetical to the principle of faith-inheritance (denial of this biblical truth results in the commingling of law and grace, faith and works in justification – precisely what occurs in the Shepherd-Gaffin theology); and (6) the Mosaic law brings the principle of works-inheritance to bear in the administration of temporal life in the land of Canaan (at the same time, the principle of faith-inheritance governs entrance into the heavenly, eternal kingdom).

**NOTES**

[1] Richard B. Gaffin, Jr., the Charles Krahe Professor of Biblical and Systematic Theology, stands at the very center of the doctrinal

controversy, still unresolved at Westminster Seminary. For this reason we are appending this brief overview of his views. It is not simply a matter of poor judgment on the part of Gaffin in endorsing the heretical teachings of Norman Shepherd and John Kinnaird, but of active promotion of this deviant theology, of which he is the co-author. Subtlety of expression can very easily mislead the uninformed reader in thinking that what Gaffin is saying is nothing different from what has already been said by the Reformed scholastics. The differences between the Gaffin-Shepherd theology and Protestant-Reformed orthodoxy, however, are real and substantive. More than thirty years of false teaching at Westminster Seminary have made their impact upon evangelical-Reformed churches for the worse. See my exchange with Scott Clark, John Frame, and Doug Barnes posted on The Trinity Foundation's website: www.trinityfoundation.org (appended to the March/April 2001 issue of *The Trinity Review*).

[2] Although Shepherd explicitly denies the idea of the "covenant of works" and the idea of "merit" in connection with the obedience of Christ imputed to believers, Gaffin's view does not differ substantially from Shepherd's. The Shepherd and Gaffin formulations are essentially identical. At times Gaffin employs traditional terminology, but imposes new or different meaning to his terms. Gaffin's distinctive formulation has given the impression to many that his position differs from Shepherd's. That is mere illusion. The fact remains, Gaffin heartily endorses Shepherd's theology, because it is his theology. Together they have crafted this new teaching at Westminster Seminary.

# Appendix B

**Book Review**
Michael S. Horton, *Covenant and Eschatology: The Divine Drama*. Louisville, London: Westminster John Knox, 2002.

The author, Michael S. Horton, has produced here a kind of theological prolegomenon that employs Reformed covenant theology as the entrance into the field of biblical interpretation and church doctrine. Horton is a gifted writer and a popular communicator. This book represents his first attempt at constructing a weighty tome in theological system, what constitutes merely the first in a series. *Covenant and Eschatology* is the introductory volume in a new project, a fresh presentation of Reformed federalism for the third millennium. How well does Horton succeed in restating the tradition? That is the question for his readership.

There is a great deal of good insight and interaction with contemporary theology, notably, the narrative theology associated with Yale University and Divinity School. In fact, Horton indicates that the major aim of this study is to engage the Yale school by means of a sympathetic, yet searching, critique of narrative theology, that school of contemporary interpretation which may benefit most, Horton hopes, from serious dialogue with (modified) Reformed federalism. (Horton was for two years a research fellow at Yale.) Regrettably, Horton's presentation, in my reading, is marred by a significant degree of inconsistency and contradiction. This leaves the reader in a quandary. Exactly what shape does Horton want Reformed covenant theology to take? His ties to the (new) Westminster school only underscore the gravity and importance of his undertaking.

Nine chapters are divided into two parts: "God Acts in History" and "God Speaks." The extended metaphor for Horton's brand of covenant theology is reflected in the subtitle of the book – in a word, it is *drama*. Though fresh and contemporary, Horton's accent on drama, in my judgment, tends to trivialize both the biblical narrative and the worship and witness of the church. More substantively, it entails a false understanding of the role of faith and life, doctrine and experience, in the interpretation of Scripture (specifically, in the mistaken notion of theology as *application*). A student of John Frame (though his name does not appear in the book), Horton has been heavily influenced by his Westminster professor, one who has, in turn, been shaped by the school of linguistic analysis associated with Hans-Georg Gadamer. (In this formative period of his theological education Horton is also indebted to the teaching of Yale professor Nicholas Wolterstorff.) The problem in much of contemporary theological interpretation is the urge to be creative, to say something new and intriguing. It is the aspiration on the part of church theologians to gain the attention of sleepy parishioners, while catching the eye of secular academicians. One may ask whether it is realistic to think that these two – church and public university – can ever meet. Horton yearns for "imagination" in theological discourse and interpretation of the Bible (244). Rather than viewing the hermeneutical enterprise as creatively imaginative, as Horton recommends, interpreters within the tradition of historic Reformed Protestantism down through the ages have insisted that theology be constructively reinterpretive: we think God's thoughts after him. There is no room for creative thinking (in terms of new ideas). Rather, what we find in the history of Reformed doctrine is the *recovery* of biblical truth in the life and mind of the church. If Horton agrees, then that needs to be clarified in this book.

The opening "Introduction" lays out the program and goal of Horton's study in covenant theology. The aim is "to integrate biblical theology and systematic theology on the basis of scripture's own intrasystematic categories of covenant and eschatology" (1). Horton looks to the sixteenth- and seventeenth-century federalists as guiding lights, but is insistent that he does not favor a mere repristination of their thinking. "Our precritical forebears will be treated here as important, though not definitive. Much has happened since Ursinus and Turretin, and these erudite Christian thinkers would be among the first to insist that we take account of progress in relevant disciplines" (4). Well and good. Then the question is: what shape does Horton wish to give to the theological system? And what is to be said of modern-day biblical criticism? Here Horton blurs the picture and confounds issues in his argumentation. A large part of the problem is Horton's reading of modern Dutch and Dutch-American covenant theology (including the biblical theology movement in Calvinist circles). Here lies the major flaw in Horton's study, namely, the confutation of two opposing theologies, Calvinism and neo-Calvinism (including Barthianism). Horton fails to distinguish properly between the views of theologians like G. C. Berkouwer, Herman Ridderbos, and Richard Gaffin, on the one hand, and those of Herman Bavinck, Geerhardus Vos, and Meredith Kline, on the other. The former repeatedly emphasize dialecticism with regard to the believer's present experience of salvation, the soteric benefits associated with individual union with Christ in the (traditional) *ordo salutis*. In this view, for example, the truth of the definitive, once-for-all justification of the saints is severely compromised, if not denied. Invariably, the traditional Reformed federalists and their modern-day practitioners are accused of separating the application of salvation (*ordo salutis*) from the accomplishment of salvation (*historia salutis*). "The result," writes Horton, "is that we often fail to recognize the revolutionary logic of biblical (especially Pauline) eschatology, in which the future is semirealized in the present and the individual is included in a wider eschatological activity" (6-7). Does Horton really believe that Protestant-Reformed Orthodoxy missed this basic teaching? If not, the author must exercise far greater care and provide specificity in his challenges to and modifications of traditional covenant theology. (See further Chapter 7 in this volume.)

Of course, there is plenty of room for improvement and clarification within the Reformed theological tradition. One area concerns the subject of the relationship between cult (the worship and faith of the church) and culture (the common-grace institution, more broadly speaking). But even here, more reflection and interaction with opposing views are required on the part of our author. Horton favors the church's engagement in the public arena, encouraging the church to implement social programs and ministries to the poor and disenfranchised. Here it would do well for Horton to interact with the insightful teaching of Meredith Kline, among others, as regards the covenantal distinction between cult and culture. In this connection, there is – contrary to Horton's suggestion – little in liberation theology to warrant sympathetic embrace. The goal of the Reformed ministry in Word and Sacrament is not the transformation of communities, but the cultivation of a sanctified people, a kingdom wherein righteousness and truth prevail. Such a spiritual kingdom transcends all social and geo-political entities. Another element in Reformed theology demanding clarification and, in some cases, reformulation concerns the application of the classic Protestant Law/Gospel antithesis in its doctrine of the covenants, notably, in its interpretation of the Mosaic covenant. Even here, concern needs to be expressed over Horton's analysis. He writes: "In his active obedience as the Second Adam, the Servant fulfills the law on behalf of his new humanity, rather than abolishing it; redeems nature instead of eradicating it" (33). Later in the book he makes the claim that "Both Luther and Calvin insisted upon the distinction (though not separation) between law (command) and gospel (promise)" (136). What must be asserted in bold and unambiguous terms is the truth of Christ's fulfillment of all righteousness in the accomplishment of salvation for the elect of God. The legal demand of the original Covenant of Works set before the First Adam was fully satisfied by the Second Adam. That demand upon those united to Christ through faith has been abrogated, pure and simple. Such is the justice of God in justifying sinners. Regrettably, Horton's view of the Mosaic covenant is much closer to that of the dispensational school (in which he was reared) than the Calvinist. Despite the peculiarities of the old dispensation of law, the Mosaic economy is part of the single, ongoing Covenant of Grace. The Mosaic covenant itself is a *renewal* of the Abrahamic covenant. The law-principle operative in the symbolico-typical sphere of life in the land of Canaan, what distinguishes the old covenant from the new, terminates with the establishment of the new and better covenant; in so doing, shadow gives way to reality. Accordingly, when Horton asserts that "law and gospel, wrath and love, [are] in both testaments" (237), there is need of further amplification and clarification. On this and other facets of current theological study and debate, see my *Covenant Theology in Reformed Perspective: Collected Essays and Book Reviews in Historical, Biblical, and Systematic Theology* (Eugene, OR: Wipf and Stock, 2000).

Then there is the dispute concerning the nature of theological (and moral) discourse itself. In the first place, how do we come to a knowledge of God? Here we meet Horton the apologist (a position recently assumed by Horton on the faculty of Westminster Seminary in California). Horton contends that "the only knowledge of God that could be gleaned apart from God's own gracious initiative would be confused and utterly equivocal apart from God's initiative in self-communication. . . . After all, it is not God's inner essence but God's revealed character, intentions, and actions made explicit in Christ that concern humanity in its concrete situation" (8). More than once Horton asserts that revelation is subservient to redemption. This conceptualization leads to a christomonistic understanding of covenant and revelation. Horton's formulation also perpetuates the faulty nature/grace dichotomy so deeply embedded within federal scholasticism. Analogical (eschatological) discourse, according to Horton, provides the bridge between nature and grace, reason and revelation. Additionally, we are told, "Analogical thinking is necessarily dialectical thinking" (ibid.). Here again we note the convergence in Horton's thinking of covenant eschatology with dialecticism. He writes: Barth and his postliberal ("narrative") heirs have indicated the right direction in this whole matter of translation. . . . Christians live in this world, not in a text. That is to say, they live on a public stage and not in a private realm of textual world-projection. . . . As Calvin demonstrates in his dialectic between the creator and the creature in his opening to the *Institutes,* all knowledge of God – and indeed of all reality – is always a personal knowledge, a knowledge-in-relationship. . . . Since the creator of all reality is a person, all of that reality that God voluntarily produces exists in relationship"(14, 16). Let it is said, genuine Reformed interpretation has no affinity to the Barthian hermeneutic. While the creator/creature distinction does mean that human knowledge is analogical in nature, it is not dialectical (there is no conflict between opposing realities). Furthermore, Reformed theological interpretation acknowledges the priority of doctrine over life, enlightened (regenerated) reason over experience. The historicity of God's action and speech and the historicity of human life in the confines of a particular time and place are not of equal, "dramatic" weight in the interpretation of Scripture. At the root of Horton's theologizing is a misappropriation of biblical theology (redemptive revelation in its historical unfolding) in the system of Reformed doctrine. As saints redeemed by Christ and regenerated by his Spirit, we are to be transformed by the renewing of our minds. This – what Horton wrongly caricatures as "the static view of textual meaning" (139) – stands in opposition to his "holistic" model of drama, one which gives equal place to reason and experience. (Horton commends the moral and philosophical views of Alasdair MacIntyre.)

Finally, Horton's apologetic misplaces emphasis on probability theorizing, rather than certainty based upon the self-attesting Scriptures. Perhaps in his zeal to be a "conversation partner" among university academicians Horton does not want to come across "preaching" to his audience, and so he favors an apologetic that will appeal to those on other side of the theological spectrum. (Horton's apologetical stance thus differs sharply from that of Cornelius Van Til, who held tenaciously to the fundamental antithesis between Christianity and secularism in all its forms.) The best case for which Horton can argue is "the possibility of determining the [biblical] author's intentions *in so far as those intentions are embedded in the text itself*" (155). The underlying problem, as I see it, is that Horton's apologetic (mis)places emphasis on the biblical narrative – as an isolated object of study – rather than on the foundational doctrine of Reformed epistemology, what was the strength in Van Til's apologetical defense of the gospel and of the Calvinistic world-and-life view.

These criticisms of Horton's theological proposal should not in any way be interpreted as deprecatory of the project in hand. They are intended to elicit refinement and modification in critical places. There are sections of discussion in this book which offer an alternative reading of Horton's theology. These need to be taken into account; however, there must also be consistency in presentation. Perhaps another reading of *Covenant and Eschatology* on the part of Horton will result in a happy resolution and conclusion.

# Appendix C

**Book Review**
Willem J. van Asselt, *The Federal Theology of Johannes Cocceius (1603-1669)*. Trans. by Raymond A. Blacketer. Studies in the History of Christian Thought, vol. 100. Leiden, Boston, Köln: Brill, 2001.

Professor Asselt has produced an exceptional study in Reformed covenant theology by way of summarizing – and commending to the churches – the teaching of one of its most distinguished and prominent post-Reformation systematicians (and biblical theologians), Johannes Cocceius, one who was not well understood or appreciated in his own day. The reasons for this are many and varied. Van Asselt offers some perspective concerning this widespread misunderstanding. Most importantly, however, the author of this one-hundredth volume in *Studies in the History of Christian Thought* has performed an invaluable service in faithfully re-presenting the covenant theology of Cocceius.

Though weak on American Reformed scholarship, this study will unquestionably stand the test of time. It serves well as a compendium on Reformed covenant theology in a critical period of Reformation/post-Reformation thought (more specifically) and on Reformed dogmatics (more generally). Virtually every *loci* in Christian dogmatics is touched upon to one extent or another. In all essentials, Cocceius' theology embodies standard Reformed teaching, claiming nothing original in its breadth and depth of formulation. Comments van Asselt: "His work, of course, had its limitations – a fact of which he himself was well aware. Accordingly, two years before his death, he wrote to [Johann Heinrich] Heidegger in Zürich, 'All my work is unremarkable' (*Omnia mea sunt mediocra*). Such was the modesty with which Coccieus was graced" (33). To the credit of our present author, he has shown discrimination and discernment in summarizing accurately so vast a theological output as that produced by Coccieus. Additionally, van Asselt has mastered both the history and theology of the Reformed covenantal tradition, evident in his judicious handling of important doctrinal elements within scholastic orthodoxy.

As made crystal clear in this study, the warp and woof of Coccieus' covenant theology is the traditional Protestant Law/Gospel antithesis, what van Asselt identifies as "the hub upon which the whole wheel of dogmatics turns" (1). Unquestionably, the Law/Gospel contrast is the central plank in Protestant-Reformed theology, especially in the doctrine of the covenant(s), the *principium* of Coccieus' theology (143). At the same time, van Asselt rightly points out that this theological interpretation of the Bible is decidedly practical and devotional in orientation (which may explain, in part, the appeal of covenant theology to the English Puritans and the Dutch precisionists). "Above all, the interpretation of the Scripture is to be undertaken by and for the church. For this reason, there must not be an absolute separation between exegesis and proclamation" (134). There are, observes van Asselt,

> two factors to which we must pay attention in our analysis of Coccieus' theological method. The first is the doctrine of the covenant and the pinnacle or crown, the epitome, and the goal of the whole of the theological enterprise (*totius theologiae apex, consummatio et finis*); the second is the concept of the twofold knowledge of God. These two aspects are the two factors which together characterize the structure of Coccieus' theology.

Essential for the interpretation of Coccpius' theology is the role that the interpreter assigns to each of these factors in elucidating Coccpius' theological system. [143]

We begin by commenting briefly on Coccpius' doctrine of the knowledge of God in relation to the divine covenants. The idea of covenant as relationship with God (though broken by virtue of the sin of our first parents in the Garden of Eden) is innate. All humankind has some sense of and longing for relationship with God (39, compare 151; see also the discussion of Jürgen Moltmann's analysis of the concept of *amicitia* in Coccpius' theology, 311-12). One of the unsettled, contentious questions relating to Coccpius' thought is the matter of the relation between theology and (Cartesian) philosophy, more specifically, the place of natural theology in his dogmatics. (This is perhaps the least satisfying section of van Asselt's presentation, in that it leaves the reader with many unanswered questions, especially with regard to Coccpius' use of the "proofs" for the existence of God. Among other things, this reviewer would like to have seen some interaction with the incisive critique of the traditional proofs found in the work of the American-Dutch theologian Cornelius Van Til.) Van Asselt states that "natural knowledge of God and revelation are not mutually exclusive; they complement each other" (69), without ever defining precisely what he means by the term "natural revelation" or "natural theology." There is a right and a wrong interpretation and employment of such revelation from God. In the first place, we do recognize that there are those truths which God has implanted within the human heart, truths which are universally suppressed in unrighteousness, to one degree or another. But secondly, these remnants of truth – what constitutes, in part, the grounds for human accountability and obedience to God – are never the *source* of theology, simply because they are insufficient and unreliable in the repristination of divine revelation (including redemptive revelation now necessary for our salvation). Concerning the views of Cocceius, Van Asselt concedes: "The real truth about salvation must be drawn from the word of revelation. Reason (*ratio*), therefore, cannot be the *principium fidei*" (69). He ends this section on the knowledge of God by asserting: "[Cocceius'] 'epistemology' has a theological purpose, but he also includes Christology in this discussion; nor is the pneumatological element lacking from the mix. Without the love and fear of the Lord, which are bestowed by the Holy Spirit, none of the areas of theology can be properly studied" (71). The reader is still left with a number of unanswered questions. It is not sufficient to say that "external factors brought Cocceianism and Cartesianism together" (83). Why did Cocceius resort to its use? Nor is it an adequate or compelling reason to conclude that "There were common enemies to be fought, and thus the two systems were, so to speak, driven into an alliance" (83). I would agree with van Asselt, in any case, that the question of the relationship between philosophy and theology in Cocceius thought is not finally answered by reference to the larger issue of the relationship between Protestant-Reformed orthodoxy and scholasticism (viewed as a theological methodology). One can employ the scholastic method without confounding speculative natural theology and revealed theology.

Just a further word on hermeneutics: van Asselt notes that "There is in fact a certain amount of tension in the *Summa Theologia* between these two aspects [what we would call the biblical-theological and the systematic], particularly in the doctrine of God and the divine attributes; but considered as a whole, the perspective of salvation history is not obscured by Cocceius' complementary use of the loci method" (61). What faced Cocceius in his interpretation of Scripture, written for the benefit of the church, is true for every theologian, past and present.

Whatever "tensions" exist between the two disciplines – biblical theology and systematics – they are not insuperable, nor are they to be avoided at all cost. The two interpretive approaches to the Word are genuinely complementary; more than that, the one impacts the another, and that reciprocally. Christian theology must necessarily employ both approaches, each of which are found in the Bible itself. Lastly, "systematic theology for Cocceius means reflection upon the results of exegesis" (139). The point to be made here is that exegesis *requires* of the interpreter that he or she give adequate attention to both the history of redemption (with special attention to the single, unifying Covenant of Grace spanning the entire period of redemptive history, from the Fall to the return of Christ) and doctrinal systematization (emphasizing the unity of biblical teaching). One other regret in this regard is that van Asselt did not interact more substantially with the work of Geerhardus Vos, a modern-day exponent of Cocceian biblical theology.

Before drawing this review to a close, we must return to what is the pivotal doctrine in Cocceius' theology, namely, the doctrine of the covenants, beginning with the prelapsarian Covenant of Works. Nothing out of mainstream federal thinking is to be found here, with the exception of Cocceius' doctrine of the progressive abrogation of the Covenant of Works in the course of redemptive history. Even here, Cocceius' views – with some additional clarification and nuancing – have much in their favor. The climax of the Covenant of Grace, to be sure, is the atoning work of Christ, which fulfills all righteousness for the sake of God's elect.

> Briefly stated, this doctrine depicts five stages (*gradus*) through which God leads humanity to eternal life, and in which the consequences of the violation of the covenant of works through sin are gradually nullified. [271]

Van Asselt urges the churches to reclaim Cocceius' federal interpretation of the Bible – and for that (in most respects) we are very thankful, given the posture now assumed by many contemporary theologians in their forthright repudiation of the teaching of classic federalism. Van Asselt argues (inconsistently throughout the book) that "From the very beginning the relationship of God with humanity is viewed in the light of the covenant (of works). By virtue of creation, and as the bearer of the image of God, primordial humanity is inclined toward a covenantal relationship with God" (58). Later he explains:

> The covenant of works does not follow automatically from creation. Humanity is created *for* a covenantal relationship, but does not immediately stand in this relationship. . . . It is not a natural "given" with creation, but rather a "second miracle of the love of God," the first being the act of creation itself. In their created being as such, human persons do not have, by virtue of creation, any claim to the enjoyment of the blessed friendship of God. On the other hand, we must think that Cocceius sees two states of humanity before the Fall into sin: first a natural state, followed by a covenantal state. Cocceius' concept of the covenant of works avoids both of these two extremes: that of identifying creation and the covenant of works, and that of positing a duality of creation and covenant. [259-60]

> The relationship of peace and friendship with God, however, is not simply part and parcel of the divine-human relationship that exists by virtue of creation. Instead, such friendship is a gift of God's goodness (*bonitas Dei*) above and beyond that mere Creator-creature relationship. [268]

Following Cocceius and the scholastic federal tradition, Van Asselt mistakenly views all God's works in creation and recreation in terms of divine grace – "grace" in the broadest, nonsoteric sense (more on this below). More significant and crucial, however, is the emphasis upon Law as *legal demand,* first set forth in the original covenant with Adam as federal head. Nothing could be more important in biblical theology than the acknowledgment of the biblical distinction between the Law and the Gospel of free grace in Christ Jesus, mediator of the Covenant of Grace. The demand for perfect, personal obedience is foundational for understanding humanity made in the image of God and Christ as reconciler between God and humankind (the doctrine of substitutionary atonement). Succinctly stated, Law "rewards obedience." In (soteric) justification, Christ's obedience is the *meritorious grounds of life and salvation* (220).

> The character of the eternal pact (and of the covenant of works) is thus one of obligation, not of grace, as is the case in the covenant of grace. The eternal pact is a description of the legal position of Christ as Sponsor, just as the covenant of works describes the legal position of humanity in the state of rectitude. The parallel between Christ and Adam, as first and second Adam, finds its origin here. [242 - Note the different reference in van Asselt's use of the term "grace" in this context, one which contemplates *redemptive* provision.]

One nagging issue in Reformed federalism, already alluded to above, is the (commonplace) misapplication of the biblical term "grace" to the pre-Fall epoch. Here, once again, van Asselt is thoroughly inconsistent with his own analysis and critique of Coccceius' teaching, whose teaching is representative of federal theology as a whole. In this connection also it is highly misleading to speak of "salvation" prior to the Fall. Underlying all this discussion is van Asselt's reluctance to identify the legal demand of the covenant of works as *meritorious*. On this point of doctrine van Asselt is thoroughly inconsistent in his argumentation. Another related issue requiring further reflection (and reformulation) in this book is the role of the Spirit of God in both the creation and recreation epochs and in the old and new covenants. Our author is not entirely clear in expounding upon the similarities and differences of the Spirit's working in the creation/recreation epochs and in the two economies of redemption, the old and the new. Additionally, van Asselt mistakenly restricts the mediatorial role of the second Person of the Trinity to the provisions of redemption. The Son is not seen as mediator of the covenant between God and man established at creation. (Of course, there is no need before the Fall for the messianic ministry of the Son of God with respect to the accomplishment of humanity's redemption from sin.)

One of the appendices takes up the question of the origins of the doctrine of the Covenant of Works. Though brief, it is extremely well stated and well answered. In van Asselt's opinion (with which I am in full agreement), federalism is a later maturation of early covenant theology, the latter development standing in continuity with the preceding period of doctrinal formulation. Essentially what we have in the Reformation, post-Reformation age are not two divergent streams, but rather two *convergent* streams of covenantal thinking, each bearing all the essential elements necessary for the exposition of the doctrine of the Covenant of Works. In sharp contrast to the thesis advanced by Peter Lillback our present author rightly assesses Calvin's place in the history of covenant theology. Far from being the first (serious) attempt to evaluate Calvin's teaching, Lillback's study, *The Binding of God: Calvin's Role in the Development of Covenant Theology* (Grand Rapids: Baker Academic, 2001), falsely aligns Calvin's doctrine of the covenant with the teaching of medieval voluntarism, specifically, the nominalist doctrine of congruent merit, and in so doing dissolves the crucial

Law/Gospel antithesis so crucial in Calvin's thought and those in his theological tradition. (The Law/Gospel contrast is writ large across the pages of Scripture.) For further analysis of the teachings of Reformed theology, see my *Covenant Theology in Reformed Perspective: Collected Essays and Book Reviews in Historical, Biblical, and Systematic Theology* (Eugene, OR: Wipf and Stock, 2000).

There are many other facets of Reformed doctrine – restated by Cocceius in his writings – that could be accented in this book review, such as the origins of the biblical doctrine of eschatology in the creation account (surprisingly, van Asselt omits explicit mention of the doctrine of probation, an important element in a mature statement of the doctrine of the covenants), typological interpretation of the Bible as a distinguishing feature of covenant theology, the relationship between the covenant and the decrees of God (including double predestination, seen as a process of differentiation between the elect and reprobate in the gradual unfolding of history), and developments among later disciples of Cocceius (wherein a psychologizing of salvation history in the doctrine of the Christian life surfaces in some Calvinistic quarters, for example, in English puritanism and Dutch precisionism, schools of pietistic federalism). Reformed covenant theology stands as a persuasive and convincing alternative to the Lutheran tradition which has no comprehensive doctrine of the covenants (or doctrine of eschatology rooted in the biblical account of creation). Van Asselt concludes his treatment with the following remarks:

> Cocceius is a wonderful friend and companion for any one seeking a deeper spiritual life at the heart of the Church and world. He lived his life of teaching, preaching, and writing, not from his own empty resources but from the well-spring of the Holy Spirit: he discovered that "the most beautiful thing that can happen, is to be

called a Christian and that the rights and the duties entailed by this name are a magnificent thing. For a Christian is ultimately. . . a friend of Christ. [321]

It is thus no exaggeration to say that the study of Cocceian theology in relation to the rest of Reformed theology and piety still remains an underdeveloped area. A detailed study, oriented toward the history of doctrine, should be able to shed some light on these matters, as well as on the more important question of how the students of Cocceius within the Reformed tradition differed among each other, and who were the closest in their thinking to Cocceius himself. [339]

# Appendix D

# FIGHTING THE GOOD FIGHT: A BOUT WITH JOHN FRAME

In "Studying Theology as a Servant of Christ" (*Reformation & Revival Journal: A Quarterly Journal for Church Leadership* 11 [2002] 45-69) John M. Frame expostulates on the relationship between student and teacher in the seminary context. This essay was originally published as a booklet by Reformed Seminary in Orlando. Contrary to Frame's subtle and not-so-subtle comment, the teaching authority of the church resides in the Word of God, not in seminary faculties. We do not hold the doctrines of the faith to be true because Frame or some other like-minded church theologian sanctions a particular reading of doctrine.

In recent years, Frame has yielded to the impulse to defend in writing his position on theology and the ministry of the Word. The writing of this present essay provides Frame the occasion to attack those who reject his theological method, known as multiperspectivalism – a method he (erroneously) views as consistent with Reformation hermeneutics. Sad to say, Frame has shown himself to be readily prone to misrepresentation of truth and distortion of fact. There is a direct tie between these two – namely, Frame's proclivity towards misrepresentation and his theological hermeneutic, one that blurs the picture and confounds the issues. Multiperspectivalism can be thought to succeed only when one's perception of truth is clouded, a condition that surely infects Frame's thinking on a number of subjects.

Our author defines theology as "application" (46). He abhors the notion of "objective truth." For him truth is what it means to the regenerated believer. Truth, in Frame's thinking, rests upon subjective appropriation. This is false and unorthodox thinking. Truth resides exclusively in God, not in human (albeit enlightened, sanctified) understanding. Frame likewise undermines Christian theology's *systematic* restatement of biblical teaching. He objects to the efforts of Charles Hodge – illustrative of the Reformed orthodox dogmaticians as a whole – to "put the truth in 'proper order' [on grounds that] Scripture already does those things perfectly well" (46). According to Frame, faith and practice – doctrine and life – inform each other correlatively. That is to say, they are of equal weight in the exegetico-theological enterprise. Frame asserts:

> We are sometimes inclined to say that "doctrine is the basis of the Christian life." That's a true statement, if by "doctrine" we mean the teaching of Scripture itself. But if "doctrines" are human theological formulations, human understandings of biblical teachings, then they are not the singular basis for the Christian life. [47]

Two comments here by way of response: Firstly, Frame is in error distinguishing between doctrine (the teachings of the Bible) and dogma (the teachings of the church). How precisely does Frame think we access the teaching of Scripture, except by the Spirit's illumination of the text to believing hearts and minds (see Rom 10:17 and 12:2; compare Heb 6:1-3)? Frame's notion leads a false bifurcation between biblical statement and theological formulation – with the implication that only the exact words of Scripture (in their original language) are authoritative and infallible. Students of the Bible, in Frame's thinking, can only have an approximate understanding of divine truth. *Contrary to Frame's opinion, to the extent that Christian doctrine and ethics faithfully (re)present the teaching of Scripture, to that extent Christian teaching bears the stamp and authority of Scripture. Such doctrine is to be believed and obeyed.* Frame's interpretation undermines the Scripture's authority, clarity, and sufficiency to make known the truths of God. Secondly, the Christian life does not precede doctrine and ethical instruction, but rather follows. Doctrine has precedence over life, which is equivalent to saying that Scripture is the foundation for Christian living. More exactly, it is Christ speaking through the Scriptures by his Spirit. The meaning of the text of Scripture is not its application in the interpreter's life-experience. (This is not to disparage the necessity that Scripture be applied to all of life.)

As has been pointed out in my exposé *The Changing of the Guard: Westminster Theological Seminary in Philadelphia* (Unicoi, TN: The Trinity Foundation, 2001),[1] the faculties of Westminster Seminary have failed to uphold in clear and unambiguous terms the Reformation doctrine of justification by faith alone. It is not sufficient – as in the case of some members of the faculty – to denounce the teachings of Norman Shepherd, yet endorse the teachings of Dick Gaffin (co-architect of Westminster's new theology) as orthodox expressions of the biblical, Reformed faith.[2] Frame offers this statement of faith:

> Salvation is a gift of God, the gift of Jesus' perfect righteousness in place of our sin, which he bore for us on the cross. We receive that gift through faith alone, by trusting Jesus as Lord and Savior. [52]

Two observations are again in order: In the first place, Frame's statement fails to bring clarity to the modern-day dispute, wherein some have undermined the truth of Scripture concerning the perfect righteousness of Christ which not only stands in place of our sin, but also cancels out our obligation to render full and perfect obedience as required in the prelapsarian covenant (the Edenic covenant). In the second place, according to the teaching of all the Protestant reformers – Lutheran and Reformed alike – the sole instrumentality of faith is intended to exclude human works of any kind, not just works performed with expectation of earning or meriting reward from God. Good works, which flow from true, saving faith (what the apostle Paul calls the "obedience of faith"), are likewise excluded. This latter aspect is at the heart of the ongoing Shepherd-Gaffin controversy, a controversy having ties more broadly with the dispute in present-day biblical and theological studies concerning Paul's understanding of the law of God.

Much of Frame's erroneous thinking is to be attributed to his practice and promulgation of multiperspectivalism, a theological method and hermeneutic which undermines – implicitly and explicitly – the perspicuity and sufficiency of Scripture in biblical, churchly interpretation. It is unclear where in Frame's experience – whether his teaching tenure at Westminster or his studies at Yale University (or both) – he acquired his distaste for traditional Reformed dogmatics. For those who differ with Frame, he opines: "You probably have very little idea how complicated the [theological] questions are, how many facets of them need to be considered" (55). He adds, as a warning to novices of Bible interpretation (those less learned than he!):

> Don't act like the great expert on difficult and controversial issues like exclusive psalmody, the regulative princi-

ple, confessional subscription, theonomy, supralapsarianism, common grace, infant communion, apologetic method, etc. . . . There is far too much cocksureness in Reformed circles, too many easy answers to difficult questions. Let us not be guilty of so trivializing the gospel of Christ. [56]

Frame's essay closes with a misdirected attack upon "partisanship," as the author views it. This is nothing other than a swipe against all those who do not share his thinking (on whatever it is that Frame propounds).³ Frame confuses the factions Paul castigates in his first letter to the Corinthians with divisions arising out of ongoing defense of the gospel against any and all attempts to undermine the teaching of God's Word. (Here, John, I cite Paul's letter to the Galatians. Check it out.) Among issues which Frame deems of lesser import are the following: the incomprehensibility of God, the place of the law, the place of the confessions (and churchly tradition), the nature of biblical covenants, and the relation of works to justification (63). I could not differ more vigorously with Frame. These are vital and essential issues in theological interpretation.

Frame confesses: "I have tried to search my own heart-motives in writing this essay" (66). This is good, John. It is something we must all do. But I counsel you to study more carefully the teaching of Scripture and the history of Reformed doctrine. If there is reason to challenge the teachings of our theological forebears, then let's do so with care and with humility. But don't undercut the Reformation teaching by careless and inaccurate readings of the Bible and the Protestant tradition. Be direct, straightforward, and truthful. Curiously, Frame remarks in one of his endnotes:

> The Reformed have often been known for the quality of their scholarship, to the extent that other branches of the evangelical church have often depended on them. Per-

haps we (and I speak as a Reformed confessionalist [so he says!]) have been a bit too prideful about our scholarship, indeed about our supposed intellectual superiority to other Christians. That kind of boasting is never appropriate, but in my view it is less plausible today than it ever has been. [68, n.5]

Such reasoning as this has helped redirect Frame's theologizing, especially with a view to his peculiar concoction, multiperspectivalism, his remedy for theological division and strife in the church, past and present.

Frame himself did not find Westminster West to be congenial or hospitable to his theological ruminations. This factor and the strong criticism he has received within the wider seminary community led him to move on to his new home at Reformed Seminary.[4] Frame's accusation against Mark Karlberg as having a "movement mentality" could not be further from the truth (69, n.11). If by "movement" Frame means commitment to historic Reformed orthodoxy – in the line of J. Gresham Machen, Cornelius Van Til, Geerhardus Vos, and Meredith Kline (to name only a few) – I plead guilty. But the facts are that Frame's assessment of church and seminary is false and inaccurate, even illusionary. Frame can only see things his way; he eschews traditional orthodox polemics. Frame is a polemicist of a different kind. Multiperspectivalism is inherently eclectic in its approach to theological interpretation. It stands in sharp conflict with Reformational hermeneutics.[5]

Frame's reasoning (in places) can simply be nonsensical. My advice is the same as that given by Richard A. Muller of Calvin Seminary: "John, don't stand too long in Elmer's shoes" ("*The Study of Theology* Revisited: A Response to John Frame," *WTJ* 56 [1994] 409-17). Despite its pious claim to Christian virtue, Frame's teaching is characterized by arrogance and pride – he's a seminary professor and therefore we are obliged to listen and learn from him! Lurking beneath the surface of Frame's thinking is a spirit of elitism. He knows more than others. (This may well be the reason why Frame never obtained his doctorate. Doubtless, at every turn he knew more than his Yale professors.) By way of a closing rejoinder, I again offer these words of exhortation and admonition to Frame: What is required of him – and those of his theological ilk – is a spirit of repentance for the grave doctrinal error that has so widely infiltrated our churches. Here we are talking about doctrinal teaching that pertains to the very essence of the Gospel, justification before a holy God on the grounds of the merits of Christ's righteousness alone, received through the sole instrumentality of saving faith. Nothing less than a renunciation of deviant, heretical teaching is demanded – something Frame and those in his camp are unwilling to produce. May God's grace prove stronger than the human sin and hardness of heart that has settled so pervasively upon the church today.

**NOTES**

[1] Republished here as Chapter 6.

[2] In the case of Frame, he supported Shepherd's teaching from the very outset of the controversy, and he continues to regard that view as fully orthodox and scriptural. He does believe that an injustice was done to Shepherd, rightly observing that Gaffin should also have been dismissed from the faculty, since their views are the same. (What does that say about Frame as a supporter of this deviant teaching?) See my "Current Theological Trends in Reformed Seminaries: The Dilemma in Ministerial Education," read at the Eastern regional meeting of the Evangelical Theological Society in Lancaster, PA (April 3, 1998).

[3] Richard Horner, OPC minister and former classmate of Frame, received an angry, vicious letter from Frame after his review of Frame's book on Van Til appearing in the pages of the OPC denomination's periodical *New Horizons*. Frame does not take kindly to criticism, a disposition he shares with many of his former faculty colleagues.

[4] Perspectivalism and the New Westminster theology have greatly impacted the teaching at Reformed Seminary. Former President Luder Whitlock was unwilling or unable, whatever the reasons, to address this problem within the faculty at Reformed Seminary. The decision to enlist John Frame and Richard Pratt for revision of *The New Geneva Study Bible* (Nashville: Thomas Nelson, 1995; later renamed *The Reformation Study Bible*), to become the *Spirit of the Reformation Study Bible* (Grand Rapids: Zondervan, 2003), is most lamentable. The commentary by Frame and Pratt is, in places, decidedly *anti-Reformational*. The issue of readability aside, the substitution of the New International Version for the New King James Version only serves to introduce erroneous teaching into the text of Scripture, as regards, for example, the apostle Paul's view of the Mosaic law. In many respects, the NIV is inferior among modern translations serving the Protestant-Reformed community.

[5] For additional evaluation of Frame's theology and methodology, see my essays "On the Theological Correlation of Divine and Human Language: A Review Article," *JETS* 32 (1989) 99-105, and "John Frame and the Recasting of Van Tilian Apologetics: A Review Article," *Mid-America Journal of Theology* 9 (1993) 279-296.

# Supplemental Bibliography
[To my previous study, *Covenant Theology in Reformed Perspective*]

Beach, J. Mark. "The Doctrine of the *Pactum Salutis* in the Covenant Theology of Herman Witsius," *Mid-America Journal of Theology* 13 (2002) 101-142.

Beale, G. K. *The Book of Revelation: A Commentary on the Greek Text* (The New International Greek Testament Commentary; Grand Rapids: Eerdmans, 1999).

Berends, William. "The Obedience of Jesus Christ," *Vox Reformata: Australasian Journal for Christian Scholarship* 66 [2001] 26-51).

Carson, D. A., P. T. O'Brien, and M. A. Seifrid. *Justification and Variegated Nomism: Vol 1, The Complexities of Second Temple Judaism* (Wissenschaftliche Untersuchungen zum Neuen Testament 2, Reihe 140. Tübingen: Mohr Siebeck; Grand Rapids: Baker Academic, 2001.

Colyer, Elmer M., ed. *Evangelical Theology in Transition: Theologians in Dialogue with Donald Bloesch* (Downers Grove: InterVarsity, 1999)

Dorrien, Gary. *The Remaking of Evangelical Theology* (Louisville: Westminster John Knox, 1998)

Gaffin, Richard B., Jr. "Biblical Theology and the Westminster Standards," in *The Practical Calvinist: An Introduction to the Presbyterian and Reformed Heritage in Honor of Dr. D. Clair Davis on the Occasion of His Seventieth Birthday* (Ross-shire: Christian Focus, 2002) 425-442.

_____. "The Obedience of Faith,"*Israel and the Church: Essays in Honour of Allan Macdonald Harman on his 65th Birthday and Retirement* (ed. D. J. W. Milne (Melbourne: The Theological Education Committee of the Presbyterian Church of Victoria, 2001) 71-85.

Green, J. B. and M. Turner, eds. *Between Two Horizons: Spanning New Testament Studies and Systematic Theology* (Baker: Grand Rapids, 2000).

Grenz, Stanley J. *Renewing the Center: Evangelical theology in a Post-Theological Era* (Grand Rapids: Baker, 2000).

Grenz, Stanley J. and John R. Franke. *Beyond Foundationalism: Shaping Theology in a Postmodern Context* (Louisville: Westminster John Knox, 2001).

Griffith, H. and J. R. Muether, eds. *Creator, Redeemer, Consummator: A Festschrift for Meredith G. Kline* (Greenville, SC: Reformed Academic Press, 2000).

Hafemann, Scott J. *The God of Promise and the Life of Faith: Understanding the heart of the Bible* (Wheaton: Crossway, 2001).

Hamilton, James M. (Jr.). "God with Men in the Torah," *The Westminster Theological Journal* 65 (2003) 113-133.

_____. "Old Testament Believers and the Indwelling Spirit: A Survey of the Spectrum of Opinion," *Trinity Journal* 24 NS (2003) 37-54.

Hart, D. G. *Recovering Mother Kirk: The Case for Liturgy in the Reformed Tradition* (Grand Rapids: Baker, 2003).

"Historic Documents of American Presbyterianism: The Justification Controversy" (PCA Historical Center: www.pcanet.org/history/documents/shepherd/justification.html).

Hodges, Louis Igou. *Reformed Theology Today* (Columbus, GA: Brentwood Christian Press, 1995).

Horton, Michael S. *Covenant and Eschatology: The Divine Drama* (Louisville, London: Westminster John Knox, 2002).

_____. "Law, Gospel, and Covenant: Reassessing Some Emerging Antitheses," *The Westminster Theological Journal* 64 (2002) 279-287.

Karlberg, Mark W. "John Frame and the Recasting of Van Tilian Apologetics: A Review Article," *Mid-America Journal of Theology* 9 (1993) 279-296.

_____. "On the Theological Correlation of Divine and Human Language: A Review Article," *Journal of the Evangelical Theological Society* 32 (1989) 99-105.

Kline, Meredith G. *God, Heaven, and Har Meggedon: A Covenant Theology Primer* (Overland Park, KS: Two Age, forthcoming).

Leith, John H. *Crisis in the Church: The Plight of Theological Education* (Louisville: Westminster John Knox, 1997).

_____. *From Generation to Generation: The Renewal of the Church According to Its Own Theology and Practice* (Louisville: Westminster John Knox, 1990).

_____. *Introduction to the Reformed Tradition: A Way of Being the Christian Community* (Atlanta: John Knox, 1977).

_____. *The Reformed Imperative: What the Church Has to Say That No One Else Can Say* (Philadelphia: Westminster, 1988).

McKnight, Scott. "From Wheaton to Rome: Why Evangelicals become Roman Catholic," *Journal of the Evangelical Theological Society* 45 (2002) 451-472.

Mohler, R. Albert. "Evangelical Theology and Karl Barth: Representative Models of Response" (Ph.D. dissertation, Southern Baptist Theological Seminary, 1989).

Moore, T. M. *I Will be Your God: How God's Covenant Enriches Our Lives* (Phillipsburg: Presbyterian and Reformed, 2002).

Muller, Richard A. *Post-Reformation Reformed Dogmatics: The Rise and Development of Reformed Orthodoxy, ca. 1520 to ca. 1725* (4 volumes; Grand Rapids: Baker, 2003).

Osbourn, Grant R. *The Hermeneutical Spiral: A Comprehensive Introduction to Biblical Interpretation* (Downers Grove: InterVarsity, 1991).

Piper, John. *Counted Righteous in Christ: Should We Abandon the Imputation of Christ's Righteousness?* (Wheaton, IL: Crossway Books, 2002).

Riddlebarger, Kim. *The Case for Amillennialism: Understanding the End Times* (Grand Rapids: Baker, 2003).

Robbins, John. *A Companion to the Current Justification Controversy* (Unicoi, TN: The Trinity Foundation, 2003).

Robertson, O. Palmer. *The Current Justification Controversy* (Unicoi, TN: The Trinity Foundation, 2003).

Schreiner, Thomas. *Paul: Apostle of God's Glory in Christ: A Pauline Theology* (Downers Grove: InterVarsity, 2001).

Silva, Moisés, "Abraham, Faith, and Works: Paul's Use of Scripture in Galatians 3:6-14," *The Westminster Theological Journal* 63 (2001) 251-67.
    This essay also appears (slightly changed) as an appendix in *Interpreting Galatians: Explorations in Exegetical Method* (second edition; Grand Rapids: Baker, 2001).

Spykman, Gordon J. *Reformational Theology: A New Paradigm for Doing Dogmatics* (Grand Rapids: Eerdmans, 1992).

Stam, Clarence. *The Covenant of Love: Exploring our relationship with God* (Winnipeg: Premier, 1999).

Stuhlmacher, Peter. *Revisiting Paul's Doctrine of Justification: A Challenge to the New Perspective* (Downers Grove,IL: InterVarsity, 2001).

Trumper, Tim J. R. "Covenant Theology and Constructive Calvinism," *The Westminster Theological Journal* 63 (2002) 387-404.

_____. "An Historical Study of the Doctrine of Adoption in the Calvinistic Tradition," (Ph.D. dissertation, University of Edinburgh, 2001).

Van Asselt, Willem J. *The Federal Theology of Johannes Cocceius (1603-1669)* (trans. by Raymond A. Blacketer; Studies in the History of Christian Thought, vol. 100; Leiden, Boston, Köln: Brill, 2001).

Van Vliet, Jan. "Decretal Theology and the Development of Covenant Thought: An Assessment of Cornelis Graafland's Thesis with a Particular View to Federal Architects William Ames and Johannes Cocceius," *The Westminster Theological Journal* 63 (2001) 393-420.

_____. "From Condition to State: Critical Reflections on Cornelius Van Til's Doctrine of Common Grace," *The Westminster Theological Journal* 61 (1999) 73-100.

Ward, Roland. "Some Thoughts on Covenant Theology and on Justification (Part 1)," *The Presbyterian Banner* (March 2002) 11-12; "Some Thoughts on Covenant Theology and on Justification (Part 2)," *The Presbyterian Banner* (April 2002) 10-11.

\_\_\_\_\_. *God and Adam: Reformed Theology and the Creation Covenant* (published by the author; Wantirna, Australia: New Melbourne, 2003).

Warfield, B. B. *The Plan of Salvation: A Study of the Basic and Essential Differences Between Various Interpretations of the Christian Religion* (revised edition; Grand Rapids: Eerdmans, 1970).

Webber, Robert E. *The Younger Evangelicals: Facing the Challenges of the New World* (Grand Rapids: Baker, 2002).

Wells, David F. *God in the Wasteland: The Reality of Truth in a World of Fading Dreams* (Grand Rapids: Eerdmans, 1994).

\_\_\_\_\_. *Losing Our Virtue: Why the Church Must Recover Its Moral Vision* (Grand Rapids: Eerdmans, 1998).

\_\_\_\_\_. *No Place for Truth: Or Whatever Happened to Evangelical Theology?* (Grand Rapids, Eerdmans, 1993).

# Author Index

**A**myraldus, M. 74
Aquinas, T. 75
Augustine 113

**B**arnes, D. 271, 285
Barker, W. 201
Barth, K. 16, 17, 24, 25, 94-95, 113, 173, 191, 193, 202, 208, 213, 226, 231, 245-246, 267, 268, 292
Bavinck, H. 54, 181, 289
Beach, J. M. 54
Beale, G. K. 18, 92
Beeke, J. 55
Berends, W. 119
Berkhof, L. 18, 57, 95
Berkouwer, G. C. 5, 194, 213, 289
Blaising, C. 14, 19, 131-132
Bloesch, D. 231-232
Boice, J. M. 195
Bray, G. 67

**C**alvin, J. 24, 26, 27, 55, 60, 64, 67, 86, 94, 100, 107, 109, 128, 140, 148, 153, 213-216, 226, 227, 232, 258, 263, 265, 292
Carpenter, C. B. 270
Carson, D. A. 19
Clark, R. S. 55, 211, 223, 285
Clowney, E. P. 182-184, 220, 221, 262, 274
Cocceius, J. 295-304
Cullmann, O. 52

**D**avis, D. C. 6, 258
Dennison, J. 220
Dillard, R. B. 26, 51
Dorman, T. M. 52, 55, 222, 233
Dorrien, G. 52, 84
Dunn, J. D. G. 93, 130, 224

**E**dwards, J. 139
Elliott, J. P. 271
Eveson, P. 91

**F**erguson, S. 6, 16, 50, 179-180, 195-196, 199, 201, 208, 222, 258
Foraker, C. 6
Frame, J. M. 19, 62, 85, 98-99, 117, 118-119,

198, 199, 202, 223, 268,
274, 285, 288, 305-312
Franke, J. R. 18, 116
Fuller, D. 20, 54, 71, 131,
138, 143, 149-151, 187,
202, 250

**G**adamer, H-G. 288
Gaffin, Jr., R. B. 3, 4, 6,
15, 16, 21, 22, 24-26, 52,
54, 55, 118, 157-204,
205-233, 255-264, 268,
270-272, 274, 275, 279-
285, 289, 307
Garlington, D. 14, 19, 229
Gerstner, J. 75
Godfrey, W. R. 90, 201,
263-264, 276
Gootjes, N. H. 231-232
Grenz, S. 18, 19, 52, 84
Gundry, R. 251

**H**afemann, S. 54, 117,
268-269
Hagner, D. 135
Hamilton, J. M. 50
Hart, D. 6, 7, 50
Hart, T. 99-100
Heidegger, J. H. 296
Heynes, J. A. 91
Hodge, C. 57, 147, 191,
306
Hodges, L. I. 43-45, 48,

53, 120
Hoekema, A. A. 90, 92
Horner, R. 312
Horton, M. S. 119, 198,
231, 264, 276-277, 287-
294

**I**rons, L. 199-200, 231

**J**eon, J. K. 258, 263
Jewett, P. K. 87

**K**innaird, J. 3, 4, 6, 256,
270, 285
Kline, M. G. 4, 25, 53, 86,
87, 162, 188, 198, 199-
201, 208, 211, 257-264,
267, 274-275, 289, 290,
310
Krahe, C. 3, 6, 258
Küng, H. 194

**L**eith, J. H. 1, 52, 85
Letham, R. 201
Lillback, P. A. 54-55, 118,
201, 219, 232, 258, 271,
302
Lints, R. 84, 202
Logan, S. 20, 22, 187,
223, 270
Longman III, T. 51
Luther, M. 55, 107-109,

124-127, 130, 181, 205-206, 232

**M**achen, J. G. 173, 197, 255, 310
MacIntyre, A. 293
McGrath, A. E. 52
McKim, D. 84
McKnight, S. 55
McWilliams, D. 22, 201, 220, 223, 272
Miller, E. 7
Mohler, R. A. 22
Moltmann, J. 297
Moo, D. 14, 19
Moore, T. M. 21
Mote, E. 155
Muether, J. 6, 7
Muller, R. A. 18, 87, 120-121, 310
Murray, J. 2-5, 24, 26, 45, 48, 57, 70, 73, 74, 76, 88, 90, 114, 161, 202, 207-211, 215, 258-262, 265, 268, 273, 275

**N**iemczyk, C. 7
Noll, M. 7, 157, 197

**O**'Brien, P. T. 89
Old, H. O. 91
Osborne, G. R. 53, 84

Osterhaven, M. E. 52

**P**acker, J. I. 76
Parker, T. H. L. 88
Pinnock, C. 68, 82, 84
Piper, J. 14, 15, 20-22, 54, 137-155, 200, 222, 249-255, 256, 268, 269
Poythress, V. 202
Pratt, R. 312

**R**eymond, R. 13, 18, 57-92, 119, 187-188, 200
Ridderbos, H. 5, 26, 52, 62, 198, 213, 289
Riddlebarger, K. 18, 88
Robbins, J. 14, 20, 204
Robertson, O. P. 20, 26, 200, 204
Rogers, J. 135

**S**anders, E. P. 93, 130, 170
Schreiner, T. 54, 233
Shepherd, N. 2, 4-6, 14-16, 19, 20-22, 25, 26, 54, 71, 118, 128, 157-204, 205-233, 251, 269-272, 275, 279-285, 307
Silva, M. 54
Spykman, G. J. 53, 84
Stam, C. 45-48, 55

Stone, S. J. 49
Strimple, R. 198, 211, 223, 271
Stuhlmacher, P. 135-136, 222

**T**ertullian 113
Thielman, F. 89
Thomas, G. M. 90, 195
Torrance, J. B. 275
Torrance, T. F. 16, 24, 25, 201, 207-208
Trueman, C. 201
Trumper, T. J. R. 15, 16, 21, 22, 24-27, 223, 257-264, 271-276
Turretine, F. 95, 289

**U**rsinus, Z. 289

**V**an Asselt, W. J. 119, 295-304
Van Til, C. 20, 21, 25, 62-63, 84, 88, 117, 173, 211, 223, 226, 236, 264, 268, 269, 293, 297, 310, 312
Van Vliet, J. 55
Van Buren, P. 224
VanDrunen, D. 223
VanGemeren, W. 136
Venema, C. 19, 118

Vos, G. 5, 24, 54, 87, 111, 198, 211, 229, 289, 310

**W**all, R. W. 96-98
Ward, R. S. 54
Warfield, B. B. 51, 53, 57, 67, 88, 90
Webber, R. E. 52
Wells, D. F. 1, 60, 85
Whitlock, L. 21, 312
Wolterstorff, N. 288
Wright, N. T. 19, 52, 130, 224

**Z**ens, R. M. 200, 203
Zwingli, U. 237

www.ingramcontent.com/pod-product-compliance
Lightning Source LLC
Chambersburg PA
CBHW071231230426
43668CB00011B/1385